A People's History
of World War II

Remembering Slavery: African Americans Talk About
Their Personal Experiences of Slavery and Emancipation
(with Ira Berlin and Steven F. Miller)

A People's History of World War II

The World's Most Destructive Conflict,
as Told by the People Who Lived Through It

Edited by
Marc Favreau

THE NEW PRESS

NEW YORK
LONDON

Compilation © 2011 by The New Press
All rights reserved.
No part of this book may be reproduced, in any form,
without written permission from the publisher.

Requests for permission to reproduce selections from this book should be mailed to:
Permissions Department, The New Press, 38 Greene Street, New York, NY 10013.

Published in the United States by The New Press, New York, 2011
Distributed by Perseus Distribution

CIP data is available
ISBN 978-1-59558-166-2 (pb)

www.thenewpress.com

Composition by dix!

Printed in the United States of America

2 4 6 8 10 9 7 5 3 1

Contents

Series Preface

Turning history on its head opens up whole new worlds of possibility. Once, historians looked only at society's upper crust: the leaders and others who made the headlines and whose words and deeds survived as historical truth. In our lifetimes, this has begun to change. Shifting history's lens from the upper rungs to the lower, we are learning more than ever about the masses of people who did the work that made society tick.

Not surprisingly, as the lens shifts the basic narratives change as well. The history of men and women of all classes, colors, and cultures reveals an astonishing degree of struggle and independent political action. Everyday people played complicated historical roles, and they developed highly sophisticated and often very different political ideas from the people who ruled them. Sometimes their accomplishments left tangible traces; other times, the traces are invisible but no less real. They left their mark on our institutions, our folkways and language, on our political habits and vocabulary. We are only now beginning to excavate this multifaceted history.

The New Press People's History Series roams far and wide through human history, revisiting old stories in new ways, and introducing altogether new accounts of the struggles of common people to make their own history. Taking the lives and viewpoints of common people as its point of departure, the series reexamines subjects as different as the American Revolution, the history of sports, the history of American art, the Mexican Revolution, and the rise of the Third World.

A people's history does more than add to the catalogue of what we already know. These books will shake up readers' understanding of the past—just as common people throughout history have shaken up their always changeable worlds.

Howard Zinn
Boston, 2000

Editor's Note

The title of this book takes its cue from Howard Zinn's *A People's History of the United States*. Prior to his death in early 2010, Zinn was the longtime editor of The New Press People's History Series. It was at his urging that we decided to assemble this "greatest hits" collection of first-person testimonies from World War II, drawing on The New Press's extensive published work in this area, as well as from sources beyond our own list.

Zinn's influence is not incidental to the pages that follow. Nearly seventy years after the end of World War II, our collective memory of the world's most destructive conflict seems to have narrowed to a select few events and characters, all of them heavily filtered through commercial movies and television. The experience of ordinary people threatens to be lost—particularly as the generation that experienced the war directly fades from the scene—and with it a proper sense of the astonishing range of human experience, struggle, and suffering.

This book is the kind of history Howard Zinn championed: it samples from the rich outpouring of personal testimony and literary expression captured by a gifted set of historians and writers, including especially Studs Terkel, Haruko Taya Cook and Theodore Cook, Nelson Peery, David Wyman, Mark Anderson, and many others. It is our hope that this extraordinary body of writing—and the experiences and memories it contains—will inspire further exploration and reading.

—Marc Favreau
June 2011

Part I

Beginnings: Pearl Harbor

On the morning of December 7, 1941, the Imperial Japanese Navy made a devastating surprise assault on the United States Naval base at Pearl Harbor, on the Hawaiian Island of Oahu, where the U.S. Pacific Fleet was based. The attack killed over 2,400 American servicemen, wounded more than 1,300 others, and sank or damaged a large number of ships and aircraft—including three battleships. It was a major and risky move on the part of the Japanese, whose armies had advanced swiftly across East Asia in the preceding years, and whose military leaders hoped to neutralize any American opposition to their push into Southeast Asia. Pearl Harbor was quickly followed by attacks on other American military installations in the Pacific.

The "day that will live in infamy"—President Franklin Delano Roosevelt's stirring phrase in a speech to the American people on December 8—shook the American psyche to its foundations. The United States declared war on Japan hours after Roosevelt's speech. On December 11, following a declaration of war on the United States by the Axis powers Germany and Italy, the U.S. declared war on those countries as well, marking its full entry into the Second World War.

"U.S.S. *Shaw* exploding during the Japanese raid on Pearl Harbor, December 7, 1941." (Still Picture Branch, National Archives and Records Administration, Record # 80-G-16871)

"Captured Japanese photograph taken during the December 7, 1941, attack on Pearl Harbor. In the distance, the smoke rises from Hickam Field." (Still Picture Branch, National Archives and Records Administration, Record # 80-G-30550)

"[U.S. Navy Submarine Base] Pearl Harbor, T.H., taken by surprise during the Japanese aerial attack. U.S.S. *West Virginia* aflame, December 7, 1941." (Still Picture Branch, National Archives and Records Administration, Record # 80-G-19947)

"Captured Japanese photograph taken aboard a Japanese carrier before the attack on Pearl Harbor, Hawaii, December 7, 1941." (Still Picture Branch, National Archives and Records Administration, Record # 80-G-30549)

"December 7, 1941"

John Garcia and Anton Bilek

In an excerpt from his acclaimed oral history *"The Good War"*, Studs Terkel interviews American witnesses to the Japanese attacks on Pearl Harbor, and on the U.S. military installation at Clark Field, in the Philippines.

JOHN GARCIA

A huge man, built along the lines of a sumo wrestler. He manages a complex of apartment buildings in Los Angeles. He could quite easily be the bouncer, too. He is resigned to the assortment of illnesses that plague him; his manner is easygoing. "With my age, my love for food, that's caused diabetes, the whole bit." He is a Hawaiian.

I was sixteen years old, employed as a pipe fitter apprentice at Pearl Harbor Navy Yard. On December 7, 1941, oh, around 8:00 A.M., my grandmother woke me. She informed me that the Japanese were bombing Pearl Harbor. I said, "They're just practicing." She said, no, it was real and the announcer is requesting that all Pearl Harbor workers report to work. I went out on the porch and I could see the anti-aircraft fire up in the sky. I just said, "Oh boy."

I was four miles away. I got out on my motorcycle and it took me five, ten minutes to get there. It was a mess.

I was working on the U.S.S. *Shaw*. It was on a floating dry dock. It was in flames. I started to go down into the pipe fitter's shop to get my toolbox when another wave of Japanese came in. I got under a set of concrete steps at the dry dock where the battleship *Pennsylvania* was. An officer came by and asked me to go into the *Pennsylvania* and try to get the fires out. A bomb had penetrated the marine deck, and that was three decks below. Under that was the magazines: ammunition, powder, shells. I said, "There ain't no way I'm gonna go down there." It could blow up any minute. I was young and sixteen, not stupid, not at sixty-two cents an hour. (Laughs.)

A week later, they brought me before a navy court. It was determined that I was not service personnel and could not be ordered. There was no martial law at the time. Because I was sixteen and had gone into the water, the whole thing was dropped.

I was asked by some other officer to go into the water and get sailors out that had been blown off the ships. Some were unconscious, some were dead. So I spent the rest of the day swimming inside the harbor, along with some other Hawaiians. I brought out I don't know how many bodies and how many were alive and how many dead. Another man would put them into ambulances and they'd be gone. We worked all day at that.

That evening, I drove a truckload of marines into Palolo Valley because someone reported that the Japanese had parachuted down there. Because of the total blackout, none of the marine drivers knew how to get there. It was two miles away. There were no parachuters. Someone in the valley had turned their lights on and the marines started shootin' at that house. The lights went out. (Laughs.)

I went back to my concrete steps to spend the night there. Someone on the *Pennsylvania* was walking along the edge of armored plate. He lit a cigarette. All of a sudden, a lot of guns opened up on him. I don't know if he was hit.

The following morning, I went with my tools to the *West Virginia*. It had turned turtle, totally upside down. We found a number of men inside. The *Arizona* was a total washout. Also the *Utah*. There were men in there, too. We spent about a month cutting the superstructure of the *West Virginia,* tilting it back on its hull. About three hundred men we cut out of there were still alive by the eighteenth day.

How did they survive?

I don't know. We were too busy to ask. (Laughs.) It took two weeks to get all the fires out. We worked around the clock for three days. There was so much excitement and confusion. Some of our sailors were shooting five-inch guns at the Japanese planes. You just cannot down a plane with a five-inch shell. They were landing in Honolulu, the unexploding naval shells. They have a ten-mile range. They hurt and killed a lot of people in the city.

When I came back after the third day, they told me that a shell had hit the house of my girl. We had been going together for, oh, about three years. Her house was a few blocks from my place. At the time, they said it was a Japanese bomb. Later we learned it was an American shell. She was killed. She was preparing for church at the time.

My neighbors met me. They were mostly Japanese. We all started to cry. We had no idea what was happening, what was going to happen.

Martial law had been set in. Everyone had to work twelve hours, six to six. No one on the streets after 6:00 P.M. No one on the streets before 6:00 A.M. The military took over the islands completely. If you failed to go to work, the police would be at your door and you were arrested. You had to do something, filling sandbags, anything. No one was excused. If you called in sick, a nurse would come to your house to check on you. If you failed to be there or were goofing off, you went to jail. All civil liberties were suspended.

There was no act of treason by anyone that I know of. There were spies, but they were all employed by the Japanese embassy. If they had arrested the ordinary Japanese, there would be no work force at Pearl Harbor. There were 130,000 Japanese on the islands. There'd be no stores, no hotels, nothing. You'd have to shut the city down. They suffered a lot of insults, especially by the servicemen. They took it without coming back.

I tried to get in the military, but they refused. They considered my work essential for the war effort. I was promoted to shop fitter and went from $32 a week to $125. But I kept trying for a year to get in the fight. Finally, I wrote a letter to President Roosevelt. I told him I was angry at the Japanese bombing and had lost some friends. He okayed that I be accepted. I went into the service and went down to $21 a month. (Laughs.)

My grandmother signed for me because I was only seventeen. She said she would never see me alive again. It turned out prophetic because she died one day before I got home. January 1946.

They wanted to send me to Texas for training. I got on the stick and wrote to the President again. I wasn't interested in Texas, I wanted to go into combat. I got an answer from the White House requesting that I be put into a combat outfit. I got thirty days washing dishes for not following the chain of command. (Laughs.)

ANTON BILEK

He's still wiry, with just a slight touch of middle-aged flab. His appearance is that of an old-time welterweight fighter. Or an Eddie Stanky-type infielder.

He runs a greenhouse and flower shop in Rantoul, Illinois, near the Chanute air base. "Nothin' but you and the flowers, and they don't talk back to you.

"Prior to the war, I was a go-getter. Now, I live on the only hill in town. I very seldom leave the place. I get up in the morning, tend my flowers, and I go back to sleep at night. I have my shot of bourbon and beer at night and stay away from people.

"I'd like to go back to the Philippines again. I got a lotta memories there. They've got the most beautiful cemetery in the world for our boys."

A lotta friends I lost. We had 185 men in our squadron when the war started. Three and a half years later, when we were liberated from a prison camp in Japan, we were 39 left. It's them I think about. Men I played ball with, men I worked with, men I associated with. I miss 'em.

I got in the Philippines in 1940 for a two-year term. I enlisted in 1939. I was nineteen. Jobs were hard to get. I was always interested in building things, especially aircraft. I wanted to pursue that, but I didn't have money for school. I found a little brochure: join the air corps and learn a trade. So I joined, went down to Chanute, went through sheet-metal school. After I graduated, they shipped me to the Philippine Islands. I went right to Clark Field, about sixty miles due north of Manila.

He shows me a photograph of Clark Field in 1939. It is startlingly plain and bare.

There were only about 250 men there at the time. We had only one bomb squadron, the Twenty-eighth. I worked repairing the old B-10s. Things were real slow then. In mid-1941, they started bringin' in the troops.

We could never believe that the Japanese would attack the United States of America. That was out of the question. So we didn't pay too much attention. We were going through alerts, starting in November. I was assistant machine gunner to old Sergeant Amos. It was an old Lewis machine gun from World War One, an air-cooled job.

On December 8—that's December 7 here—an alert sounded around nine o'clock. All the fighters and all the B-17s took off. We thought, Gosh, General MacArthur's payin' us a visit and we're showin' him. Soon all the airplanes came back. It was about eleven-thirty or so. I got through eating and went into the dayroom. I was thumbin' through a sports magazine and the radio was playin'. All of a sudden, the newscaster from Manila stops the music: "Clark

Field's been bombed." He starts shouting: "The Japanese have at-tacked Clark Field."

I got up, looked out the window, and I didn't see any bombers. Everything's real calm. I sat down and told the guy next to me, "D'ya hear that?" He said, "Oh, Jesus, some of that crap." There's all kinda rumors floatin' around. I thought this is a good time for me to start writing down all these rumors and the date I heard 'em on. In a coupla months, it would be a good laugh. I went back to my bunk, had a little black address book, and I started writing the rumor of Pearl Harbor being bombed in the morning. We couldn't believe that. And now we're hearin' that Clark Field's been bombed. I'm sittin' here and there's nothing dropped. (Laughs.)

Just then the first sergeant ran in, shouting, "It's the real thing. Here they come!" I grabbed all my gear, a Springfield riffle, a World War One model, and threw my helmet on, my gas mask, and I ran out of the barracks.

As soon as I hit our little machine-gun pit, the bombs started droppin'. I stood up and says, "So that's what it sounds like." Amos grabbed me by the back of the pants and pulled me back. 'Cause I'd been seein' a lot of that stuff on newsreels, about what's goin' on in Poland, what's goin' on in Europe. The real thing is kinda surprising.

They leveled the whole field. Tremendous bombing. They didn't miss anything. All our airplanes had just come in and were being refueled.

When our airplanes first took off that morning, the Japs did come in. They hit the city of Baguio in the northern part of Luzon, and then went back to Formosa. Our planes couldn't find 'em, so they come back and were outa fuel. They didn't see the bombing, they were twenty thousand feet up. So they went to chow and got some lunch. And that's when the Japs come in to Clark Field. As they left, after leveling us, Amos and I got out of the pit. We were flabbergasted.

We look around and see all this devastation, airplanes burning, hangars burning, gas trucks burning. Men yelling and screaming.

Wounded and dead all over the place. Jap fighters followed 'em in, about eighty of 'em. Just strafed everything that stood. Amos started shootin' at 'em with our little old putt-putt. (Laughs.) I stood by with the ammunition box. After it was over, we were kinda in shock.

This shouldn't have happened to us. We were Americans, they were Japanese. They weren't supposed to bomb us. This is the way we were talkin' about it. (Laughs.) We were always told that they all wore glasses and they didn't have a decent bombsight. And they didn't have any navy to amount to anything. They were usin' all our scrap metal, all our oil. You always thought that way. Jesus Christ, how the hell'd this happen?

For the next month, there wasn't much to do. We did help some of the squadrons repair their aircraft and make one good one out of maybe three or four bombed ones. Then they started shippin' the men out. We had nothing left any more, see? We lost a lotta men.

We flew the bombers down to the Del Monte pineapple plantation on Mindanao, oh, seven hundred, eight hundred miles south. It was the only other air base in the Philippines that could hold a B-17. We had about sixteen B-17s left out of thirty-five. And our P-40s, we had about fifty percent of those left. We had nothin' left to fight 'em with. We tried to use our planes strategically, but the Jap Zero was a better maneuverable aircraft than our P-40.

One thing that hurt us, we knew of Pearl Harbor, we had eight hours to do something and we didn't. We had airfields where we could have dispersed our craft. I've loaded fifty-five-gallon drums at different air bases throughout the Philippines. Consequently, we lost 'em. The Japanese had the run of the land.

We stayed there till Christmas Eve, 1941. We were thinking, Hell, we're gonna get the troops in here. They're gonna fly in supplies, stuff. We heard of a convoy that was coming in with fifty-four A-24 dive bombers. We didn't have a single dive bomber. We heard artillery was comin' over. That was the war plan, see? Battleships and everything. The navy would protect a convoy to come to the Philippines. But here was our navy resting on the mud flats of Pearl

Harbor. We didn't know the damage inflicted on Pearl Harbor, how bad it was.

Christmas Eve, we get orders: retreat to the Bataan peninsula. About a hundred miles. The first sergeant said, "I need five volunteers. You, you, you—" the five of us he pointed at were the volunteers. (Laughs.) "You're gonna stay here at Clark Field while the rest of the men move out."

On December 22, General Homma's forces landed at Lingayen Gulf on the northern part of Luzon. Another force landed on Lamon Bay. They formed a pincer movement on Manila. MacArthur had about seventy thousand Filipino troops but no equipment. General Wainwright was at Lingayen, but he had just one little regiment of American infantry and some Filipinos. He didn't have any aircraft, no dive bombers. So they landed without opposition.

We five guys are still at Clark Field. Our shavetail, a second lieutenant, just came into the army out of college. A slim Jim. He didn't know what he was there for, either. Next morning, Christmas Day, Major Johnson pulls up in a staff car: "Lieutenant, this is your air base. This is your staff, these five privates. You have a gas truck and an oil truck." The gas truck is full of three thousand gallons of high-octane gasoline. "You will service any of our P-40s that makes a forced landing here. When you think it's fit to leave Clark Field, that's entirely up to you." And the major took off for Bataan.

We were there for four days. We could hear the fighting at Tarlac, about twenty miles north. We slept on mattresses on the airfield, in case aircraft did come in. We could see the flashes from the artillery and hear the boomin'. I nudged the lieutenant: "Don't you think it's time to leave?" (Laughs.) The shootin's gettin' pretty close, with three thousand gallons of gasoline. That's a big bomb in itself. All it takes is one tracer bullet into that thing. We gotta get that down to Bataan.

He says, "Tomorrow morning." We had our last meal—cleaned everything up. We had our last bacon and eggs for the next three and a half years.

He gently holds forth an old photo: men in baseball uniforms at Clark Field. He points to each man as he tells of him.

We had a ball club there. We played in Manila every weekend. Filipino teams, American teams, one Jap team. I pitched ball—I had a pretty good arm. At first base we had Max and O'Connell, they used to alternate. Both those men died at Cabanatuan. At second base was Andy Olds from Milwaukee. He was a Polack, a lovable guy. Andy made it back and he died of a heart attack shortly after he returned. At shortstop we had Armando Viselli. He was from Connecticut. Armando died in a reconnaissance flight over Lamon Bay on the twenty-second of December, 1941. At third base was Cabbage Clan, a Pennsylvania Dutchman—we called him Cabbage. He died when his ship was torpedoed off Mindanao. Torpedoed by a U.S. Navy submarine. We had two catchers. We had Beck. He was hit on the first day the Japanese bombed at Clark Field and his leg was badly mangled. He was shipped out on a hospital ship, and I don't know what happened to him. The other catcher was Dumas. He was from Massachusetts. Dumas was killed on the first day at Iba.

I'm the only one left out of the whole infield, the only one that came back. That's why I treasure that picture.

"December 8, 1941"

Itabashi Kōshū, Yoshida Toshio, and Noda Mitsuharu

In an interview with historians Haruko Taya Cook and Theodore F. Cook from *Japan at War,* three former members of the Japanese armed forces offer different perspectives on the Pearl Harbor attacks—part of the first oral history to capture the Japanese experience of World War II.

ITABASHI KŌSHŪ

He entered the naval academy in late 1944. The war ended before he could graduate. "I was there only ten months, but the impression it made on me was very powerful. Were I young and able to live my life over again, I would still want to go. That kind of education—rigid discipline—is no longer available anywhere in the world. Everything was in order. You acted flat-out, with all your power, every day for one goal. I was full of ardor to abandon my life for the sake of the nation."

Today, he is the Head Priest at Daijōji temple of the Sōdōshū sect of Zen Buddhism, located on the outskirts of Kanazawa City. He wears the full paraphernalia of his office. A heavy rain beats down on the roofs of the enormous temple. Despite the summer season, the dampness is carried in on a chill breeze from the moss gardens below.

14

I was in the second year of middle school that day, Pearl Harbor Day. "Well, we really did it!" I thought. The sound of the announcement on the radio still reverberates in my ears. [*He hums a few bars from "The Battleship March," the unofficial navy anthem played on the radio to set the tone for victory announcements.*] "News special, News special," high-pitched and rapid. "Beginning this morning before dawn, war has been joined with the Americans and British." I felt as if my blood boiled and my flesh quivered. The whole nation bubbled over, excited and inspired. "We really did it! Incredible! Wonderful!" That's the way it felt then.

I was brought up in a time when nobody criticized Japan. The war started for me, in the brain of this middle-school student, as something that should happen, something that was natural. Every day, we sent warriors off with cheers of *"Banzai! Banzai!"* War was going on in China. "Withdraw your forces," America ordered Japan. If a prime minister with foresight had ordered a withdrawal, he probably would have been assassinated. Even I knew that withdrawal was impossible! There was the ABCD encirclement—the Americans, British, Chinese, and Dutch. They wouldn't give us a drop of oil.

The Japanese had to take a chance. That was the psychological situation in which we found ourselves. If you bully a person, you should give him room to flee. There is a Japanese proverb that says, "A cornered mouse will bite a cat." America is evil, Britain is wrong, we thought. We didn't know why they were encircling us. In Japan, nobody was calculating whether we would win or not. We simply hit out. Our blood was hot! We fought. Until the very end, no one considered the possibility that Japan could lose. We were like Sergeant Yokoi and Lieutenant Onoda—the men who emerged from the jungles, one in Guam, the other in the Philippines, in the 1970s—who couldn't imagine Japan had been defeated. That's the way the whole country felt. Today's youth can't conceive of such feelings.

I was at the First Middle School in Sendai, the best school in Miyagi prefecture. I never really thought about becoming a military man. I was thinking about being a doctor. But the whole nation was at war, everyone was for the war. You don't feel that you want to preserve your own life in such an atmosphere. I guess I was simple-minded, but I thought if you have to go into the military anyway, better to go someplace good. I didn't think I'd make it, but the naval academy was smart, attractive. I took the entrance exams in my fifth year of middle school. Until then, only two hundred or three hundred were taken from the whole nation each year, but in our time, two or three thousand were admitted. It was as if they were using a bucket to scoop us up.

There was no sense that you personally might be hit by a bullet. You fought for the sake of the nation, for the sake of justice, whenever or wherever the Imperial Standard led. We didn't even think of the pain of being blown to pieces. The objective of war is always these things. No wars have ever been fought for any other reasons. "For the sake of His Imperial Highness" seemed to embody everything—nation, history, race, and peace. That's why it served to inflame passions and cause everyone to seethe with fervor. For Japan, that was a sacred war. Japan claimed it would unite the eight corners of the world under one roof. If Japan had declared it was fighting only to add territory, I don't believe we ever could have gone as far as Borneo.

YOSHIDA TOSHIO

Tōgō Jinja, the Shintō shrine dedicated to Admiral Tōgō Heihachirō, naval hero of the Russo-Japanese War, is a green refuge at the end of a warren of trendy Tokyo back-street hangouts for young Japanese at Harajuku. Behind the shrine is the Suikōkai, the former navy officers' club. Today, officers of the Maritime Self-Defense Force are numbered among its members along with former Imperial Navy officers. Inside, a large painting of the super battleship Yamato *hangs near the entryway. By the receptionist's window is a small stand selling replicas of the painting, naval hats, nautical books, and models of Tōgō's flagship* Mikasa.*

"My father was in the navy. I was crazy about battleships as a kid and was raised in Sasebo, the great naval base. So I ended up an officer without really thinking much about it." He wears a jacket the color of young leaves, and dark green trousers. He exudes scholarliness and certainly looks as if he could have written his thirty books. As we talk, he sometimes nods to other graduates of the Imperial Naval Academy passing through the lobby.

"The Imperial Japanese Army and Navy have opened hostilities with the United States and England in the Western Pacific." I was on my way to my office at the Navy Ministry when I heard that announcement. That was how I learned of war for the first time. I, a full lieutenant in the Intelligence Department, Navy General Staff, assigned to the English Section, didn't even know they were planning it. I got off the train at Shimbashi Station. From a restaurant called the Shimbashitei, a radio was blaring the news. I felt like someone had poured cold water on my head.

I knew Japan shouldn't fight a war. I looked at Japan like an outsider. A chill cut right through me. I can feel it now. I ran to the Navy Ministry. Those who had known about Pearl Harbor were all smiles. The people in my section didn't know anything.

Every time I remember that day I am seized with the same feeling of disappointment. In the next couple of days, information about the attack on Pearl Harbor, that afternoon of December 8, came pouring in. Soon everyone knew. "Victory, victory!" Things became raucous with the news. But people like me thought from the beginning that Japan would be completely defeated. I was stunned by our success. Those in the Operations Section told us, "*We* planned this!" They were swaggering up and down the halls, swinging their shoulders. Full of pride.

I was supposed to be an insider. I was in a section which had to have a critical mode of thinking, which had to try to look into the future. For about seven months just prior to the outbreak of the war

I had been in Indonesia, in Surabaja and Batavia, trying to purchase oil. Japan had been cut off by America, so we were trying to get some petroleum from the Dutch East Indies. But Japan's authorities failed in "risk management." You can say that just by looking at that time with what passes for common sense today. The leaders looked only at their pluses and paid no attention to minuses. When looking at weapons systems, they only measured offensive capabilities, not defensive requirements. They held that if you attack, the path of opportunity will open up naturally. If you try to defend yourself, you will lose. "Advance, advance" therefore became the only objective. But what would happen when you advanced? What situations would arise? These things were not in their minds. It was almost a philosophy. Manage risks to prevent a collision between countries? Protect your interests by preventing risks? That was not something they cared about. As in *bushidō*, whether you lived or died was not crucial. Individual autonomy or independence? *Not* important.

Our stock of petroleum was kept completely under wraps. It was an absolute secret. Where we obtained oil, how much, and at what price, were also kept Top Secret. The section that had that data was the Fuel Section in the Navy Ministry. We on the Navy General Staff couldn't get that data. They just told us to go to the East Indies and buy oil. I was part of a delegation led by Yoshizawa Ken'ichi, an envoy from the Foreign Ministry. There were five or six from the Foreign Ministry and attachés with staffs from the army and navy. I was the bottom-most member of our naval group of four. The attachés each had residences in the capital of Batavia, so from time to time we'd get together there and talk, and once in a while we all met together at the consulate general in Batavia. But I hardly knew anything about how events were moving. It was just "Hey, Yoshida, do this," or "Take care of that, Lieutenant."

There wasn't any chance at all that the Dutch governor general of the East Indies was going to agree to sell us oil after all these negotiations. The war in Europe had already begun. If the Dutch sold petroleum to Japan, the American embargo on oil sales to Japan would have become meaningless, so the American consul general was right on top of events, making sure they didn't. But I guess even we who were there didn't fully realize that at the time. "Somehow things will work out for Japan"—that's what we thought. That was because Japan saw itself as so strong. It was more over-confidence than self-confidence: "If we go to Indonesia, everyone will tremble in fear and awe and bow down before us. All we have to do is say 'This is necessary for Japan. Moreover, this will make you happy, too.'" We tried to cover our desires with talk of the Greater East Asia Co-Prosperity Sphere.

We had plenty of intelligence information. I got information from the Foreign Ministry, from newspapers, and we received telegrams. People brought back information from many places. We had lots of files. But nobody looked at them. We didn't have much of a staff. The navy didn't spend money on intelligence. Nobody really looked into these things. I wonder why that was the case? Everybody there was a graduate of Etajima, the naval academy. These men were considered qualified to be vice admirals or full admirals. They had all made their way to the Center—as we called the heart of the navy—since they'd finished at the top of their classes at the academy, taken the exams for the naval staff college, passed, and been there for two years. Everybody said these were the most "excellent" officers in the Imperial Navy. I've often wondered since what that word *excellence* meant to them.

NODA MITSUHARU

While the majority of the warships of the Imperial Japanese Navy were steaming toward their battle stations, Admiral Yamamoto Isoroku, Commander-in-Chief of the Combined Fleet, was aboard his flagship, the battleship Nagato, *riding at anchor in Japan's Inland Sea, preparing to give the final order that would commit Japan to war and the navy to the attack on Pearl Harbor.*

Present at the beginning, Noda Mitsuharu was a sailor during the war. He ended up ashore on the island of Saipan and took part in the

*Japanese garrison's final "banzai" charge July 7, 1944. Wounded, he was
one of the few survivors. When he returned home after the war, his grave-
stone had already been erected.*

I was assigned to the Headquarters Combined Fleet as a scribe first
class, a clerk in the paymaster's branch of the navy in April 1941.
I don't know why I was assigned to headquarters, except that my
record at naval training school was good. When I graduated in June
1939, I was sent around the world, or at least half of it, on a training
cruise. When we got to Honolulu they didn't let us into Pearl Harbor, but we did go ashore for a one-day "home stay." The crew of the
ship was taken care of by the various Japanese prefectural associa-
tions on Oahu. I'm from Ibaragi, which unfortunately had no group,
so the one from neighboring Fukushima prefecture took care of me.

That day, the daughter of the host family came to meet me in a
car! She was a high-school graduate working at the Dole pineapple
factory, like her father and her elder brother. What surprised me
most when I got to her house was that there were two other cars!
That was astounding. Just laborers at a pineapple factory—not noble
offspring of immigrant barons—but each had his own automobile!
What a grand country, I thought! In those days, in my hometown
of Mito there was only one taxi company with about ten vehicles.
Town hall and the police station each had a few more, and maybe
one or two families in the whole city had private cars. The roads we
took on Oahu were all paved. In Mito there was only a single hard-
top road. When the family took me back to my ship, they dropped
off cases of Dole pineapple cans for us sailors to take with us.

December 8, 1941, I was serving aboard the battleship *Nagato*,
flagship of Admiral Yamamoto Isoroku. We were still in the Inland
Sea, in touch with the whole fleet by wireless. Orders and commands
to the fleets at sea were all in special codes. If it was *"Niitakayama
nobore"* [Climb Mount Niitaka], it meant war with America was going to begin and the attack on Hawaii should proceed. There were
all kinds of four-digit numbers with special meanings listed on a

mimeographed sheet, so that if they were sent by telegraph the officers would know their meanings. We scribes were the ones who made up those lists, duplicated them, and then distributed them.

That day was a very special one for us. We were authorized to purchase saké at the canteen. In the navy, on special days like the Emperor's Birthday, we used to have a special feast, with every sailor receiving fish and celebratory red rice, but that day, with fighting still going on, we didn't have the food. Telegrams of celebration and congratulations poured in from the entire nation addressed to Admiral Yamamoto Isoroku personally. Letters and encouraging postcards came to the *Nagato* by the sack. I took care of them, opening every letter and handing them over to the admiral personally. He ordered me to have extra-large name cards made up bearing the inscription: "Combined Fleet Commander-in-Chief Yamamoto Isoroku." On each, he wrote, in his own brush hand, "I swear I shall conduct further strenuous efforts and shall not rest on this small success in beginning the war." His handwriting was truly exquisite.

Even when the chief of staff and the other senior officers had retired to their cabins, the Commander of the Combined Fleet's office light still burned. I wondered what he was doing, until I realized he was still writing those responses. As long as the admiral was up, we sailors couldn't go to bed! After December 8, I'm sure he wrote hundreds—no, thousands—of letters. I respected him greatly for this. I put them into envelopes after affixing the admiral's official seal.

Yamamoto Isoroku had been naval attaché to Washington when he was still a captain. He himself wrote how foolish it would be to fight a war against America, particularly after he saw the automobile plants in Detroit and the oilfields of Texas. I served him up close. He loved gambling, cards in particular. He sometimes lost his whole uniform at the table, as the other officers bet for saké. Yamamoto loved *shōgi*—Japanese chess—and he played that constantly. We nicknamed one officer on his staff "the Staff Officer for Chess" because it seemed he was there far more due to his ability to play *shōgi* than for knowledge of logistics, his official assignment.

The admiral also loved women. He was famous for his geisha lover from Shimbashi. Everybody knew about it. We knew her, too. When the *Nagato* was anchored in Yokosuka, she and her friends all came aboard the battleship. A launch was sent to convey them to the ship and the ship's captain went to the gangway to meet them. The ship's band played popular folk dances. If the army had ever seen that, it would have caused quite an incident! Yamamoto was really a worldly man, flexible, and approachable.

I know these things, really. I knew him, his personality, well. That "sneak attack" was not his intention. We had a special liaison staff officer, Fujii Shigeru, responsible only to the Combined Fleet staff. When they emerged from the operations room after drafting that final order for the general offensive across the Pacific, I witnessed Yamamoto confirming once again: "Without fail, the Americans have been given notice, have they not?" I saw that with my own eyes. This was not supposed to be a sneak attack. The proof of that is the special liaison officer. He was there to keep us in contact with Imperial General Headquarters and the Foreign Ministry. The Americans were supposed to get our note just before the attack.

After the successful attack on Pearl Harbor, we sailors talked about the opportunities we might get. My dream was to go to San Francisco, and there head up the accounting department in the garrison unit after the occupation. All of us in the navy dreamed of going to America. I don't think anybody wanted to go to China.

"Austin, Texas, December 9, 1941"

Joe Jirosik

The day after the Pearl Harbor attacks, Alan Lomax—noted folklorist and then-head of the Library of Congress' Archive of American Folk Song—arranged for fieldworkers across the United States to record "man on the street" interviews, to capture ordinary Americans' responses to the momentous turn of events. Here, John Henry Faulk, a folklorist and storyteller who went on to become a popular radio and television entertainer after the war, speaks with Joe Jirosik of Austin, Texas.

AUSTIN, TEXAS

John Henry Faulk: Mr. Jirosik, what do you think about Japan's action last Sunday?

Joe Jirosik: I think they were all wrong.

Well, for what reason? Do you think it was any justification whatever on the part of Japan in making that attack?

I don't think there's any.

What do you think the United States should have done then?

Declare war on them.

In other words, you're behind Roosevelt's resolution?

Hundred percent.

Well, that's good. Do you think that all America has fallen, I mean all of your associates have fallen, in pretty well behind him?

As far as I can see, all of them.

Do you hear much talk around your job? You're a carpenter, aren't you?

Yes.

A finisher.

There is right smart talk (?)

What seems to be the general opinion amongst the carpenters' union, then?

Well, they all about like me. They think it's right for the United States to declare war on them.

Mm, hmm [affirmative]. Do they seem to have any opinion as to who's going to win and who's going to lose?

Well, some of them seems to think that won't last long, but I'm of a different opinion. I think it's going to last quite a while.

How come?

Well, because the United States is going to first have to corner it.

[*Laughs*].

Just like a dog catching a rabbit, you've got to catch him before you can kill him.

That's right. It's going to be some problem catching out there in the Pacific Ocean. ???

That's right.

Do you think maybe Germany had any hand in this?

I believe Hitler had a direct contact in it.

He's the one that instigated it?

I believe that's right.

What do you think about Russia's part in it?

Well, I don't think Russia's got anything to do with it.

I mean though, do you think Russia's going to give us a hand? Do you think she's going to support us or she's going to . . .

Well, to be honest with you, I wouldn't trust them too far.

Wouldn't trust Russia?

Not too far.

Well, why do you reckon Japan wanted to do such a cruel thing as to attack the United States?

[*Pause.*] Listening to Hitler, that's my opinion.

In other words, it wasn't their own deciding?

Not totally.

I don't believe that . . . what do you think about Japan's preparation? Do you think—I'd like you to kind of summarize that. By that, I mean, how is Japan—is Japan prepared for such a war as this, do you think?

I don't think they are prepared. They might think they are, but I don't think they'll last over two years.

You mean they'll collapse then economically?

I believe they will.

Well, what about the United States then? How well prepared is she?

Well, I believe she is as well prepared as Japan and she can prepare faster now than Japan can.

What do you think the labor ought to do about this? You know labor has been, in the opinion of some people, getting kind of a raw deal. And they're fixing to get a pretty raw deal at least, at least before the war was declared.

Well, that's my opinion. I think they didn't. I don't believe in strikes during this . . .

Emergency.

This emergency, but at the same time, I don't believe in the capitalists tromping on the laboring man.

Well, I like that. I like that, I like that opinion all right and I think that—do you think that labor is going to come out though ahead after this war? Do you think that, in other words, her rights will be protected? The labor man's rights will be protected properly?

I believe they will.

Well, how about Roosevelt, is he a friend or not to labor?

He's a laboring man's friend, at least that's the way I take him.

What about Mr. O'Daniels, senator from Texas, and Tom Connally?

Well, I don't think very much of Senator O'Daniels.

He's the one that's gotten bad with the labor here in Texas some time ago.

Well, I think very little of him and I'd rather not even discuss him. [*Interviewer laughs.*] That's right.

Well, that's good. A minute ago you said you thought that all your fellow workers out there on jobs—where about you working?

Working on the music hall in the University of Texas.

They're all in behind the president. Have you heard anybody dissent? Have you heard anybody that's not with the United States ???

I haven't heard a soul. Not a one.

In other words, labor got right in behind Mr. Roosevelt when he declared war.

I believe the labor is a hundred percent behind him.

Here in Austin anyhow.

Yeah.

Well, that's interesting because goodness knows he'll need that support. Everybody needs the labor support [for] this country to go on. How about South Americans? What do you think they're going to do? What about South American countries?

Well, to tell you the truth, I don't know much about this.

Think they'll be any help?

Well, yes, they'll be some help. No doubt about that.

Might give a hand in [helping us] get on our feet [laughs] then while we're trying to catch the Japanese. How about Japan's preparation, do you think they're pretty well-prepared?

I believe they're prepared to last two years.

I mean you think they've been preparing for this very thing?

Oh yes. All this scrap iron they bought from the United States. That's all went in the war machinery.

Do you reckon the people that sold them that scrap iron knew about it? What do you think the laboring man thinks about that?

Well, I guess the laboring man is of the same opinion I am.

Sure you—

Yes, it was the capitalists that sold this stuff to them, they knew what they was using it for. But that wasn't a question at that time, it was money, greed for money.

Mm hmm [affirmative]. ??? What about the oil that was sent to them? Do you have any opinion?

Well, I believe they knew that they were storing up for the very purpose.

Last ship back on to the United States and bomb us.

That's it.

I wouldn't be surprised if that's not a very sound opinion, Mr. Jirosik.

That's exactly what I believe.

Part II

The War in Europe

From September 1939, when Hitler's armies invaded Poland, to the final Allied defeat of Germany in May of 1945, every European country—citizens and soldiers alike—was swept up in the total war brought on by the Nazi regime. The fighting itself claimed millions of lives, as German "lightning war" or *blitzkrieg* offensives pressed in nearly every direction. Victory for Hitler's armies came swiftly: only the fierce opposition of the Soviet Red Army in the east and Great Britain's Royal Air Force (RAF) in the west managed to contain Germany's advances.

But the long periods of occupation—of Poland, France, the Ukraine, and elsewhere—were equally a defining experience of World War II for untold millions of civilians. Under the new Nazi overlords, civilian populations were ruthlessly oppressed and exploited, many of them as slave laborers forced to support the German war effort. Resistance movements, in France, Italy, Greece, the Balkans and elsewhere, were met with vicious reprisals.

Above all, under Hitler's "Final Solution," over six million European Jews, along with Roma, homosexuals, and communists, among others, were systematically murdered in the Nazi concentration camps, and in a campaign of mass slaughter in Eastern Europe.

Any account of this era must also grapple with the

destruction visited on civilians by urban aerial bombing on the part of both Germany and the Allies. In the early years of the war, German air attacks on Great Britain resulted in over 60,000 casualties; Allied saturation bombing of Germany's civilian centers—including the city of Dresden, which was completely flattened by fire-bombing in February 1945—killed an estimated 600,000 people in the final years of the war.

"War"

Eric Hobsbawm

One of the most distinguished and prolific historians of our time, Eric Hobsbawm was a student at the University of Cambridge when World War II broke out. This excerpt from Hobsbawm's memoir *Interesting Times* offers a fascinating account of life on the British home front during the war.

I

I arrived back in England just in time for the war to start. We had expected it. We, or at least I, had even feared it, though no longer in 1939. This time we knew we were already in it. Within a minute of the prime minister's old, dry voice declaring war, we had heard the wavy sound of the sirens, which to this day brings back the memory of nocturnal bombs to any human being who lived through the Second World War in cities. We were even surrounded by the visible landscape of aerial warfare, the corrugated iron of shelters, the barrage balloons tethered like herds of silver cows in the sky. It was too late to be afraid. But what the outbreak of war meant for most young men of my generation was a sudden suspension of the future. For a few weeks or months we floated between the plans and prospects of our pre-war lives and an unknown destiny in uniform. For the moment life had to be provisional, or even improvised. None more so than my own.

Until my return to England I had not really come to terms with the implications of the family's emigration. I now discovered myself not only without a known future for an unpredictable period, but also without a clearly discernible present, unanchored and alone. The family home was gone, and so was the family. Outside Cambridge I had nowhere in particular to go, though I would not be short of comrades and friends to put me up, and I was always welcomed in the only available household of London relatives, the ever-reliable Uncle Harry's. I had no girlfriend. In fact, for the next three years, when I came to London I lived a nomadic sort of existence sleeping in spare beds or on the floors of various flats in Belsize Park, Bloomsbury or Kilburn. From the moment I got called up, my only permanent base was in a few crates of books, papers and other belongings which the head porter of King's allowed me to store in a shed. I packed them after my call-up. I thought of them reemerging after the war, with luck, like a Rip van Winkle whose life had stopped in 1939 and who now had to get used to a new world. What world?

The war had begun to empty Cambridge. As the former staff of *Granta* had already dispersed, I asked the printers to close the journal down for the duration, thus formally burying an essential component of pre-war Cambridge. Research on my proposed topic of French North Africa was now pointless, though I went through the motions, background reading, hitchhiking to the British Museum when necessary and when the snowdrifts of an unusually freezing winter made it possible.

What is more, since the line-change of the autumn of 1939, it was not the war we had expected, in the cause for which the Party had prepared us. Moscow reversed the line which the Comintern and all European Parties had pursued since 1935 and had continued to pursue after the outbreak of war, until the message from

Moscow came through. Harry Pollitt's refusal to accept the change demonstrated that the leadership of the British Party was openly split on the issue. Moreover, the line that the war had ceased to be anti-fascist in any sense, and that Britain and France were as bad as Nazi Germany, made neither emotional nor intellectual sense. We accepted the new line, of course. Was it not the essence of "democratic centralism" to stop arguing once a decision had been reached, whether or not you were personally in agreement? And the highest decision had obviously been taken. Unlike the crisis of 1956 most Party members—even the student intellectuals—seemed unshaken by the Moscow decision, though several drifted out in the next two years. I am unable to remember or to reconstruct what I thought at the time, but a diary I kept for the first few months of my army service in 1940 makes it clear that I had no reservations about the new line. Fortunately the phoney war, the behaviour of the French government, which immediately banned the Communist Party, and the behaviour of both French and British governments after the outbreak of the Soviets' winter war against Finland made it a lot easier for us to swallow the line that the western powers as imperialists were, if anything, more interested in defeating communism than in fighting Hitler. I remember arguing this point, walking on the lawn in the Provost's garden in King's with a sympathetic sceptic, the mathematical economist David Champernowne. After all, while all seemed quiet, if not somnolent, on the western front, the only plans of the British government for action envisaged sending western troops across Scandinavia to help the Finns. Indeed, one of the comrades, the enthusiasic public school boy and boxing half-blue J. O. N. ("Mouse") Vickers—he actually looked more like a large weasel than a mouse, thin, quick and mobile—was due to be sent there with his unit when the Russo-Finnish war ended. For communist intellectuals Finland was a lifeline. I wrote a pamphlet on the subject at the time with Raymond Williams, the future writer, critic and guru of the left, then a new, militant and obviously high-flying recruit to the student Party. Alas, it has been lost in the course of the alarums and excursions of the century. I have been unable to re-discover a copy. And then, in February 1940, I was at last called up.

The best way of summing up my personal experience of the Second World War is to say that it took six and a half years out of my life, six of them in the British army. I had neither a "good war" nor a "bad war," but an empty war. I did nothing of significance in it, and was not asked to. Those were the least satisfactory years in my life.

Although I was clearly not the military type, and still less a potential commander of men, the main reason why I wasted my country's time and my own during most of my twenties was almost certainly political. I had, after all, some qualifications relevant to a war against Nazi Germany; not least a native knowledge of German. Moreover, as a rather bright history student at King's, whose intelligence veterans of the First World War were given the responsibility of recruiting for the future staff of Bletchley, and which sent seventeen of its dons there, it is inconceivable that my name would not have crossed the mind of one of these. It is true that I lacked at least one conventionally accepted qualification for intelligence work, namely doing the *Times* crossword puzzle. As a central European I had never grown up with it, nor did it interest me. It is also true that I did not rate highly on the other traditional qualification, the one that had got my uncle Sidney into codebreaking in the First World War, namely chess. I was an enthusiastic but very far from distinguished player. Still, had I not been quite so public and prominent a bolshevik as an undergraduate, I rather think that I would not simply have been left in Cambridge to await the decisions of the East Anglian call-up authorities.

On the other hand, the official view that someone of such obvious and recent continental provenance and background could not, in spite of his and his father's passports, be a 100 percent *real* Englishman, may well have played some part. (Such a sentiment was far from uncommon in the Cambridge of the 1930s and was shared perhaps by my supervisors.) After all, plenty of Party members did serve in intelligence during the war, including some who made no secret of their membership. Certainly my nomination a few weeks after call-up for what turned out to be a divisional cipher course (two officers, seven NCOs, three other ranks) was aborted for this reason. "Nothing personal, but your mother was not British," said the captain as he told me to take the next train from Norwich back to Cambridge. "Of course you're against the system now, but naturally there's always a bit of sympathy for the country your mother belonged to. It's natural. You see that, don't you?" "Yes, sir." "I mean I have no national prejudices. It's all the same to me what the nations do, so long as they behave themselves, which the Germans aren't doing now." I agreed. He promised to recommend me for an interpreter's job. Nothing further was ever heard about it. Curiously enough, my memory completely wiped out this episode, although I recorded it at the time.

Did I already have an intelligence file when I was at Cambridge? There is no way of knowing. I had certainly acquired one by the middle of 1942, when a friendly sergeant in Field Security told me that I was supposed to be watched. It is possible that I acquired one in 1940 shortly after I was called up, for as a good communist I made arrangements to stay in contact with the Party, which meant that when in London, I met Robbie (R.W. Robson), a sallow, lined, hard-smoking working-class full-time cadre since the early 1920s, in one of those small, dusty, second-hand-looking offices up a dark staircase in WC1 or WC2, in which such people were to be found. These were very likely bugged by Security.

Whenever I acquired my file, I was clearly seen as a suspicious character, to be kept out of sensitive areas such as abroad, even after the USSR became Britain's ally and the Party devoted itself to winning the war. While the war lasted (and indeed from 2 September 1939 until my first postwar visit to Paris in 1946) I never left the soil of Great Britain—the longest unbroken period I have ever spent without crossing some sea or land frontier. Nobody after May 1940 appeared to take an interest in my languages. At one moment I got as far as an interview on the subject in what I took to be a secret service office at the top of Whitehall, but nothing came of it. Reluctantly I got used to the idea that I would have no part in Hitler's downfall.

What could the officers do who found themselves lumbered with an intellectually overqualified and practically underqualified oddball with minimal gifts for the military life? Since I could drive a car I was called up as a driver, but I did not take to the company's requisitioned 15-cwt- and 3-ton trucks, or to motorbikes, and soon became merely a pair of unskilled arms. What could be done with such a figure? I was presumably regarded as unpromotable. In the end the 560th Field Company of the Royal Engineers found a way of getting rid of me. I was recommended for transfer to the Army Education Corps, which—since this was a people's war—was being rapidly expanded. I was sent on the required course to a building behind the jail in Wakefield, taking with me—why should I still remember this so vividly?—Thomas Mann's *Lotte in Weimar*. There I discovered the enormous superiority of northern fish-and-chips to what I had hitherto been used to, and passed [the time] in the company of another historian and future vice-chancellor of London University.

My transfer came through some time later, in the early autumn of 1941, a few days after we had moved to Hay-on-Wye, on the Welsh border, near which, exactly fifty years later, I found myself buying the Breconshire cottage in which I write these lines. It may well have saved my life, for in the meantime the unit had been ordered abroad, and we already had our embarkation leave behind us. As usual, I spent it among the bombs in London. Naturally nobody told us where we were bound for, though the Middle East seemed the most likely. But the 15th East Anglian Division, including the 560th Field Company RE, did not set sail for the Middle East, but via Cape Town and Mombasa for Singapore, where they were captured by the Japanese in February 1942. Those who survived spent the next three years building the Burma railway. About a third of them did not. I never saw my mates again. Would I have survived?

Who knows. In any case, I did not find out how lucky I was until much later.

II

My army career thus falls into two sharply distinct parts. The first of these, my time with the Royal Engineers, was by far the more interesting. As might be expected, a field company of sappers was a purely working-class unit, except for its few officers. I was the only intellectual in it, indeed almost certainly the only other rank in it who habitually read the news pages of the daily newspaper before or instead of the racing pages. This unusual habit gave me my nick-name during the weeks when France collapsed: "Diplomatic Sam." For the first time in my life I found myself a member of the proletar-iat whose emancipation was to bring freedom to the world, though an uncharacteristic one. To be more precise, I found myself living in the country in which the majority of the British people spent their lives, and which had only a marginal contact with the world of the classes above them. Being called up in Cambridge dramatized the contrast, since for two or three months I lived in both worlds. After duty (i.e. mainly learning the elements of drill on the green turf of Parker's Piece) I moved from one to the other as I walked to the centre of university Cambridge from the working-class street where the military authorities had quartered me and a barber's assistant and former hotel porter from Lowestoft called Bert Thirtle, on an elderly widow, Mrs Benstead. We shared what had been the Ben-stead matrimonial bed, which was fortunately a wide one. It was not an ideal introduction to the world of the proletariat, since Thirtle lacked the social reflexes which I found so striking in my otherwise politically disappointing mates, and which explains so much about British trade unionism. Most of my mates saw themselves essen-tially as civilians who put on uniforms as their dads had done in 1914–18. They saw no special virtue in the martial life or look: civvy street was where they hoped to go back to as soon as possible. But Thirtle had always secretly dreamed of wearing a uniform, although it did not get him far with the girls (any girl was a "tart" in our jargon) he picked up in Petty Cury. His fiancée, a seventeen-year-old who worked in a kitchen, wrote him daily letters and sent parcels containing the local papers, *The Wizard*, *Comic Cuts* and American strip cartoons.

In retrospect I am amazed how powerful an instinctive sense or tradition of collective action was in a bunch of young working men, ranging from the unskilled to some apprenticed tradesmen, mostly builders, assembled in the same NAAFI canteen or games room by the accidents of conscription. This struck me less at the time than their wavering uncertainty—and indeed my own—about what we should all do at moments that called for some action, and the general sense of helplessness in the face of authority. And yet, as I read the notes of my diary, what impresses me is the familiarity with the procedures of collective action, the constant, almost intuitive, potential for militancy. They were at home in the "public sphere" of the British working class. Had not someone, during one protest, suggested that we should organize a proper meeting at The Locomotive like a real union, with a table and a bell and a glass of water?

The proletarian experience was novel in other respects. I think it is safe to say that in 1940 few Kingsmen had had occasion to operate a road drill, and I found the experience of doing so tiring but exhilarating. The Sappers were essentially a formation of workers skilled and less skilled, more from general manufacture and the building trades (for a lot of metal workers were in reserved occupations and those needed by the army went into other, more specialized corps) from many parts of Britain—the Black Country, London, Nottingham, a sprinkling from the Northeast and Scotland—but mainly from the eastern counties, since ours was essentially an East Anglian division. A few anomalous Cantab recruits found themselves in its ranks—myself, slightly older friends and acquaintances such as Ian Watt, later a distinguished professor of literature, whose work on the origins of the English novel the student Marxists were already discussing, and slightly younger ones such as the witty graphic satirist, *Granta*'s cartoonist Ronald Searle. Both returned, marked for life, from Japanese gulags. Ronald, whom I occasionally saw during our common time in the division, was already being discovered by the admirable Kaye Webb, then commissioning editor at *Lilliput*, a pocket-sized and very hip magazine founded by an emigrant Mitteleuropean, and much appreciated by our generation, who later married him. (She also took a few articles from me during and after the war, until the magazine disappeared.) Meanwhile, he became one of the most successful cartoonists of his time, thanks largely to the invention of St Trinian's, a girls' school peopled by the most appalling pupils, inspired, one understood, by the small terror-bringing Japanese of his wartime prison camps.

By and large in my days as a Sapper I lived among workers—overwhelmingly English workers—and in doing so acquired a permanent, if often exasperated, admiration for their uprightness, their distrust of bullshit, their sense of class, comradeship and mutual help. They were good people. I know that communists are supposed to believe in the virtues of the proletariat, but I was relieved to find myself doing so in practice as well as in theory.

Then Hitler invaded Norway and Denmark and the war really began. As soon as the Germans—we could hardly believe it—began to overrun the Low Countries, the 560th Field Company had something real to do. For anything up to fourteen hours a day, virtually isolated from the civilian life of Norfolk which went on around us, we improvised defences for East Anglia against a potential invasion. We shifted sandbags, revetted the walls of giant anti-tank trenches round the town that were being dug ahead of us by a civilian excavator, inexperienced, clumsy and above all utterly unconvinced that the ditch would stop any tanks, especially since there were no anti-tank guns or anything else, but our main work was mine-laying and attaching explosive charges to bridges, ready to blow them in case of need. As spring turned into summer, we had absolutely miraculous weather for this work. I can still feel the wonderful elation of climbing (a bit nervously) up the sides of the girders of the great bridge across Breydon Water, just outside Great Yarmouth, to work on the high span between blue sky and salt water, the (deceptive) sense of power that comes from the routine handling of explosives, fuses and detonators. I can remember the holiday idleness of lazing in small detachments of three or four posted to some remote lock or bridge with a tent and 200 lb of explosives, waiting for the invaders. What would we have done, had they come? We were raw, without military experience or even arms: in addition to our clumsy Lee-Enfield rifles the company had exactly six Lewis guns with which to keep enemy aircraft at bay. We would not have made an impressive first line of defence against the Wehrmacht.

The lads' reaction to the German invasion of Denmark and Norway was a confident indignation. Gloom, depression and even defeatism had been the mood by the time they invaded the Low Countries, in the middle of the political crisis that finally threw out Neville Chamberlain. "What kind of English soldiers are you?" said the company Irishman, Mick Flanigan, surrounded by barrack-room talk about how much better the German army obviously was than ours, and what things might be like under a German government. Chamberlain's fall cheered them up again, for he had obviously been a major cause of the general depression. Patently the new Churchill government was welcomed by our company. (I noted at the time how strange it was that the heroes of the British workers were Churchill, Duff Cooper and Eden, "aristocrats, not even demagogues.")

Discouragement grew again in the next few weeks of backbreaking physical work and virtually complete isolation in our camps. Whatever the effect on civilians of Churchill's famous radio addresses, the one on "We shall fight on the beaches," including presumably those of Norfolk, was given at a time when we could not have heard it. Indeed, at the time I described the mood of the lads as "terrible." We were working all hours of day and night, virtually confined to barracks and workplace ("our biggest entertainment," I wrote, "is going to have the weekly shower"), without explanation, recognition or appreciation and, above all, ordered about, anonymous and inferior. Middle-class recruits dreamed of getting to the front where "they'd forget about blanco and polishing cap-badges and we'd all be in it together." Most of my mates simply concluded: "This is no life for a human being. If the war finishes, OK. I want to get out of this and back into civvy street." Did they mean it? Plainly they did not, as their reaction to the fall of France on 17 June was witness.

I heard the news on a trip to a nearby pub from our post by the small bridge we were guarding on the table-flat road to Great Yarmouth. None of us had any doubt about what it meant. Britain was now alone. Let me transcribe what I wrote a few hours later in my diary:

> "Who was responsible?" Half an hour after the radio announcement the English are already asking the question. In the pub where I heard the news, in the car that gave me a lift back to the bridge, in the tent with the two mates. Only one answer: it was old Chamberlain. The unanimous view: whoever is guilty must pay for it somehow. It's something, even if it should turn out to be just a passing impulse . . .
>
> A car stops at our bridge. I'd guess the driver, specs and false teeth, is a commercial traveller. "Have you heard the news on the radio?" I say, "Yes, we have." "Bad, bad," says the man shaking his head. "Bloody bad, terrible." Then he drives on. We call after him, "Thanks, anyroad" and go back to lying on the bank in the long grass and talking things over, slowly and in dismay.
>
> The other two cannot believe it.

Not only could my mates not grasp what had happened. They could neither take in nor even imagine that this might mean the end of the war or making peace with Hitler. (Actually, reading my own immediate reactions to the fall of France, and in spite of the official Party line since September 1939, neither could I. A victory for Hitler was not what we had had in mind.) They could envisage defeat at the end of a fighting war—nothing was easier in June 1940. It was also clear to anyone near the East Anglian coast that, if Hitler invaded, as everyone expected him to, there was nothing much to stop him. What they could not envisage was not going on with the war, even though it was plain to anyone with a sense of political realities (even one reduced to an occasional sight of the *Daily Telegraph* on the East Anglian marsh), that Britain's situation was desperate. This feeling that Britain was not defeated yet, that it was *natural* to go on with the war, was what Winston Churchill put into words for them, though with a tone of heroic defiance which, pretty certainly, none of my mates felt. He spoke for a British people of ordinary folk, such as those of the 560th Field Company, who (unlike many of the better-informed) simply could not imagine that Britain might give up.

As we now know, in the words of Hitler's Chief of General Staff, General Halder, "the Führer is greatly puzzled by England's persistent unwillingness to make peace," since he believed himself to be offering "reasonable" terms. At this point he saw no advantage in invading and occupying Britain which (to quote Halder again) "would not be of any benefit to Germany. German blood would be shed to accomplish something that would benefit only Japan, the United States and others." In effect, Hitler offered to let Britain keep her empire as what Churchill, writing to Roosevelt, correctly described as "a vassal state of the Hitler empire." In the 1990s a school of young Conservative historians argued that Britain should have accepted these terms. If Lord Halifax and the powerful peace party in the 1940 Conservative Party had prevailed it is not impossible— indeed, it is not unlikely—that the bulk of Britons would have gone along with them, as the bulk of Frenchmen went along with Marshal Pétain. Yet nobody who now remembers that extraordinary moment in our history could believe that the defeatists had a real chance of prevailing. They were seen not as the peace-bringers but as the "guilty men" who had brought the country to this pass. Confident in this massive popular backing, Churchill and the Labour ministers were able to hold their own.

We knew none of this—neither of the peace party in Churchill's government (though the left suspected there was one), nor of Hitler's offers and hesitations. Luckily in August 1940 Hitler began the mass aerial attack on Britain, which became the nightly bombing of London in early September. From being a people that went on with the war because we could not think of anything else to do, we became a people conscious of our own heroism. All of us, even the ones not directly affected, could identify with the men and women who continued with everyday life under the bombs. We would not have put it in Churchill's bombastic terms ourselves ("This was their finest hour"), but there was considerable satisfaction in standing up to Hitler alone.

But how were we to go on? There was not the slightest chance of returning to the continent within the foreseeable future, let alone winning the war. Between the Battle of Britain and the time the East Anglian division was sent to its doom, we moved across vast stretches of Britain, from Norfolk to Perthshire, from the Scottish Borders to the Welsh Marches, but during this entire period nothing that the 560th Field Company did appeared to its members to have any bearing on fighting the war against Germany, except the time in 1941 when we found ourselves stationed on Merseyside during the great German raids on Liverpool and consequently mobilized to clear up among the ruins on the mornings after. (A picture of myself in a tin hat being fed tea at a Liverpool street canteen by friendly ladies may well be my first appearance in a newspaper.) On the other hand, there was no way in which Hitler could get Britain out of the war either. Nor could he simply leave things as they were. In fact, as we now know, the failure to defeat Britain in the west decided him to turn east against the Soviet Union and, in doing so, to make the war winnable again for Britain.

At all events, from the summer of 1940 one thing was clear even to Party members as passionate and devoted as myself: in the army nobody would listen to the official Party line against the war. It made increasingly little sense and, from the moment when the Germans swept into the Balkans in the spring of 1941, it was clear to me (and indeed even to most in the Party leadership) that it made no sense at all. We now know that Stalin became the chief victim of its unrealism, stubbornly and systematically *refusing* to accept the accumulation of detailed and utterly reliable evidence of Hitler's plan to attack the USSR, even after the Germans had crossed its borders. The probability of Hitler's attack on Russia had been so great that even the British Party appears to have expected it by early June 1941, worried only about Winston Churchill's reaction to it.

Both communists and non-communists, therefore, felt the same sense of relief and hope when Hitler invaded the USSR on 22 June 1941. In what was essentially a working-class unit like our company, there was more than relief. Generations brought up during the Cold War are not aware how widely British workers and even Labour leaders before the war had thought of Soviet Russia as in some sense "a workers' state," as well as the one great power committed to opposing fascism, as it were *ex officio*. And, of course, everybody knew that its support against Hitler was indispensable. There was no shortage of deeply hostile observers and critics, but until the Cold War the dominant image of the USSR in the British labour movement was not that of totalitarianism, mass terror and the gulag. So in June 1941 Party members, sighing with relief, returned to what they had been saying before the war, and rejoined the masses of ordinary Britons. On my suggestion, I got a football signed by every member of the 560th starting with the company sergeant-major, and sent it to the Soviet Embassy in London for transmission to an equivalent engineers' unit in the Red Army. I think the *Daily Mirror*, already very much the forces' paper, published a photo. After 22 June 1941 communist propaganda more or less made itself.

III

However little I contributed to Hitler's downfall or to the world revolution, there was a lot more to be said for serving in the Royal Engineers than in the Army Education Corps. It is far from clear what the traditional army thought of an outfit that claimed to teach soldiers things they did not need to know as soldiers, and to discuss nonmilitary (or any) matters. It was tolerated, because its head, Colonel Archie White, was a professional soldier who had won a vc in his time and because most serving soldiers in the war were undeniably past and future civilians, whose morale required more than the inculcation of regimental loyalty and pride. The army did not like the AEC's link with the new Army Bureau of Current Affairs (ABCA), which issued regular monthly discussion pamphlets on political subjects, as like as not written by Labour sympathizers. Conservative politicians were later to hold ABCA responsible for the radicalization of the armed forces who, in 1945, massively voted Labour.

This is to overestimate the interest of the bulk of servicemen and women in specifically political literature. ABCA appealed to and aimed at the reading minorities, but did not excite the masses. If any reading-matter shaped the squaddies' politics, at all events in or within reach of the UK, it was the *Daily Mirror*, a brilliantly produced and certainly Labour-sympathizing tabloid more widely read and discussed by the troops than any other. Nor can I claim to have made any greater contribution to the political radicalization of the British army's Southern Command than to the defeat of Hitler. After June 1941 the Party line was winning the war, and this aligned communists with everyone else, though it made them more reluctant to criticize the government than less aligned and disciplined leftwingers, except on issues suggested by the USSR, such as demanding an invasion of western Europe much sooner than Roosevelt and the even more reluctant Churchill wanted. Public opinion did not need the Party to arouse passionate admiration

and enthusiasm for the Red Army and Stalin. During the war my
then father-in-law, a retired and non-political sergeant-major in the
Coldstream Guards (though a Labour voter in 1945), liked to remind visitors proudly that he looked like Vishinsky, the notorious
prosecutor in the Stalinist show trials of the 1930s.

Since the army did not quite know what to do with them, AEC
sergeant-instructors like me (the lowest rank in the Corps) found
themselves in a curious military limbo, rather like military chaplains, except without the officers' pips and the ritual occasions for
which the padre's presence was mandatory. They were distributed
in ones and twos throughout the training camps or base camps, or
attached, without any very clear function, to operational formations.
We did not really belong to the outfits that were technically responsible for our rations, quarters and pay; nobody troubled us much. We
had arms, but they were so irrelevant that, when I was finally demobilized, there was no available mechanism for handing in my rifle.
On the other hand, wherever stationed, I had no difficulty finding a
place for my typewriter and a few books. I cannot recall that anyone
in the Guards Armoured Division, to which I was attached for a
while, ever commented on the appearance of a sergeant whose dress
and bearing made no serious attempt to live up to the notoriously
exigent requirements of the Household Brigade. Nobody but an
Education sergeant would have got away with it. At least until we
went overseas, the army allowed us to live a life of semi-detachment.
I cannot remember how often I went to London from the various
places in southern England to which the AEC took me, but in the
end—and particularly after I married in the spring of 1943—I spent
practically every weekend there.

So, for practical purposes I increasingly found myself living like a
civilian weekend commuter. Indeed, there were times when even my
daily life was hard to distinguish from that of civilians, except for the
fact that I wore a uniform. Thus in my last eighteen months I lived
in Gloucester, billeted on a Mrs Edwards, an agreeable middle-class
lady, friend and supporter of past and future Labour MPs in the

area, whose sitting room contained a Matisse of medium quality which her financial adviser—evidently a good one—had persuaded her to buy for investment in 1939 for £900. In the election campaign of 1945 I even canvassed there for the Labour Party, amazed like so many others at the unexpectedly massive support I encountered on the doorsteps. I even found myself, representing the army, addressing the workforce at one of the great aircraft plants along the road from Gloucester to Cheltenham, which were the strongholds of the local CP. I concluded that I was not a natural mass orator.

Nevertheless, London was where I really lived as an adult human being. That is where I had spent all my leaves anyway, in the days of the Blitz of 1940–41, discovering on night-time walks that only a degree of desensitized fatalism ("it will only hit you if it's got your name on it") makes it possible to conduct the usual activities of life under bombardment. That was also where, since I could now get there so often, a less irregular and unpredictable private life became possible. In May 1943 I married Muriel Seaman, whom I had vaguely known as a very attractive LSE communist girl, and who was now working in the Board of Trade. This enables me to say that I was once married to one of the few literal Cockneys ("born within the sound of Bow bells"), for she was born in the Tower of London, her mother the daughter of a Beefeater (the Wardens of the Tower), her father a sergeant of the Coldstream Guards detachment detailed to guard its treasures. It also helped to clarify my postwar future. As someone married to a full-time senior civil servant, I would have to change my postwar field of research, or face leaving a wife in London while I spent a couple of years in French North Africa. After consulting my old teacher Mounia Postan, now also a temporary civil servant in London, I hit on the history of the Fabian Society, practically all of whose sources were in the metropolis. The subject turned out to be disappointing. But then, so also did my own marriage, like a number of other wartime marriages, although I did not think so at the time. Fortunately, we had no children.

I had met Muriel again through my main London friends,

Marjorie, an old flame from the LSE, and her partner, the charming economist Tedy Prager, another old LSE red, who had returned from the temporary exile (Isle of Man, Canada) to which the British government had almost automatically sent so many of the passionately anti-Nazi young Austrian and German refugees. After his Cambridge doctorate he worked in what would today be called a think-tank, PEP (Political and Economic Planning), before returning to Austria in 1945 as a loyal Party member; by then with another wife. From the point of view of his career, professional or perhaps even political, he would have done better to stay. They were among the rare couples of my student generation or age group who lived and worked permanently in wartime London—my cousin Denis Preston's ménage was another—for most of the physically fit men were in uniform, and only a few servicemen, mostly in staff and intelligence work, were based in the metropolis. On the other hand, the place was full of women one had known in student days, for the war provided far more significant jobs for women than before. By age, health and gender, one's London friends and contemporaries were thus a curiously skewed community. The men blew in and out, visitors from outside, as I was myself. The regular residents were the women, and those unfit and past military age. But there was one more constantly present scene: the foreigners, which, so far as I was concerned, meant those who operated in the German language. So it was natural that Tedy Prager should bring me into the broad ambit of the Free Austrian Movement, in which, of course, as a communist he was deeply involved.

I expect that, at a loose end and a regular visitor to London, I would sooner or later have found my way into the refugee milieu. Indeed, I had come across them from the start in the course of my military duties on Salisbury Plain, for nobody was more likely to be found in restrooms and libraries than the miscellaneous collection of musicians, former archivists, stage-managers and aspirant economists from central Europe whom Britain was employing as unskilled labourers in the Pioneer Corps. (In due course many of them were more rationally employed in the armed forces.) Although I had absolutely no emotional tie to Germany, and little enough to Austria, German had been my language, and since leaving Berlin in 1933 I had made enormous efforts not to forget it in a country where I no longer had to use it. It still remained my private language. I had written my voluminous teenage diaries in it, and even in wartime the diaries I occasionally kept. While English was my regular literary idiom, the very fact that my country refused to make any use of my bilinguality in the war against Hitler made me want to prove I could still write the language. In fact, in 1944 I became a freelance contributor to a poorly printed German exile weekly, financed by the Ministry of Information, *Die Zeitung,* for which I wrote various literary pieces. Whatever the political or propagandist object of this journal was, it failed to achieve it, and so its disappointed backers shut it down immediately [after] the war ended. The paper was bitterly opposed both by the German social-democratic and socialist exiles and by the communist émigrés. From this I infer that I cannot have consulted the Party about it, or, in other words, that I did not think of it as "political" at all. I had written out of the blue to the paper's literary editor "Peter Bratt," who turned out to be one Wolfgang von Einsiedel, a wonderfully cultured, soft-faced, homosexual relative of Bismarck and numerous Prussian generals, literary editor on the *Vossische Zeitung* before 1933. He treated me with exemplary kindness, understanding and friendship, no doubt correcting my German. We used to meet and talk in wartime Soho pubs. I lost contact with him after he moved to Munich, but perhaps this book is a suitable place to give thanks to one of the few persons in wartime outside my family and the Communist Party to whom I owe a personal debt.

The Free Austrian Movement, into which Tedy Prager brought me, was a much more serious matter, politically and culturally. Though behind the scenes it was organized by the communists, and therefore run with great efficiency, it succeeded in mobilizing the great bulk of the not very heavily politicized Austrian emigrant community (including my future father-in-law in Manchester), on the basis of a simple and powerful slogan: "Austrians are not Germans." This was a dramatic break with the tradition of the first Austrian Republic (1918–38) in which all parties, with the exception of the handful of surviving Habsburg loyalists—and since about 1936 the communists—assumed the opposite and emphasized that their country was *German* Austria, and (until Hitler) looked forward to an eventual unification with Germany. Ideologically Hitler's Anschluss in March 1938 therefore disarmed its opponents: the old socialist leader Karl Renner (who was to become the first President of the second Austrian Republic in 1945) had even welcomed it. The communists had for some time developed an interesting argument in favour of the historic and even cultural separateness of Austria from Germany, for which I was also eventually mobilized, being both a communist and an available qualified historian. (From April 1945 to the time I was demobilized in 1946 I wrote a series of historical articles along these lines in the Free Austrian journals, probably my first published historical work.) Not being Germans was a line that naturally appealed to the overwhelmingly Jewish Austrian emigrant community, which, with all its gratitude and admiration for Britain, in any case seems to have found it harder to assimilate to local society than the emigrant Germans. It also fitted in with the postwar policy of the Allies, which meant that the Free Austrian Movement—by far the best-organized section of the continental refugees—enjoyed some official respect and was largely free from the more public squabbles so typical of émigré politics. It was also unusually successful in giving the Austrian child and teenage refugees of the 1938–9 *Kindertransporte* a sense of community and future in its "Young Austria." At all events, they returned to Austria with the warmest memories of their British exile. Several of my later friends, notably the poet and translator Erich Fried and the painter Georg Eisler, came from this milieu.

Life in semi-detachment from the army was thus acceptable enough, even if hardly demanding. I had a wife, friends and a cultural scene in London, and (thanks to my cousin Denis, who was associated with a tiny periodical for intellectual and mostly left-wing aficionados, *Jazz Music*) I got to know and learn from the small community of serious jazz and blues fans in and out of London. Indeed, one of my more successful army educational enterprises was a jazz record class I organized for a so-called Young Soldiers training unit in deepest Dorset, for which I travelled regularly to Bournemouth to borrow records, and improve my own knowledge from one of them, Charles Fox. Moreover, though I was not formally organized in any Party branch, as far as I recall, there was plenty of politics to discuss, since in 1943 Moscow seemed to put the entire future of the communist movement into question. It dissolved the Communist International. In the same year the Tehran meeting between Stalin, Roosevelt and Churchill moved Stalin to announce the prospect of a continued postwar collaboration between capitalism and socialism. The Communist Party of the USA was consequently dissolved. The American communist leader Earl Browder announced that "Capitalism and Socialism have begun to find a way to peaceful coexistence and collaboration in the same world"—a proposition no communist would have maintained in public without prior clearance with Stalin—and the British CP based its plans for the future on the assumption that this is what "the Tehran line" meant. Indeed, someone at King Street—I suppose it must have been Emile Burns, the culture commissar at the time—actually asked me to prepare a memorandum for their discussions on the economic possibilities of postwar capitalist–communist development. Loyal and disciplined as we were, not all revolutionaries found these "new perspectives" easy to swallow, even when we could see why it might be sensible to dissolve the Comintern, and had no doubt that socialism was not going to come to the USA in anyone's lifetime.

And yet, not surprisingly, every day of this existence was a reminder that I was doing nothing to win the war, and that nobody would let me near any job, however modest, where my qualifications and gifts, such as they were, might have been of some use for this

purpose. The division to which I was attached prepared to go overseas, but without me. From the cliffs of the Isle of Wight I could
see what was clearly the gathering of the invasion fleet for France,
while I had nothing better to do than to play the uniformed tourist
in Queen Victoria's camp residence Osborne, and to buy a second-
hand copy of Hazlitt's *Spirit of the Age* in a bookshop. I volunteered
to go abroad, but nobody wanted to know. I was sent to Gloucester.
As far as the greatest and most decisive crisis in the history of the
modern world was concerned, I might as well not have been there.

And yet, although I did not realize it, I was to see something in-
directly of the war after all. I was posted to the Military Wing of the
City General Hospital, Gloucester, where I acted as a sort of general
welfare officer or liaison with civilian bodies offering help. It specialized in serious casualties, increasingly the battle casualties from Normandy, and especially in the treatment of severe burns. It was a place
of penicillin, blood and skin transfusions, limbs wrapped in cello-
phane and men walking around with things like sausages suspended
from their faces, dressed in the curiously strident "hospital blue" with
the red ties of military patients. It dealt with everybody, even with
wounded Germans (one officer explained to me that he had not been
a Nazi, but he had given a personal oath of loyalty to the Führer)
and Italians (one of them, in bed and reading Strinberg in an Italian translation, talked and talked and would not let me go, though
I could barely understand Italian: about Italian officers, Britain
and Italy, the future of Italy, the war, anything). We were naturally
prouder of our "Allies," whom I recorded in a fortnightly bulletin: the
Pole from Torun, who had fought in both armies, deserting from the
Germans in Normandy and back there again with the Poles after a
night in Edinburgh; and the ward's showpiece, the little Moroccan,
with his thin, high-cheeked Berber face, in bulging hospital blues
with a much-unfolded citation for exemplary bravery of "*le jeune spahi
Amor Ben Mohammed*" at Himeimat, who communicated with us
via a French Algerian, Private Colleno of the Free French.

It was a place of disaster. And yet, the most extraordinary thing about this place of blood was that in it a death surprised us. It was a place of hope, rather than tragedy. Let me quote what I wrote at the time:

> The unexpectedness of seeing people with only half a face and others rescued from burning tanks, has now passed. Occasionally someone comes in whose mutilation is a shade more gruesome, and we hold our breath when we turn to him, for fear our face might give away our shocked repulsion. We can now reflect at leisure that this is how Marsyas looked when Apollo had finished with him; or how unstable the balance of human beauty is, when the absence of a lower jaw will completely unhinge it.
>
> The reason for this callousness is that mutilation is no longer an irrevocable tragedy. Those who come here know, in general, that they will leave in the end as, approximately, human beings. It may—it will, in fact—take them months or even years. The process of completing them, a delicate living sculpture, will take dozens of operations and they will pass through stages when they will look absurd and ridiculous, which may even be worse than looking horrific. But they have hope. What faces them is no longer an eternity shut away in some home, but human life. They lie in saline baths because they have no skin, and joke with one another because they know they will get some. They walk round the ward with faces striped like zebras and pedicles dangling like sausages from their cheeks.
>
> It is only in a hospital such as this that one begins to realize the meaning of Hope.

And not only hope for the body. As the end of the war, and certain victory, drew nearer, hope for the future was in the air. Here are two news items from the bulletin I published for the Military Wing.

> I used to be in agricultural work, but my feet are gone, and I can't do it any longer. Mr Pitts asked me what I wanted to do and I said, having been a motor-mechanic in the Army, how about it? So I'm

going to a training school in Bristol . . . to polish up my i.c. en-
gines, 45/a week if I live at home, and I'm not forced to stick to the
job . . . I think this plan for setting disabled soldiers on the road is
pretty good.

And again: "The ABCA Discussion on Friday will be opened by
Sgt Owen RA of Hut 9 who will give his idea of 'How I'd set about
rebuilding.'" And Sgt Owen, a foreman bricklayer and once TUC
delegate for his union, wondered whether "any other men in Building have any ideas to bring forward." The end of the war was near,
there would be a General Election (some wards actually asked for
the voting forms before they had been distributed) and things would
be different. Who did not share this belief in 1944 and 1945, even if
the first of our worries after the end of the war was naturally when
we would get demobilized?

It was mine too. Pointless as my military service was, while the
war lasted it was both normal and necessary. I had no complaints.
Once the war was over, as far as I could see, every day in the army
was a day wasted. As the summer of 1945 turned to autumn and
then to winter, I was approaching the end of my sixth year in uniform, but the army showed no sign of wishing to get rid of me. On
the contrary. Early in 1946, to my utter astonishment, it proposed
to send me, attached to, of all things, an airborne unit, to, of all
places, Palestine. The army seemed to think being sent to fight Jews
or Arabs was a compensation for not being sent to fight Germans.

This, finally, was the straw that broke the camel's back. Communist Jews were, of course, anti-Zionists on principle. And yet,
whatever my sympathies, antipathies and loyalties, the situation of
a Jewish soldier dropped into the middle of a tripartite dispute between Jews, Arabs and the British was filled with too many compli-
cations for me. So, for the first time I pulled strings. I telephoned
Donald Beves, the Tutor at King's, saying I wanted to get out of
the army to take up my 1939 research studentship. He wrote the
necessary letters, saying how indispensable it was for me to return

to Cambridge, and they did the trick. On 8 February 1946 I handed in my uniform, though keeping a gas mask case, which turned out to be a useful shoulder bag, received my civvie clothes and fifty-six days' demobilization leave. At the age of twenty-eight and a half years, I returned to London and to human life.

"Flight"

Elisabeth Freund

Between Adolph Hitler's rise to power in 1933 and the final defeat of Germany by the Allied forces in 1945, hundreds of thousands of Europeans were forced to emigrate—many of them to the United States—for reasons of religious or political persecution. In this piece (from the book *Hilter's Exiles*), Elisabeth Freund, a German Jewish émigré, recounts her flight from Nazi Germany.

Born in Breslau, Elisabeth Freund (1898–1982) studied economics in Breslau and Berlin, where she lived in the house of her uncle, the Nobel Prize winner Fritz Haber. After the emigration of her three children, she was forced by the Nazis to work in a large laundry and in an armaments plant. She and her husband succeeded in emigrating to Cuba just before [Nazi Interior Minister Heinrich] Himmler suspended all emigration from Germany in October 1941.

We were so sure that we would now [May 1941] receive the visas for the United States, but we still have not heard anything about them. Our brothers and sisters in America write that we should inquire of the American Consul, that they had taken care of everything, that our affidavits were at the consulate and were proper and adequate. Even a bank deposit was made for us, and a certification by the shipping line was sent, stating that the tickets were already paid for. Our waiting number, which we had applied for in November 1938, should have come long ago. But it seems like a disaster; we still do not have the summons to the consulate. If we only knew why we are not making any progress! Unfortunately, at the consulate no information is given about the state of matters pertaining to emigration. We are completely at a loss. What if some day America really enters into a war with Germany—everything does seem threatening enough—and then all contacts to foreign countries are barred and we have not received our visas in time! It is simply inconceivable. Then we will not be able to see our children ever again.

It is really enough to drive one to despair. We've already done so many things in order to get away from Germany. We have filed applications for entry permits to Switzerland, Denmark, and Sweden. It was all in vain, though in all these countries we had good connections. In the spring of 1939, from an agent we obtained an entry permit for Mexico for 3000 marks. But we never received the visa, because the Mexican consulate asked us to present passports that would entitle us to return to Germany, and the German authorities did not issue such passports to Jews. Then, in August 1939 we did actually get the permit for England. But it came too late, only ten days before the outbreak of war, and in this short time we were not able to take care of all the formalities with the German authorities. In the spring of 1940 we received the entry permit for Portugal. We immediately got everything ready and applied for our passports. Then came the invasion of Holland, Belgium, and France by the German troops. A stream of refugees poured to Portugal, and the Portuguese government recalled by wire all of the issued permits. As it happened, we were lucky that we had not given up our apartment and not yet sold our furniture. It was also good that in December 1940 we had not already paid for our Panamanian visas, for we noticed that the visas offered us did not at all entitle us to land in Panama. Things can again work out for us in such a way that we will no longer be able to leave.

We are convinced that in reality America wants to help and is receiving the European refugees in the most generous manner. But they do not know there how difficult the situation is; otherwise they would permit these poor and tortured people to get there quickly, while it is still possible. They could lock them up in a camp there until the situation of every individual is clarified, and the relief committees could bear the costs for it. But we had better get away from here, and as quickly as possible; otherwise we will meet the same fate as the unfortunate people who were deported from Stettin to Poland, or as the Jews from Baden, who were sent to France and who are being held captive there in the Pyrenees.

[On June 22, 1941, Germany attacks the Soviet Union. Shortly thereafter Elisabeth Freund collapses doing forced labor at the steam press.]

I was sick for over three weeks and lay in bed practically the whole time. Our old Hedwig looked in on me every few days and tended to me in a touching way. She is an Aryan woman who has been with our family for more than forty years. As a young girl she was a domestic at my parents'. She knows every member of the family, and practically knows more about all of them than I. She also saw my children growing up and worries about them. Her husband works for the postal service and her son is already married. She never lost touch with us and says again and again that she will never forget that without my parents' help her boy would have probably died many years ago from a serious illness. She is such an upright, faithful human being; I can discuss everything with her and confide everything to her.

How she continues to stick by us amid the greatest difficulties is touching. For the risks that she takes upon herself for our sake are actually so great that I myself should dissuade her from coming to us. At the postal authorities all employees, thus also her husband, have just had to declare under oath once again that they no longer have any connections with Jews. Naturally, this declaration also applies to the acquaintanceships of the wife. If it comes out that she visits us, her husband will lose his position and therewith his livelihood. She herself is in a terrible conflict between fear and conviction. On the one hand, she explained to me that it was all the same to her whether a false declaration under oath was made or not: "One is being virtually trained to commit perjury. What things my husband has to constantly swear to, every week something else! One can no longer have any respect for it." On the other hand, she is terribly afraid that she could be caught. She told her Nazi sister-in-law, who asked about us schemingly, that she did not know where we have emigrated. She is very proud of this diplomatic answer. Early in the morning she scurries into the house and is constantly worried that she could be seen, perhaps through the window or when she leaves. When the doorbell rings, she hides. And in spite of this fear and nervous strain she still comes and hauls food, which I cannot even take because I know that she is depriving herself of it, and that it endangers us both. It is admirable how this simple woman has the courage that so many of the "educated" people do not summon. In such a time of distress the true essence of a person proves itself. Unfortunately, we were mistaken about some of our so-called friends. That much the more one must acknowledge old Hedwig's behavior.

She urges us all the time finally to emigrate. As if that were not our most fervent wish. The bystanders, the Aryans here, and people abroad can probably not understand at all why we are still here. They don't know that it does not at all depend on us, but rather that unfortunately we simply do not get admission to any other country. There are no more visas for the United States. My husband has made one last attempt and asked our relatives in America by wire for the entry visas for Cuba. That is the only possibility that still exists. No other country gives an entry permit to German Jews any longer, or is still reachable in any way.

Hopefully, we will succeed this time. The difficulties are already piling up again. The costs for such a visa are very high. Large sums of money have to be deposited for us. I hope that my brother-in-law will raise the money for us. The United States has introduced an exchange embargo and, besides, the rush for these Cuban visas is very great at the moment, so that three to four weeks are necessary for transfer of the deposits. At best we can expect the visas by the middle of August. Hopefully, nothing unexpected will again interfere. After our failures we have become very pessimistic about all matters concerning emigration.

[*Elisabeth Freund now has to work in an armaments plant.*]

It is fortunate for me that I have landed here. Here the heat is not so terrible. When I hear how things still are in the laundry, then I have to be most content that I'm no longer there. No doubt the work is difficult everywhere. The worst thing is the situation of our boy workers. We have a large number, starting at the age of fourteen. I often talk with them when I meet them on the way. My own son is also almost fourteen now. I wonder if he is already as tall as these boys here. I hope that he will not be so embittered and serious. After all, he has it good in his English school. He has the chance to learn something and is growing up as an equal in a big group of comrades. For him it is bad only that he has to be separated from his parents.

The poor Jewish boys here in the factory! The worst thing is not the difficult work, it is the hopelessness. There is one fellow, Kurt, a tall and lanky boy in breeches that are much too short; his arms stick way out of his sleeves. Even the young people do not get ration coupons for clothes! Kurt worked for a year in a training center of the Jewish community, is very interested in technology, and wanted so much to become an electrical engineer. "Then isn't it actually quite interesting for you here, isn't there a great deal to learn?" I ask him. "Oh, that's what you think. Only the Aryan boys are apprentices; they are shown things. We Jewish boys are not allowed to learn anything here. At best we are allowed to work at a machine once in a while, and then we're shown the operation that's needed for that one machine. But that's really all. That's just it—we're supposed to remain unskilled workers." [. . .]

The poor fellows. Everything is hopeless for them. No diligence, no energy, no matter how great, helps any; they can learn nothing. They have a terrible youth. Under these conditions, how long will the educational level of the Jews, which until now was always so high, be maintained at all? The door to every possibility is closed to them. They are not allowed to attend either the theater or concerts. Museums, libraries, even the zoo are forbidden to them. The few Jewish schools still existing suffer from an insufficient number of teachers and insufficient teaching materials. In general, there is only one secondary school for Jewish children left in Berlin, and it, too, will probably not exist much longer. The good school buildings have long since been seized by the party.

I'm always hearing so much about all these hardships because I am friends with a Jewish school teacher. The financial means of the community for all its purposes are becoming more and more tight, the need greater and greater, the difficulties and the pressure more and more insurmountable. This summer, for example, one of the greatest problems was what to do with the school children during the vacation. In almost all families the parents are working in the factories; thus the children were unsupervised at home. Where was one to put them, these poor, overly nervous children, who after these last years with their terrible experiences needed a holiday rest especially badly? In earlier years the Jewish school administration had organized excursions for the children to the forest, with immense difficulty, for the Gestapo had declared that the children are allowed on the streetcars or city trains or subways only in small groups of no more than six. Just imagine how hard it is under these conditions to take even only a hundred children anywhere with supervision. Quite apart is the problem of finding a suitable and undisturbed place for playing, where the children will not be assaulted and beaten up by some ruffians.

This year, however, the Gestapo has also strictly forbidden these excursions to the forest. What was left! The parks are also forbidden. Many of the Jewish day nurseries do not even have a yard, let alone a garden, and if they have one, the children are not allowed to play in it—because of the neighbors, who complain about the noise. Finally, the Jewish community hit upon the solution of transforming every free spot in the Jewish cemeteries into playgrounds with sand boxes for the smaller children. And the bigger children, class by class, had the duty to clear the graves and paths of weeds, and to maintain them in good condition. In this way the children were occupied and out in the fresh air, and at the same time the graves were kept in order, which curiously enough the Gestapo had suddenly demanded and for which otherwise, naturally, there would not have been workers or the financial means. This is what things have come to now: in Germany the cemeteries are not only the final resting place for the old people, but also the only spot where Jewish children can play.

[*In September 1941, Jewish women between the ages of eighteen and forty-five are forbidden to emigrate.*]

The Gestapo has permitted me to leave Germany, in spite of the prohibition! We do not even dare to believe it yet. It came about like this: my husband met an old acquaintance quite by chance on the street, an executive in one of the major banks of Berlin, with whom he had worked together a great deal, especially at the time of the uprisings in Upper Silesia after the First World War. At that time, my husband was a senior member of the board of the Upper Silesian Iron Industry Corporation and, in constant danger of his life, he successfully saw to the provision of Upper Silesia with the financial means to pay salaries. Without that, in addition to the bloody uprisings by the Poles, there would have also been unrest among the workers. His clever negotiations with the English and French occupation authorities prevented much misfortune at that time, and have always been recognized. This gentleman, then, asked quite innocently, in a friendly manner, how we were doing, and was absolutely flabber-gasted when he heard what difficulties we were having. "But really, that just can't be! These measures are not meant for someone like you!" How often have we and a thousand other Jews heard these words already? "These measures are surely not aimed at you!" At whom, then? And if they really were not directed against "especially meritorious people"—who has the right to determine whether a man in a "high position" has greater merit than a simple worker, a hard-working merchant, or an academic? [. . .] Well, at any rate, this gentleman was very sympathetic. He asked for exact details and was going to discuss the matter with the management of his company. There they had the necessary connections to the Gestapo and would somehow fix things up for us. When my husband told me about this meeting I was so pessimistic and so tired from work that I scarcely listened. After all, we had experienced so many disappointments already; why should it turn out otherwise this time? We were also very afraid and not at all so pleased by the well-meaning offer, for after all, one does not know what could happen if something like that were passed on to the wrong place.

But the miracle happened. Things turned out well. The general on Kurfürstenstrasse* said to the bank that an exception will be made for me. We also do not have to pay anything. The Gestapo man who negotiated the matter, to be sure, would like to have a bed from us when we leave—that's all. And we will leave him this bed with the greatest pleasure. All these things are so scarce and cannot be bought in the normal way.

But we have nothing in writing on this decision. In principle, the Gestapo does not provide anything written in such cases. My hus-band immediately went to the emigration office of the Jewish Aid Society. He was congratulated there, but no one wants to take the responsibility for placing our names on a departure list. One cannot

---

*The Department for Jewish Matters, directed by Adolf Eichmann, was located at 116 Kurfürstenstrasse.

blame them for that; after all, everything is punishable by immediate deportation to a concentration camp.

There are still so many difficulties to overcome. No, I still will not believe it, otherwise there will again be a greater disappointment. We also must not talk to anyone about it. The one office of the Gestapo may have allowed it, but perhaps another one will put us in a camp for it. I must also continue to do my work in the factory, for how can I explain to the employment office for Jews that my work record can be closed for good? Without papers no one will believe me. But without termination of the work record we cannot be assigned to a departing group. We are still a long way from that.

I must go on with my work in the factory. My hours just fly by. My thoughts fly even faster. Even if I don't quite believe it yet, still, just in case, I must consider how to organize things best. A year and a half ago we were permitted to take along quite a few things as personal and household belongings for Portugal. The permission is still valid. But at that time one could still pay the transportation costs with paper marks. Now, every emigrant is allowed to take along only two small suitcases, and from the German border on one must pay in gold marks or dollars. That determines the size of our luggage. Only the most necessary things can be taken along. We will have to part with our whole household. That is bitter, especially for a woman. But I won't make it hard for myself. Three years ago I had to separate from my children—that was hard. Furniture—that's nothing to get excited about. The main thing is that we get out of Germany alive. I will give the things away to good friends; at least I will get pleasure from that. If only we were at that stage already! After all our experiences, we can give up our apartment and furniture only at the very last moment. It can happen to us again, as it did the other times, that once more at the last moment we can't get away. The best thing is to let the business of emigration simply happen, as if it did not concern us at all, as if we were acting in a film. Otherwise the tension is too difficult to bear. We still have a great deal before us: parting from our friends, leaving our old homeland.

Hitler said of the German Jews: "They are all gypsies, who feel just as well in Paris as in Budapest, London, or New York." We loved Germany as much as one can love only one's own country. We detest Hitler's Germany and everything associated with it. But we must leave the country whose language we speak, with whose songs and poems we grew up, and whose forests and mountains we have criss-crossed. For many generations, our families did their utmost for this country, and we are leaving behind their graves in this soil. Our children can grow into another future. My husband and I are no longer young enough. We are going to a foreign country, and much there will be alien and difficult for us. But once we are outside, when we are received in another country in which we are allowed to live with our children undisturbed, then, happy and grateful, we will take pains to work for this new land faithfully, as our parents and ancestors did for Germany.

Our emigration agent brings the news that there are now a number of cases in which exceptions have been made to the emigration prohibition for women. Unfortunately, not many. I also know of such a case in which the Gestapo demanded 5000 marks for it. In the main, such a permit was given if there was a gynecological certificate of infertility.

I am still working in the factory. My husband, however, now has assurance from the Aid Society that we will be put on the next departure list. However, the next groups are not leaving for three weeks. If we could only speed up our leaving. We are growing more and more frustrated.

Since last week we have been wearing the Yellow Star.* The effect on the population is different from what the Nazis expected. Berlin still has perhaps 80,000 Jews. In some sections of town one sees the Yellow Stars in very large numbers. People of whom one would not have thought on the basis of their appearance that they are Jews are wearing the Star. The population in its majority disapproves of this

*German Jews were required to wear the Yellow Star as of September 19, 1941.

defamation. Until now, all measures against the Jews occurred in the dark. Now no one can ignore them.

Naturally, there are different kinds of experiences. What I hear from other people, I experience myself: I am greeted on the street with special politeness by complete strangers, and in the streetcar ostentatiously a seat is freed for me, although those wearing a star are allowed to sit only if no Aryan is still standing. But sometimes guttersnipes call out abusive words after me. And occasionally Jews are said to have been beaten up. Someone tells me of an experience in the city train. A mother saw that her little girl was sitting beside a Jew: "Lieschen, sit down on the other bench, you don't need to sit beside a Jew." At that, an Aryan worker stood up, staying: "And I don't need to sit next to Lieschen!"

The Yellow Stars are not popular. That is a failure of the party, and then there are the failures on the eastern front. As the usual diversion, there now follows a terrible wave of anti-Semitic propaganda. In all parts of the city more than two hundred meetings are held at which the Jewish question is discussed. In the stairwells, early in the morning, there are fliers in which people are openly called upon to carry out pogroms. In the news that a soldier fell in battle, they say that the Jews are guilty of his death!

A former janitor of ours who is an army guard in a concentration camp in Poland sent his wife to us. We should see to it that we get away as soon as possible. She said that he could not bear the thought that the same could happen to us as to those poor people. Didn't we know what was in store for us? That sounds horrible. What in the world are they doing with the camp inmates? The Nazis just cannot be killing them by the thousands! That is just inconceivable—German people doing this to their fellow citizens, with whom they had fought side by side in 1914. And what is happening with the women and children? In Berlin one knows nothing about their fate. The janitor's letter to his wife does not mention any details. The army mail is probably strictly censored.

Almost every store along the entire Kurfürstendamm now has a sign: "No entrance to Jews" or "No sales to Jews." When one walks along the streets one sees "Jew," "Jew," "Jew" on every house, every windowpane, every store. It is difficult to explain that the Nazis, these fanatical Jew-haters, cover their own city completely with this word, whereas there are so few Jews left in Germany. One cannot look anywhere without coming across this "Jew." And it is not just, say, the luxury shops or cigar stores that are forbidden to Jews in the entire city; now the bakeries, the butcher, and vegetable shops are showing these signs. And no coal-ration cards were distributed to Jews for the winter. Where will it all end?

And I am still working at the factory. Until now I haven't dared to ask for my discharge there. Perhaps in the factory they know that for my age group emigration is barred. If that is the case, then there will be further inquiries and I have nothing to show from the Gestapo. All these things are so difficult. If we do anything wrong now, then everything can be put at risk.

A few days ago I asked the foreman in the propeller department to be allowed to go home an hour earlier because of emigration matters. He became furious and accused me of wanting only to avoid work; he knew very well that there was no longer any emigration and he would not let me do whatever I liked with him. I won't get anywhere with this man.

Then I am told that I am no longer listed with the propeller department, but have been transferred to the petroleum department. Now I must try it. I present my passport with the visas to my new foreman and ask him for a short leave. After five endless hours the foreman calls for me: "Here are your papers. You are dismissed. Go to the employment office and have your work record canceled."

For the last time I am taken by the Aryan escort to the factory exit. "Is it really true, are you getting away? Where is Cuba anyway? And there is really no war there?" He looks around cautiously: "Then I wish you luck. Then you are better off than all of us here."

I have actually been dismissed! Now I just have to go to the employment office. There they make things difficult for me. For people under forty-five there is no cancellation of the work record. Don't I really know that yet? Nothing helps. I have to go to the Gestapo on Kurfürstenstrasse. That is hardly pleasant, but it is the only possible way. The building of the Jewish Fraternal Society is completely empty. Besides me there does not seem to be another Jew there. I am directed into the former festival hall, along the side walls of which a few niches are fixed up as offices. An official listens to my case, but is not informed. He is very cold and quite obviously does not believe me. But he will ask his highest superior. I am told to wait. However, I may not wait by the wall, but must place myself exactly in the middle of the big hall under the huge chandelier, with strict instructions not to move from the spot. I must remain standing exactly in the middle of the inlaid floor. I had heard tell about this sadism, but had considered everything an exaggeration. But no, it was really done that way. During the three-quarters of an hour that I wait there, I am atoning for all my sins, as one says. It is difficult to stand in the middle of such a huge empty room without swaying, without getting "claustrophobic." But this is now the test: will the Gestapo stand by the authorization it granted?

I wait. I wait. Finally the man returns. Everything is all right. He calls the employment office and gives the necessary instructions. Now I am free! No, not yet, not by a long shot! I know a young girl who was all ready to depart when the prohibition to leave the country came. She was to go one day later. And now she is working in the factory again; only her parents were able to leave. Only when we are across the border, only then will I be free.

Now there comes a great nervous strain. What if in the last moment we cannot get away for some reason! In the final week, my husband pays out all we own as the Reich emigration tax,* as the tax to the Jewish community "for the promotion of the emigration of Jews" (which the community, incidentally, does not receive, but

---

*This tax was originally introduced in 1931 for all emigrants leaving with more than 200,000 marks (at 25 percent). In May 1941, for Jews it was set at 80 percent.

which goes to a blocked account!), and for our ship tickets. The price of these ship tickets is determined by the value of the assets still left us. In a certain respect, I approve of that, for how else should people without assets raise the money for the crossing? In our case, for the tickets we must pay everything that is still left in hard cash after payment of all other fees. Why is there such a great fuss being made with the calculations? Whatever we were not able to turn into money, for example, real estate and mortgages, upon our emigration becomes the property of the state anyway, since we will then be deprived of our citizenship, as "enemies of the state," and everything will be confiscated. In the end, not a penny will be left of our still sizable assets. But if we cannot get away now, we will have paid everything and at best will get a partial sum back in paper marks; we will then be completely penniless. [. . .]

Last week a large number of Jewish families in Berlin received notice to vacate their apartments—not from their landlords, to be sure, but rather on printed forms from the police. They were told not to look around for other apartments. They would be notified about what will happen with them. They were told that all their possessions were confiscated. They could regard only a limited number of things as their own, in the case of a woman, for example, two dresses, three shirts, pants, stockings, etc., and one coat.

The agitation is indescribable. What will happen with these people now? Will they be sent to the province, to barracks, or to Poland? And who has received such notices, anyway? Apparently at first the so-called "previously convicted," that is, people who had not properly observed the blackout rules, or were not at home at eight o'clock, or at whose place something had been found during a house search. Bad news keeps coming from all directions. One can hardly keep up with it anymore. A number of our acquaintances are summoned before the Gestapo and punished, partly with a fine, partly with prison, because in the telephone book they are not listed with the compulsory middle names "Sara" and "Israel." Yet none of us has owned a telephone for more than a year. Despite that, they should have immediately applied for a name change in the telephone book. A good friend of ours receives the notification that his nephew, who was in prison for two years for allegedly having had sexual relations with an Aryan, was transferred from there to a labor camp, where he "died" after two weeks.

I go to the post office to make a call from a telephone booth there. I am scarcely in the booth when a woman rips open the door and drags me out screeching: "We Aryans have to wait. The Jews are always in the booths. Out with the Jews! Out! Out with all Jews from Germany!" It is such a terrible scene that I don't know how I got out onto the dark street again. I was afraid she would rip the clothes from my body.

My husband receives a summons to appear at the Gestapo on Alexanderplatz. That is always very unpleasant. The halls leading to the offices have heavy iron bars at their entrance. Once they have closed behind you, you are never sure whether you will be let out again. Both of us had already been summoned more than once, either alone or together. It was always a question of whether we were finally emigrating. This time my husband can fortunately take along our passports with the exit permits. The official really does ask again why we are still there. When my husband presents the passports, the Gestapo official takes a slip of paper with writing on it from our file and tears it up. My husband asks very politely what this paper meant. "That was your expulsion to Poland," is his answer. "I'm glad that you are getting out of it!" He is glad! So, Gestapo men are sometimes also human beings.

That is on Thursday, and on Sunday we are supposed to go. Now everything is happening like clockwork. In the night between Thursday and Friday the Jews in Berlin are taken from their apartments for the first time. Everyone is allowed to take along only a small suitcase. The police come at night, around eleven. In the dark, just so that the population does not take sides. The poor people are taken to a transit center, the synagogue on Levetzowstrasse. The entire block there is closed off. The Jewish community had to provide nurses, doctors, and aides. In great haste provisions are prepared, for no one was allowed to take food along from home.

It is a terrible night, with rain and thunderstorms. The synagogue is not big enough. The people have to stand in the yard for hours in the rain. The scenes that took place there are supposed to have been indescribable. Families were separated, married couples were torn apart, children dragged away, parents left behind. Already during the arrests, in the apartments, people took their lives. There in the synagogue it goes on. Body searches take place, suitcases are ransacked. All must turn in their identification papers, birth certificates, passports, etc. Everything is taken from them that has monetary value, as well as soap, combs, shaving gear, scissors, brushes, everything that a civilized person needs in order to look clean and neat. They are supposed to become as neglected as the unfortunate Jews of the Polish ghettos, whose caricatures appear in the *Stürmer.*

It was only in the following two days that we heard these dreadful details from eyewitnesses. In the laundry people were picked up from the night shift by the police. So working in the factories does not protect one from deportation. A young girl whose mother was part of the transport ran from one Gestapo office to another in order to be deported together with her mother. Her request was turned down. "You are not going to Poland when *you* feel like it, but when it suits *us.*" The fear, the panic everywhere simply cannot be described. Really, we have experienced so many horrible things already. But this, this cannot be compared to anything. It is like hunting helpless animals!

One morning I ride the streetcar crisscross through the city to find out about friends and acquaintances, whether they are still there or have already been hauled off. All of us know nothing of one another; after all, we don't have telephones! Not until the very early hours of Saturday are the poor people taken to the Grunewald Station, in barred police cars. This station is so out of the way that only few people can observe what is happening there. (That is why the hospital trains from the front also always arrive there.) The people are loaded into cattle cars. Word has it that the transports are heading to Poland. Nobody knows for sure.

Acquaintances come to our place. They know that we are supposed to leave. They ask us to convey their last greetings to their relatives abroad. We should please see to it that everything is done to procure them an entry visa. We should describe abroad what is happening here, what is awaiting them. Deportation to Poland, now, in the beginning of winter, that is death by freezing, that is starvation and typhus fever, epidemics, and a miserable death. Do the people abroad suspect what is happening here? Will it be possible for help to come before it is too late? Will it be possible to raise the high sums in dollars for the visas? After all, most of the relatives abroad have no money themselves.

A few of our friends have just received visas for Cuba. They are parents or old mothers. Parting from them is easier. We hope that soon they will be able to follow us. Hopefully, they will. It cannot be that now they may no longer be able to leave, after their children procured the visas after such problems. We have to hope that they will yet succeed!

A university friend of my husband says farewell to us. His sister in Breslau just took her own life as she was about to be deported. He himself is completely calm and composed. "I've never been a coward. Until now I have endured everything and coped with it. I have no possibility of getting out. As long as I can, I will put up with things here. I will not let them torture me. If it has to be, then I will know how to die." An old teacher, who lives with an even older sister and her ninety-year-old mother, comes to us. She, too, is admirably calm. "My sister and I would take this, too, upon ourselves. But our mother! We must not subject her to these tortures. She does not know anything about these deportations yet. When we get our notice to vacate the apartment, then we will sit down in the kitchen with mother and turn on the gas. That is the only act of love that we can still perform for our mother." We dare not contradict. These poor people have to decide that for themselves.

Our seventy-two-year-old friend F. asks us to write to his daughter in Bolivia that he is healthy and doing well. Perhaps she can speed up the visa for Bolivia, which was applied for over a year ago. "But don't alarm my daughter. The poor girl cannot help me anyway." I have never seen this dear person be anything but cheerful and consistently friendly. Now, too, he speaks with us as if it were not a serious matter. "May things go well with you. I am really glad that at least you will be getting away. I am an old person. For me a few years more or less do not matter."

These terrible farewells. Don't cry, just don't cry. Once more I go through our house to take leave of the neighbors. One must not be cowardly. Perhaps they, too, have some sort of message. They can depend on us. We will pass it on immediately, as soon as we can write letters freely. If only it happens in time. I jot down addresses abroad; none of us say much, we just shake hands. Just no tears. One must not start that, otherwise one cannot stop. Who knows what will become of these people. In a situation like this, one can no longer say farewell in a conventional way. [. . .] What right do we have to leave this hell when the others have to endure it? Maybe we are only dreaming all of this. It is impossible that something so horrible exists on this earth.

For the last time we are sitting at our own table for a meal. Then we put on our coats, each one of us takes a knapsack and a small handbag, and we leave the house without looking back.

By city train we go to the Potsdam station. There, in the cellar of the station, the Jewish groups are assembled. After the examination of our papers we are let into the cellar. The door closes behind us. Thank God! The group is leaving today after all. Until the last moment we had been afraid that the journey would not be allowed. There are still many formalities with luggage and passports. We find out that last night the first groups also left Frankfurt am

Main. Three hours pass until we are finally led in complete darkness through the unlit station to the train to Paris. A sealed car is designated for our group. We get in, the doors are closed, the train begins to move. We are riding to freedom.

Four days later the German government forbids departure for all Jews, and the army command discontinues the release of freight cars for the journey through France.

But the deportation of Jews to Poland goes on.

"A Turning Point"

Mikhail Nikolaevich Alexeyev

In June, 1941, Hitler invaded the Soviet Union, opening an enormous Eastern Front in the war in which as many as 25 million Soviet citizens died. Here, oral historian Studs Terkel (from *"The Good War"*) interviews Mikhail Nikolaevich Alexeyev, Russian author and editor, about his experiences as a Soviet soldier.

He is a Russian author and magazine editor. "All my literary work is related to the war or life on the farm." He and his wife, Galina Alexeyeva, attended a Soviet–American writers' conference in Kiev in 1982. During a break, they reflected on their personal experiences in the Great Patriotic War, as they termed World War Two.

He is sixty-five, though there is as much muscle as flab. A heavy, medium-sized man, he resembles almost any older patron of any tavern in any American ethnic neighborhood.

The interpreter is Michael Kuzmenko, twenty-two.

I was born in a village in Saratov County, in a farmer's family of average income. When I was six, I began working in the fields. I went to a pedagogical high school, but I didn't manage to be a teacher. So I was enrolled in the army. From 1938 until 1955,

I served in the army. I began as an enlisted man, and at the end I was a colonel.

I faced this war here on the Ukrainian soil, near the city of Sumy. I was in the artillery when the Germans began approaching these regions. I was in a special detachment under the command of General Chesnov. This formation went to the front. In the territory of Poltava, not far from Kiev, I participated in my first combat. It was early in July 1941. The Germans were very near.

The Germans managed to encircle our troops in this region. I was heavily wounded and sent to a hospital. Later I was in a hospital in Uzbekistan. In December of 1941, I was sent to a newly formed division near Stalingrad. It has nothing to do with Stalin. This is from virgin land. I was ordered to form a company to shoot mortars at flying guns, 82-millimeter. In March 1942, this division was at Tula, a town near Moscow. We were there until July of 1942. The Germans were on the offensive in the south and captured Kharkov. They were approaching the Don River in the direction of Stalingrad. If you go up the Volga River four hundred kilometers, there is Stalingrad. It is still the low flows.

This was the time when the Germans were very sure of victory. They thought they would easily take Stalingrad on the way. It is the end of July 1942. Our division was taken to the railway station near the Don. Our regiment marched to the Don straightway without waiting for the other regiments. Our task was to defend the river and not let the enemy cross it. It is where the Don River is closest to Stalingrad. After the war, a canal was built which connected the Don and the Volga.

My mortar company was defending in the village of Nizhniy. There are defeats. Of course, there is resistance, but the Soviet army is being pushed back. We are delaying the enemy on the Don, but the forces are not even. Our army is being slowly driven back to Stalingrad. Especially hard combats have been taking place near the railway station in the village of Avgenyerova. The local people told me that for many years, they have been collecting skeletons and have been burying them. They called this the white field, because it was all white with skeletons and skulls. Of Soviet soldiers and German soldiers.

When we went to attack, the Germans were shooting us with machine guns. When they went on the attack, we did the same to them. In the beginning it had been very even ground, but as combat continued, it became steep because it was covered with human bodies.

The left wing of the German army approached Stalingrad on the twenty-third of August after a massive attack by German aircraft. During this day, the twenty-third of August, Stalingrad was practically destroyed, because of the German preponderance of aircraft. Our right wing had to retreat all the way to the suburbs of Stalingrad. There we organized our defense and never left our positions, until the twentieth of November. There were attacks and counterattacks, terrible combat. We did not give an inch.

On the nineteenth of November, the attack of the Soviet troops began. Our division joined this attack a day later. On the twenty-third of November, the Germans were encircled. Approximately 330,000 German soldiers and officers, led by General Paulus, were surrounded. As the combats continued, we were making the circle smaller, tightening the vise. General Manstein was trying to break the circle from the outside. He managed to move ahead, some thirty, forty kilometers through it. But at the Avgenyerova railway station, his tanks were defeated. There was no longer any hope to break the circle and free General Paulus and his troops.

Now the agony of the Germans began. A little before the tenth of January 1943, Soviet General Rokossovsky was proposing a surrender. Not just to continue shooting people for nothing. The proposal was rather humane. They guaranteed life to all the defeated troops, all the Germans. They offered medical aid. They promised that the officers could leave there with their hand weapons, like knives, and to keep all their military awards.

The German command refused, on orders from Hitler. On the

tenth of January, all the troops of the Stalingrad front began the big offensive. Very few of the German aircraft reached the encircled troops. By that time, we had a preponderance in the air and in anti-aircraft artillery. We destroyed enemy aircraft before they could even reach the circle.

Somewhere in the middle of January, I could not find a piece of earth for my mortar company just to shoot, so many of the German weapons lay on the ground. As the circle was becoming smaller and smaller, the mounds of German guns grew higher and higher. So many and close to one another.

By this time, the German troops numbered about 100,000. The others, about 230,000, were killed or taken prisoners of war. May I give you a detail of their losses? The night before our decisive attack, I was looking for a place to hide until morning, to get some sleep. There were many German positions safe, but nothing was available. I couldn't use them, because the bodies of the German soldiers took up all the ground. They were everywhere, piled high on the fields and in the dugouts. I could find not one piece of open field nor any unoccupied dugout. There were also so many maggots, because of the dead bodies. And oh, the lice, the lice.

I saw a dugout in the snow. I had warm clothing so I went in there and bumped against something very stiff. It was very dark, so I couldn't see what it was. I thought they were sacks of something. So I made myself comfortable lying on these sacks. In the light of the morning, I saw that I was sleeping on the bodies of killed German soldiers.

The Germans were very orderly people. When they found they didn't have time to bury these bodies, they laid them next to each other in a very neat and orderly way. I saw straight rows, like pieces of cordwood. Exact.

The most surprising thing is that I was not surprised, not shocked by this discovery, so accustomed had I become to death. Now, when you see a dead body of someone, you feel uneasy. Then, I saw it every day, everywhere and so many. I got accustomed to it.

My company was located some three hundred meters from the center, from the Paulus headquarters. We were moving in. Unfortunately, others reached these headquarters before we did. When Paulus was taken prisoner, all the German forces capitulated: on the second of February, 1943.

For many days, columns and columns of German prisoners were passing by. The length of the columns was many, many kilometers long. They seemed never to end. It was very cold and their clothing was very, very poor. They put everything they had about themselves. Women's rags, shawls, anything. They were very hungry. They had eaten all the horses from the Rumanian cavalry corps. There were no horses left. They had no other supply of food, because there was no local population. Very, very few people. The majority had been wiped out when the Germans were bombarding. Many were evacuated when the Germans were approaching. We found a few children in Stalingrad, hiding.

The Germans had committed one strategic and tactical mistake. All their best forces were concentrated on Stalingrad. In the street fights, they dispersed their forces. Their flanks were exposed, because their Rumanian and Hungarian forces were less well equipped. We concentrated on these flanks and broke through.

When this battle began, the Germans were saying in a few days the Russian forces would surrender. Then it became a few months . . . Many years after Stalingrad, I was told that under the debris of one house, they found sacks with letters of German soldiers. They didn't have time to send these letters. In the first letters, one could feel their assurance that they will capture Stalingrad in just a few days. They were very optimistic. One could feel the joy there.

I want to say the truth. When we were retreating, it was very bitter and sad for us. But we couldn't write about it to our families. Once I sent a letter home and put a piece of grass in it. Grass which smells special, a bitter smell. So my relatives who got my letter understood how bitter it was. Remember, when we encircled the Germans, our losses were also very high.

We had been very excited when the combats were actually taking place. But now as we saw these German prisoners walking by in such a pitiful way, you felt a sort of pity for them. We understood that these were people who had some families, relations who were deceived by Hitler.

When I visited West Germany for the first time in 1965, I'll never forget the welcome given us by these former prisoners of war. It was a visit of the Stalingrad veterans. Our hosts explained simply: "You fed us when you had nothing to eat yourselves. You saved our lives." It was no exaggeration. There was hunger in our people and they fed these prisoners. And they came back home alive. No one has written about this so far. If you meet former prisoners of war in Germany, they will tell you this. The Russian people cannot be angry for a long time.

"The Bombers and the Bombed"

Eddie Costello and Ursula Bender

Studs Terkel (from *"The Good War"*) interviews Eddie Costello and Ursula Bender about the Allied bombing of Frankfurt, Germany, in 1944.

Most of his work life, he had been a journalist. He is semiretired. Ever since her arrival from Germany, she has worked for a publishing house.

They have known one another for several years, but this is the first time they have talked of a city they both remember: Frankfurt, which he bombed; Frankfurt, where she lived.

EDDIE: World War Two for me is a sore asshole. World War Two for me is four years of nervous diarrhea. World War Two for me is a chance to look back on it, even now, and tell sea stories: to take what happened and enlarge it, embroider it, and come out maybe not smelling like a rose, but smelling a little better than I do.

I began as a seventeen-year-old adolescent patriot. Anything my President said was okay for me. Just before I went in the navy, I worked in an arms plant. I lied about my age when I was fourteen. I made it sixteen. I had a job straightening machine-gun barrels. '38, '39, '41. Everything is very vague now. I make it that way. When the war fever began, the manufacturer had sweepers going around with a can of yellow paint and a stencil making signs on the concrete floor of the plant: GIVE 'EM A JOLT WITH SMITH & WES-SON or SLAP THAT JAP. That was the truth.

I was second pilot on a Catalina. It was a flying boat. My first pilot was a Mustang with twenty years in. He was a great father figure. I revered him in an unhealthy way. We landed in the water and I went out on the wing to fix a pontoon that jammed. My first pilot forgot that I was out on the wing. In order to maneuver, he gunned the engine when I was directly behind it. Flew me fifty feet in the air, blew me in the water. Later, I said to him, "Aw, sure, that's okay. You forgot I was on the wing." I would have forgiven that man anything, because he was my father *in extremis*.

He taught me so well that I ended up a better navigator than he was. I could shoot, compute, and do a three-star fix in under ten minutes. But I did a lot of drinking. I learned about women and I learned how to fuck off. (A long pause.) At one point, I developed a terrible fear of the single-engine aircraft—one I was on had lost power and I went over the side at nine hundred feet. Luckily, my parachute worked. I decided to spend the rest of the war in multi-engine aircraft. I ended my days flying sector searches in the Gulf of Mexico for downed aircraft. My war was a quiet war.

The only exciting part came when my girlfriend left me and I needed a charge. I had a ten-day leave. And I got a ride over to England, where I met a guy there in a bar I'd gone to college with. He said, "Come joyriding with me tomorrow. We're gonna have a little flight." I had no idea where it was. Because I was spending all my time drunk. We had a carousing night. The next day, we were briefed and I was smuggled onto his plane. I learned that he was going to Frankfurt on an ordinary run. I had never bombed anything before. But his second pilot was hung over, so I flew in the right-hand seat. I was second pilot on a bomber.

I had never flown a bomber before. We bombed the hell out of Frankfurt.

Years later I made a business trip to Frankfurt. One evening, I was walking around the Opernplatz. It was a misty night and there was a little wind. Suddenly, I found myself downwind of this bombed-out opera house. I could still smell the burning. It was eerie, an uneasy sensation. I got back from my trip and told Ursula (he nods toward Ursula) about this weird feeling. She said she was there that very night. I was bombing somebody who was later gonna be a friend of mine. What Ursula doesn't know to this day is that I was drunk. Bombed out of my mind.

Haven't you ever smelled that smell in a neighborhood after the fire department has put a fire out? That smell. It was faint, but it was detectable.

URSULA: I will never forget that. This incredible memory is the beginning for me of the war. It lingers on till this day. I was five. I was on the toilet seat, on the middle landing. Rüsselsheim, just outside Frankfurt. It's a factory town. They were building airplanes at the time, so it was strategic bombing. The sirens went off. My mother and I were alone in the house. My sister was evacuated in the country.

I went off the pot with my pants hanging down, running into the basement. The next thing I knew, I fell asleep. I woke up and I was alone. My mother had disappeared. I wandered out into the completely burning neighborhood. The smell of burning is one of the stronger images for me of the war. It's that smell of mortar, of brick, of cement that has been hot and cooled down. Since we lived in this town that made airplane parts, we were bombed constantly.

I found her in a chain of women passing buckets from one to the other. There were no men. There were only women and old people. The whole neighborhood had really been bombed out.

I'm now six, this is '44. We were standing outside in the gardens looking at these planes flying over. I remember waving at the American pilots. They came very low and escaped the flak. Flew so low that they practically touched the roofs of the villages. I can't tell you why we weren't scared. I saw my first theater in a bunker. That was a way of life. You had your little place in the bunker, you had your dolls.

You could get there very quickly. It was not as scary as it was for the grownups. A six-year-old child has a very different perception. There was excitement, a certain adventure. Your life took place with your neighbors, with your friends. You had places where you played.

We stayed in the Rhineland for a year. Then we went to what is now East Germany, until late '45. We were with the Russians when the war ended. I remember sitting on the lap of this Russian general who gave me beer. We were in an area where the Germans had retreated, set everything on fire, and said, Take what you can carry. The population was allowed to loot as much as they could. The smart women did.

My mother took seven sacks of sugar and two little wheels from an airplane. She turned into a Mother Courage. She wheeled all her little collectings back to Frankfurt, which is about a thousand miles away. Parachute silk. For years we had blouses made of parachute silk. She bartered with that later on. She brought all this back to Frankfurt and became a merchant. Our house was never destroyed, so for years we lived on these goods.

My mother was an incredible woman. She always saw a good situation. The Russians would steal from us, we would steal from them. They would come and steal our little things that we collected. She would steal food from them. They would come and show family pictures. They would come around at night and talk about their families in very broken language. A lot of Russians didn't know what to do about the toilet and washed their heads in them. A lot of the generals with the higher ranks were very polite, but the others were raping. Every night we would sit under the roof, hiding, because they were going through the town raping anything in sight.

The Americans had been there for five days. The next day the Russians are there and that's it. I remember these two Americans knocking on the house across the street, saying, "Open the door, Richard, and let me in." Isn't that a song? I remember my sister and I giggling later on. Being afraid of these guys who were saying, "Open the door, Richard." (Laughs.)

There was a much larger fear of the Russians, because there had been rumors of Russian hordes. That was in our mind, whether it was fair or not.

There was a very eerie scene in that village. I'm going to have nightmares tonight. During the German occupation, there were prisoners behind chicken wire. They made little straw boxes. They'd sell them to the villagers. My sister still has one. When the Russians came in, they were freed. They were the worst. They were illiterate and were really for the first time in their lives let loose on the population. The Russians themselves had a hard time controlling them. They were from the Ukraine, people the German army had taken prisoners. Once they were free they came and took revenge on the population. I don't know whether in fact they did. There must have been an enormous guilt among the Germans. The panic—"The Russians are coming"—was transferred to the children.

EDDIE: I had only one experience with POWs during the war. I was in preflight school at Chapel Hill, North Carolina. Our every move was controlled from sunrise to sunset. We marched in formation to a gigantic dining hall and we were served our meals by German POWs. We were forbidden to speak to them in terms other than orders. More sauerbraten, please. No fraternization was allowed. I was—what?—seventeen, eighteen. My view of these people was that they were simply harmless captured drudges who were there to serve the *Ubermenschen*. Us. I imagine if there were German women POWs I might have gone to a government brothel for sex.

When I was eighteen, I was gung ho, completely a creature of my country's propaganda machine. There was right and there was wrong and I wore the white hat. (To Ursula) Your folks and the Japanese wore the black hats. Some of my best friends are Germans, but I still feel uneasy about the Germans as a people. I feel uneasy about rednecks, too. I really distrust Bavarians. They are the Texans of the Teutons. They have a great sense of style and they're very crude. What a silly thing. I don't know many Bavarians, maybe half a dozen. These are the guys who wear regional costumes in exactly the same way that a guy from Dallas will wear a cowboy hat and boots. They're the guys with nicknames who take you around and bullshit you and bribe you and are despicable. If they were Americans, they would chew tobacco and hang blacks.

My son is keeping company with a girl, Aki Yoshimura. When I first met her father, Mr. Jap—my son will have my head when he hears me call a Japanese person a Jap—I felt very uneasy, because he flew in the Pacific in World War Two. Before I met him, I felt like I feel about the fucking Bavarians. Very uneasy. (Laughs.) But friendship, intimacy, changes everything.

I can think back to World War Two and I can idealize the whole thing, because I don't have a guy over the back fence reminding me of the crappy way I behaved then. My leaders told me to do this because it was good. And I took their word for it, because I didn't know any better. I followed orders, it's as simple as that.

There's no such thing as a just war. Everything is perverted. Recently I heard a government official jokingly say, "Because of the financial doldrums we're in now, what we need is a good war. That's what took us out of the Depression."

URSULA: These things you live with. The word "Jew" wasn't ever mentioned. The first time I heard about concentration camps was when I found a book called *Yellow Star*. I was twenty-one, alone in this room. I'll never forget. I'm part of that generation that grew up with silence. Don't forget, Germany did not start to talk about these things in schools till into the sixties. I remember going to England and staying with educated people. They couldn't believe how ignorant I was.

There was no attempt by my parents to explain. My mother died when I was twelve. My stepmother didn't know the family history. My father suffered too much and didn't want to talk about it. My sister didn't know about it. So when I opened *Yellow Star*, which was pictures taken in a concentration camp by the Americans, I just sat there. My God, what is this? I was writing letters to my father—they lived in Cologne, I was still in Frankfurt—demanding an answer.

EDDIE: I'd rather forget about the war, except when I'm at a cocktail party and somebody gives me an opening: "Tell me about the time . . ." And I come out with these terribly well-worn stories. They bore everyone around me except the people who haven't heard them before. Sometimes I look at it as the time I had the least responsibility. And then the fun was over.

URSULA: You said the fun was over. I remember the day before the end of the war. Everything was burning. Somebody was instructing the withdrawing German troops in how to use a hand grenade. I'll never forget that. He dropped the grenade. That's the first time I'd come in touch with death really. I'd seen houses disappear, but I'd never seen dead people. This time, you see these kids under your window. Most of them killed, others crippled for life. We're talking about sixteen-, seventeen-year-old kids. About ten of them. The moaning, the screams, the blood. My mother was throwing out the gauze, rolls and rolls of gauze that she had collected. She got rid of her loot. She went down and helped. To me, that was the end of the war. I got one glimpse and my mother pulled me away: don't you dare go to that window again.

The war was mainly the territory of the grownups. Children were excluded. In all this horror, my mother tried to shelter me—from something. I was never told what really happened when my father, although he was partly Jewish, was finally allowed to go into the army in 1943. There was always this cloud. I was always kept from something.

I'll never forget in 1962 when I came home. My father and stepmother were high up, mountaineering. He was by now in his late fifties. I said I was seeing somebody and we were very friendly. I told them his name. My stepmother said, "That's a Jewish name." My father looked around and said, "Sshhh!" This is ten thousand feet up in the mountains. There is nobody near or far except this poor old schleppy couple in the ravine below us. I've never forgotten that. Ssshhhh. 1962. I felt shame for his cowardice, sad for him.

I guess we're talking about innocence, aren't we? Seeing that grenade dismember so many people, although I was allowed only a glimpse—life wasn't the same any more. No more waving. Within a week, I was sitting on the lap of these Russians and drinking beer. We still have it at home, the little aluminum can that I drank my first beer out of. I remember them as kind, good people. They wanted to be friendly with us and treated us well. This all happened within a week.

"Return to Auschwitz"

Primo Levi

Primo Levi was an Italian chemist and acclaimed author who was deported to Auschwitz, the Nazi concentration camp where over one million people were exterminated, in 1944. His memoir of this ordeal, published in the United States under the title *Survival in Auschwitz,* is considered to be among the most haunting Holocaust narratives ever written. Here, from *The Voice of Memory,* Levi is interviewed as he returns to Auschwitz for the first time in forty years.

[The interview begins in a train travelling through Poland towards Auschwitz.]

So, what effect does seeing these places again have on you?

It's all different. More than forty years have gone by. Poland then was emerging from five years of a frightful war, it was probably the country that had suffered most from the war in all of Europe, that had had the largest number of victims, and not only Jews. And then, in these past forty years, the world has changed everywhere. Also, I came through this landscape in winter, and the difference is total, because the Polish winter, then as now, is harsh, not like our Italian winters. There's snow for three or four months and we were

91

inept, we had no idea how to survive it, during and after the time in the camp. I came through these towns as a sort of missing person, disorientated, in search of a centre of gravity, someone who could take me in. And the landscape was truly desolate.

And the wheels, the goods trains that run past us, what effect do they have?

Yes, I'd say that it's the goods trains that trigger the strongest reflex, that upset me most. Even today, seeing one of these goods cars, let alone getting into one, affects me violently, reawakens strong memories, much more so than seeing these towns and places again, even, I'd say, seeing Auschwitz itself. A journey of five days shut up in a sealed cattle-car is an experience you never forget.

This morning you were telling me about the feelings you have when you hear Polish being spoken?

Yes, that's another conditioned reflex, at least for me. I am a talker and a listener: other people's language makes a great impact on me. I tend, I try to use my own Italian language as well as I can. Now, Polish was the incomprehensible language that greeted us at the end of our journey, and it wasn't the civil Polish we hear today, in the hotels, from our travel companions here. It was a rough Polish, full of swearing and imprecation that we couldn't understand; it was truly the language of hell. German was even more so, of course. German was the language of the oppressors, of our torturers, but many of us—myself included—could understand something of the German we heard, it wasn't unknown, the language of the void. Polish was the language of the void. And I was deeply struck, last night, by two drunken Poles in the hotel lift, who were speaking the language I remember, not like all the others around us: they were swearing, spitting out what seemed like a stream of consonants, a genuinely infernal language.

The same sensation, you were saying, that you get from the smell of coal.

Indeed. There's that too, perhaps because I'm a chemist. A chemist is trained to identify substances from their smell. Then, as now, as you enter Poland, Polish towns at least, there are two particular smells that you don't find in Italy: the smell of toasted malt and the acid smell of burning coal. This is a mining country; there's coal everywhere, even the heating in many homes is by coal, so in spring and autumn and all the more in winter, the smell spreads through the air. It's not even such a nasty smell, the acid smell of burning coal, but for us, for me at least, it is the smell of the *Lager*, of Poland and the *Lager*.

And the people?

No, the people aren't the same. Then we didn't get to see the people. We did see our torturers in the camp and their collaborators who were mostly Poles, both Jewish and Christian. But the ordinary people in the street, the Poles living in their own homes, we didn't see them or we saw them from afar, beyond the barbed wire. There was a country road that ran alongside the camp boundary, but hardly anyone used it. Later we found out that all the peasants had been moved out of the area. But coaches carrying Polish workers passed by and I remember that on one of these coaches there was an advertising board, just like nowadays, with the slogan "Beste Suppe, Knorr Suppe" ("The Best Soup is Knorr Soup"). It was very strange for us to see an advert for soup, as if you could choose between one soup and another.

What effect did it have coming back and leaving for this journey this morning from a luxury hotel for foreigners?

An effect of displacement, I'm tempted to say of physical dislocation, of something impossible that is nevertheless happening. The contrast is too strong. We could never have even dreamed of such a thing then, of coming back to these places as tourists in luxury (or almost luxury) hotels. Although . . .

Yes, what does this contrast, what . . .

Like any contrast, this one is partly gratifying and partly alarming, because it could all return. The inverse would have been much worse: to have come first to the luxury hotel and then later been in total despair.

Did you know where you were going, what your destination was?

Basically we knew nothing. We had seen at the station in Fossoli* a sign hung on the cars with our destination, with Auschwitz scribbled on it, but we didn't know where it was, we thought it might be Austerlitz. We thought, who knows, it must be somewhere in Bohemia. At that time, in Italy, I don't think anyone, even the best informed people, knew what Auschwitz meant.

Forty years ago, what was the first impression of Auschwitz?

It was . . . oh, well, like another planet, at night, after five days of appalling travel, during which some in the wagon had died, arriving at a place whose language none of us understood, whose purpose none of us understood. There were meaningless signs: a shower, clean side, dirty side and clean side. No one explained anything, or they spoke at us in Yiddish or Polish and we couldn't understand. It was a profoundly alienating experience. We felt we had gone insane, that . . . that we had given up all possibility of reason, we could no longer think.

After his arrest in Piedmont and before his deportation to Auschwitz, Levi was held in the prison camp at Fossoli, near Modena in central Italy, as described in the opening pages of If This Is a Man.

What had that journey been like, those five days? What do you remember most?

Oh, I remember it very well, I remember a great deal. There were forty-five of us in a very small wagon. There was just enough room for all of us to sit down, but not to lie down. There was a young mother breast-feeding her baby and they had told us to take food supplies with us, but stupidly we hadn't brought any water; we hadn't thought of it, we had a tiny amount, no one had warned us; we assumed we would find water en route. And although it was winter, the thirst was awful. Five days of thirst was really the first of many tortures. I remember that it was deep winter, that your breath froze on the wagon bolts, and we had a competition to scrape off the frozen dew—even though it was rusty, hanging off the bolts—to scrape it off to have at least a few drops of water to moisten our mouths. And the baby screamed from morning to night, because the mother had no more milk.

And what happened to the children and the mothers, when . . .

Oh, they were all killed at once. Of 650 in our train, four-fifths died the night we arrived or the night after; they were selected out immediately and taken to the gas chambers. In this grim scenario, at night, with reflector lights glaring and people screaming—screams like I had never heard before, screaming orders that we didn't understand—we left our wagons and lined up, they made us line up. Before us was an NCO or an officer—later I found out he was a doctor, but we knew none of that then—who asked each of us: are you able to work or not? I talked it over with the man nearest to me; he was a friend, from Padua, older than me and not in perfect health. I said to him, I'm going to say I can work. And he said to me, do as you please, it's all the same to me. He had already given up all hope; and in fact, he said he could not work and he never went into the camp. I never saw him nor indeed any of the others again.

What was the work like there, in Auschwitz?

The first thing to say is that, as you know, there wasn't just one camp at Auschwitz. There were many and several of them had been built to plan, as annexes to factories and mines. The camp of Birkenau, for example, was divided into a certain number of squads which worked for various factories, including armaments factories. My camp, Monowitz, with its 10,000 prisoners, was part of an industrial plant belonging to IG-Farben, an enormous chemical trust company which was dismantled after the war. The task of the plant was to construct a new factory for chemical products over an area of something like six square kilometres. The work was at an advanced stage, and everyone took part in it: English prisoners of war, French prisoners, Russians, and Germans of course, as well as free or volunteer Poles and also some Italian volunteers. There were something in the region of 40,000 individuals, of whom we 10,000 were the lowest of the low. The camp of Monowitz, made up almost exclusively of Jews, was there to provide the unskilled workforce. Despite this, however, because skilled workers were scarce in Germany at that time, since the men were all at the front, after a certain time they began to look amongst us too—in theory, labourers and slaves—for specialists . . . From the very first day in the camp at Monowitz there was a sort of census research going on: they asked everyone their age, qualifications, profession. And this was one of my great strokes of luck, because I said I was a chemist, without knowing that we were labourers in a chemical factory. Much later, this was to work to my advantage, because I was assigned to work for the last two months inside a laboratory.

And the food?

Well, food was problem number one. I can't agree with those who describe the soup and bread in Auschwitz as disgusting. As far as I was concerned, I was so starved that they seemed good to me. I never found them disgusting, even on the first day. There was very little food, the rations were minimal, roughly equivalent to 1600–1700 calories per day, in theory at least, since there were thefts along the way, so by the time it reached us there was always less than this. Anyway, that was the official allocation. Now, you know that a small man can just about survive on 1600 calories a day, but only without working, lying all day in bed. We had to work, hard labour in the freezing cold. So our ration of 1600 calories a day meant slow death by malnutrition. Afterwards I read the calculation made by the Germans. They worked out that in these conditions a prisoner might, using up this ration and their personal reserves of energy, last from two to three months.

But in the concentration camps did people adapt to everything?

The question is a strange one. The prisoner who survived adapted to everything; but the great majority did not adapt to everything, and died. They died because they couldn't adapt, even to things which seem to us today the most banal; shoes, for example. They shoved a pair of shoes at us; no, not even a pair, just two different shoes, one with a heel, one without. You almost had to be an athlete to learn to walk in them. One was too tight, the other too loose; you had to negotiate complex deals, and if you were lucky, you managed to find two shoes that went together reasonably well. In any case, all the shoes hurt your feet; and anyone with delicate feet ended up with infections. I know from experience, I still have the scars. By some miracle, mine healed on their own, without my losing a single day's work. But if you were prone to infections you died "from shoes," from infected foot-wounds which never healed. Your feet swelled up and the more they swelled the more they rubbed up against the shoes; you might end up in the hospital, but swollen feet were not sufficient an illness to get you admitted to the hospital. They were too common a complaint, so if you had swollen feet you were sent to the gas chambers.

Today, we're being taken to eat in a restaurant in Auschwitz.

Yes, it's almost laughable. That there should be a restaurant in Auschwitz. I don't know, I don't know if I will eat, it feels almost profane, absurd. On the other hand, you have to remember that Auschwitz, Oswiecim in Polish, was and is a town with restaurants, cinemas, probably even a night-club, perhaps, they have them in Poland too. There are schools and children. In parallel to the Auschwitz which is today more like a concept—Auschwitz *is* the *Lager*—there is also this civilian Auschwitz, just as there was then too.

When you left Auschwitz, your first contact with the Polish population . . .

They were suspicious. The Poles had in essence gone from one occupation to another, from the ferocious force of the German occupation to the somewhat less ferocious, perhaps more primitive force of the Russians. They were suspicious of everyone, us included. We were foreigners after all. They didn't understand us, we had on a strange uniform, the uniform of forced labour, which terrified them. They didn't want to talk to us, only a handful took pity and with them we managed to explain a little. It was very important to make ourselves understood. An abyss divides the person who can make himself understood from the person who cannot: one is saved and the other is lost. The same was true in the *Lager*: understanding and being understood was of fundamental importance.

The language problem for Italians?

This was one of the reasons for Italians having the highest group mortality rate. Italians and Greeks. Most of the Italians who were with me died in the first few days from not understanding. They didn't understand the orders and no account was taken of not understanding: an order had to be understood, it was screamed, repeated once and then no more, then came the beatings. They didn't understand when it was announced that shoes could be changed, when we were called to be shaved once a week. They were always the last, they always arrived late. When they needed something, needed to say something, even something quite simple, they couldn't say it and they were ridiculed. Even at the level of morale, they collapsed immediately. As I see it, of the many causes of ruin in the camps, language was among the worst.

A few minutes ago we passed through one of the stations you refer to in The Truce.

Trzebinia. Yes, it was a station somewhere between Katowice and Cracow where the train had stopped. It was always stopping, that train, it took us three or four days to travel 150 kilometres. It stopped and I got off and there for the first time I met a middle-class Pole, a civilian, he was a lawyer, and I managed to communicate with him as he spoke German and also French. I didn't know any Polish, as I don't today. And so he asked me where I came from. I told him that I came from Auschwitz; I was in uniform, I still had my striped rags on. He asked me why and I replied: I'm an Italian Jew. He was translating my replies for a crowd of curious onlookers that had gathered, Polish peasants, workers on their way to work, early in the morning, if I remember rightly. As I said, I didn't know any Polish, but I could work out that in his translation he had changed my reply. I had said "I'm an Italian Jew" and he had translated "he's an Italian political prisoner." So, in French, I protested. I said, "I'm not . . . I am also a political prisoner, but I was brought to Auschwitz as a Jew not as a political prisoner." And he replied to me in hurried French, "it's better for you this way. Poland is a sad country."

We're now back in our hotel in Cracow. What do you now think the Holocaust represents for the Jewish people?

It was nothing new, there had been others. As an aside, I've never liked the term "Holocaust." It is inappropriate, rhetorical and above all wrong. What it represented was a turning point: in its scale, in its modes of operation primarily, because it was the first time in recent epochs that anti-Semitism has been planned, ordered and organized by the state, not simply tacitly accepted, as had happened in the Russia of the Tsars, but actually willed. And there was no escape, the whole of Europe was turned into an immense trap. That was the novelty and that is what made it a profound watershed for the Jews, not only in Europe but in America, throughout the world.

Do you believe that another Auschwitz, another massacre like the one carried out forty years ago, could come about?

In Europe no, I don't think so, if only for reasons of what you could call immunity. There is a sort of immunization at work, so that I think it unlikely, at least for some time . . . maybe in a few decades, fifty years, a hundred years, you could conceivably find something like Nazism in Germany or Fascism in Italy. No, I don't think it could happen in Europe. But the world is much bigger than Europe alone. There are countries where you might find a desire to build an Auschwitz, where only the tools are lacking for now.

So the idea is not dead?

The idea is most certainly not dead, because nothing ever dies. Everything returns renewed, nothing ever dies.

The forms change?

The forms change. The forms are important.

Is it possible, in your view, to destroy the humanity in man?

Yes, I'm afraid so. I would say that what characterizes the German camps—I cannot comment on others, because I did not see them, perhaps the same applies to Russian camps—is precisely their annihilation of man's personality, on the outside and on the inside. This goes not only for the prisoner but also for the prison guard who loses his humanity in these places, even if along a different path. The result is the same. Only very few had the luck to keep their awareness intact during their imprisonment. Some rediscovered that sense of awareness of what had happened afterwards, but whilst there they had lost it. Many forgot everything, they never recorded their experiences mentally, they didn't engrave them on their memories, so to speak. So it did happen, yes, to all of us; a profound alteration in personality, a numbing of sensibilities; memories of home, of families, became secondary to the battle of urgent needs, to hunger, the need to protect ourselves from cold, from blows, to resist exhaustion. All this led to conditions you could reasonably call bestial, like beasts of burden. It is curious that this animal condition was even reflected in the language. In German there are two verbs for "to eat": one is "*essen*" and is used for people, the other is "*fressen*," used for animals. A horse "*frisst*," it does not "*isst*." A horse or a cat devours, you could say. And in the camps, without anyone decreeing it, the verb for eating was "*fressen*" not "*essen*," as if the perception of our regression to an animal state had spread among us all.

At the end of this second return to Auschwitz, what comes to mind?

Many things come to mind. One is this: I am rather angered by the fact that the Poles, the Polish government, have taken over Auschwitz and turned it into a memorial to the martyrdom of the Polish nation. It was that too, it was that in its first years, in 1941–2. But afterwards, with the opening of the Birkenau camp, with the building of the gas chambers and the crematoria, it became above all else the instrument of the destruction of the Jewish people. It isn't that this is denied here—we saw that there is a Jewish Block museum, just as there are Italian, French, Dutch Blocks, and so on—but the resounding fact that the overwhelming majority of victims of Auschwitz were Jews, and only in part Polish Jews, although it's not denied, is at least glossed over.

Do you not fear that others, that people today want to forget Auschwitz as soon as they can?

There are signs that it is happening—forgetting, even denial. And that is significant: to deny Auschwitz is to be ready to rebuild it.

Part III

The U.S. Home Front

The transition to wartime fundamentally changed America in the early 1940s. The 1930s had seen some of the darkest times in U.S. history, under the long shadow of the Great Depression. Almost overnight, a massive program of military spending threw the U.S. economy into high gear, effectively ending unemployment even as millions of American men and women were drafted into the armed services for the coming fight against the Axis powers.

Such profound changes resonated throughout American society. Because of a labor shortage brought on by the draft, women entered the wage-earning workforce in large numbers for the first time in American history. African Americans—the majority of whom still lived in the Jim Crow South—swelled the ranks of the still-segregated American military, throwing race relations into turmoil as thousands of black men joined the fight against fascism.

Under the intense pressure of wartime mobilization and war hysteria, American civil liberties suffered multiple blows. Japanese immigrants, most of whom lived on the west coast of the United States, were rounded up and sent to internment camps—over 100,000 in all were relocated to places like Manzanar, California, pictured in the pages that follow. Opponents of the war were often jailed and silenced.

All of these currents and countercurrents swirled around the U.S. war effort itself, by far the greatest mobilization in the nation's history. Few Americans were untouched.

"Trouble Coming"

Nelson Peery

In an excerpt from his memoir *Black Fire,* Nelson Peery describes the profound racial tensions that erupted in the southern states, as African American soldiers mobilized in large numbers.

We spent the morning of June 16 cleaning up our areas in preparation for the move to the Sabine River. After duty hours, Brad, Bunk, Lee, Jeff, Hewitt, and I got together. The position of our committees was getting dangerous. Once we left the bivouac and spread out along the Sabine, maintaining contact with the committees in the 368th and 25th would be almost impossible. We had to decide on a plan of action if rioting should break out in our area. Whatever was to be done had to be done quickly.

We agreed to try to get together the battalion and regimental leaders of the squads that night. After retreat, Brad and Bunk went to the 25th, Jeff and Lee to the 368th. Hewitt and I wandered through the 369th and found the three committee leaders from the battalions.

The seventeen of us had not been together since Nogales. There was a good bit of backslapping and handshaking. To avoid looking too conspicuous, we spread several blankets and sat together talking.

Brad and I met with the regimental committee leaders. Hewitt and Bunk met with the battalion leaders.

We could do nothing to protect an area more than twenty miles away. We were going to have to wait, no matter what happened, until we got the chance to strike. We had to keep our men ready, but they had to be cool.

The meeting had gone surprisingly well. The men well understood the dangerous position of the entire division. We were just preparing to disperse when Moore came running up to us.

"What's going on, White Rabbit?"

"There's a riot in Beaumont. The motherfuckers are burning the colored section of town."

"What happened?" "When did it start?" "Are they fighting back?"

"Wait a minute." Moore held up his hands. "I just heard it on the radio. The whites attacked the colored section. They set the place on fire."

"Well, Goddamn it. They want a war, let's give it to 'em."

"Man, this is what we were talkin' about. We can't get to Beaumont. We can't start a fight here. We got to wait until they attack us, then we can wipe 'em out."

A heavy silence fell over the group. A hundred and fifty miles away a mob with a few weapons was killing our people. We sat here—concentrated, armed, trained for combat, and unable to come to their rescue.

"Men," Brad said quietly. "My home ain't far from Beaumont. I know how every one of you all feel. The stakes are pretty big now. Everything depends on discipline. Military discipline. They're gonna hit De Ritter or Many. When they do, we'll kill every one of the motherfuckers. If we show our hand now, we ain't gonna help nobody."

The moment of tense silence hung on.

"We'd better break it up," I said. "Remember that when we get to the river, you guys are going to have to stay in touch—we won't be able to find you."

The men began to drift away toward their companies. Two of the men from the 25th hung back. I went over to them.

"Don't know if you remember me. My name's Sammy Atkinson. I was with you down in Nogales."

"Sure I remember you, Sammy." And I did. He was one of the men who had been beaten by the 8th Air Force soldiers. He seemed so calm and shy, I'd have never recognized him.

We shook hands warmly.

"I brought my home buddy up to meet you. I liked the way you guys organized things in Nogales. This here is Joe Henry Johnson."

I turned and shook hands with the lanky, smiling, dark-skinned young soldier. I recognized him too. He had taken first prize in the competition for assembly and firing of the water-cooled machine gun. I recalled how he had deftly assembled the machine gun blind-folded, recognizing the parts by touch and putting them together.

"Proud to know you, Joe Henry. I remember you and your machine gun from Huachuca."

He smiled for a moment and then said almost pleadingly, "My peoples in Beaumont. We gotta do something. I gotta do something."

I felt almost like a handkerchief head but I had to say it.

"Joe Henry, I want to fight bad as you do. But there ain't no use fighting a losing battle. We're going to have to wait. How are we going to get to Beaumont? We're going to get our chance. We've got to be soldiers and hold our fire."

"Part of me says you're right, but we can't let these white people drive us back into slavery and we got all the guns."

"Only thing I can say is, we got to have a plan and everybody got to stick to it. The plan now is to fight in De Ritter or Many and not get split up."

"We know you're right," Sammy said. "It's hard takin' low all the time. I just wanted him to hear it from you."

We shook hands again and they left for their area.

Brad had been standing quietly, listening.

"I don't think we can hold it together, Road. The men have had all they can take. If Uncle Sam got any sense, he'll get us out of here now."

"You can see the mother ain't got no sense, or we wouldn't be here."

June 19, 1943. The division loaded up into a huge convoy of trucks that deposited us along a twenty-five-mile front on the Louisiana side of the Sabine River. We immediately set about digging our latrines and garbage sumps and setting up the battalion headquarters. The men went about their tasks in sullen, ominous silence.

The rioting spread. Seven more blacks dead and 150 seriously injured that week in ten racial outbreaks. Fifty men and women injured in Mobile, Alabama. A man was lynched near Tampa, Florida. Five black shipyard workers were gunned down by Coast Guard reservists in Chester, Pennsylvania. Four black soldiers were shot in Riverside, California; three shot in Augusta, Georgia. Two more black soldiers were shot at Camp Van Dorn, Mississippi, when they refused to say "yes, sir" to a group of white men. One black soldier was shot dead at Fort Bliss, Texas.

The next morning there was a surprise inspection for ammunition. No one was caught. By limiting ourselves to two clips, we had been able to bury them the moment we arrived at a bivouac and easily dug them up just before we left.

The officers were plainly concerned by the taut silence. The news from Beaumont was horrible. It was impossible to distinguish between rumors and fact. We knew the radio and newspapers weren't telling the truth and hoped the word of mouth from Beaumont was exaggerated.

Rumor had it that the mob pinned the blacks against the river and a slaughter occurred. The papers stated that the fighting was dying down as the troops moved in. We knew, in fact, that the troops had joined the mob, and "establishing calm" meant the brutal military crushing of the resistance. Wherever men from the 93rd met in little groups, there was an exchange of rumors and a swearing of revenge.

Unbroken by the brutality of the troops, the scattered attacks by the Klan, and the constant threat of renewed mob violence, black Beaumont heroically stood firm and defiantly celebrated June 'teenth [nineteenth], the prohibition of slavery in the territories.

Tension and danger charged the air. Black Jack ladled supper from the cooking pots. The sun set into Texas. At 10:00 P.M., Harold laid aside the GI bugle and took his trumpet from the battered case. The area hushed to a surly, brooding silence as he played a mournful taps for Beaumont.

June 20. The day was especially hot and the humidity oppressive. We tried to maintain contact with our men through notes whenever a message was sent to their areas. The day wore itself out with routine chores. At 11:00 P.M. I finally got under the mosquito netting and went to sleep.

At 12:15 A.M. Lee shook me awake and motioned for me to follow him. When we were out of earshot of the headquarters tent, he whispered, "The shit is on in Detroit."

"What happened?"

"We turned the radio on in the message center and got a news broadcast. A riot started on some island near Detroit. They're killin' every colored man they can find."

"Jesus Christ, Lee. What do you think we should do?"

"Can't do nothin' 'cept what we're doin'. If I know this white man, they're gonna expect us to do something. They gonna really search for ammo."

"I think you're right, Lee. See if you can get a message to the men to get rid of the shit."

"I think Jinks is already doing that. I just wanted to check with you."

When the sharp sound of reveille pierced the woods and lagoons, I had been peering into the graying sky for several hours.

• • •

June 21. The rifle companies moved from their bivouac area to take defensive positions along the river. The 25th and 369th were on the defensive line, with the 368th in reserve. The radios switched from clear to code and imposed battle discipline.

There was little more for the operations section to do for a few hours. Captain Akeley was groggy, having been on his feet for eighteen hours. I hated myself for it, but I spread out his bedroll and told him I'd be able to handle things for a few hours if he wanted to sleep. He looked at me in absolute shock that I would do such a personal thing without an order.

"Thanks, sergeant. But wake me up in two hours."

"Yes, sir."

He pulled off his shoes and stretched out. In a few moments I could hear the gentle, deep, regular breathing.

True to their word, our committee leaders from the 25th, 368th, and 369th regiments came to the battalion headquarters to check in. It was a good feeling to know that we were maintaining good communications.

Our information was that the white mobs had killed at least twenty blacks and seriously injured many more in Beaumont. As the fighting died down there, it increased in fury in Detroit. Over thirty were confirmed dead and the injured topped seven hundred. The news fired the men into a seething, impotent rage. They wanted to march. Our little group, by urging the men to be cool, found itself in bed with the officers and Uncle Toms.

June 22. Sergeant Jackson woke me up at 5:00 A.M. The river operation was to begin. After gulping down the bitter coffee, I went to the operations tent. Captain Akeley was at work. At 6:00 A.M. he mentioned that he was going to a staff meeting at Regiment. He left and I walked up toward the message center, where I could get the reports as they came in.

The river crossing began. From our hilltop headquarters I could see the assault boats heading across the river and the combat engineers constructing a pontoon bridge.

TUM-TUM-TUM. TUM-TUM-TUM. The sound of the machine gun ricocheted across the river, through the swamps and the forest, and shattered against the hills. Forty-five seconds of sustained firing followed the two short bursts.

Holy Jesus Christ! What the fuck is going on? I ran to the Message Center.

"Jinks, what the hell is happening?"

"I don't know. Sounds like a water-cooled down in the 25th area."

"Reckon those white boys want a shooting war?"

"Could be the 25th."

The 240 radio lit up. The speed key began to sing. Jinks reached for his earphones when the message broke in clear.

"This is General Leyman. Battalions report!"

"Cobra Red."

"Cobra White."

"Cobra Blue."

We stood breathlessly as the commanding general continued. "All company commanders are to make immediate inspection for live ammunition. I will be in the company areas within the hour."

"Roger!"

"Over and out."

Jinks printed the message on the quadruple forms and called the company runners.

"Get this to the company commanders, but first tell everybody to get rid of the shit."

Within the hour General Leyman and several jeeploads of his staff had arrived in the area. They were holding full field inspections throughout the division. I waited in the operations tent, resigned to whatever might happen.

Captain Akeley, a white major, and a lieutenant entered the tent.

I rose and saluted the officers. They returned the salute.

"Rest, sergeant."

"Sergeant Peery," Akeley's face was tight and grim—"Major Thomas, from Division G-2, and Lieutenant Jefferies, from CIC, want to talk to you." Akeley's eyes were almost pleading for me to come clean. While not the target, he knew he was in the line of fire.

"Yes, sir."

The lean lieutenant's snakelike eyes were barely visible behind the air force glasses. He exuded a menacing air.

"Take a seat, sergeant."

"Thank you, sir."

"I'll come right to the point. We're fighting a war for the existence of this country and its way of life."

I breathed deeply to control myself.

"To win this war, we need the army to function as a unified command. Articles of War defend the soldier *and* the army. You understand that?"

"Yes, sir." I had to breathe deeply again.

"We have reports that you may be involved in a conspiracy."

I thought it best to be silent.

"Do you know what that means?"

"Yes, sir."

"This conspiracy now means two men have been charged with attempted murder. I want you to tell me honestly two things."

"Yes, sir."

"Were you in the riot in Nogales?"

Lay dead, play crazy. If they knew everything, they would have arrested you a long time ago. They think you're another stupid jig they can intimidate. I fought to hold back the rage.

"I didn't know there was no riot, sir. My friend and me (don't speak too good English—it'll make them suspicious) we was walking a little ways from what they called Ranchita and some white soldiers jumped us. We got in a fight and got back to where the convoy was. I heard there was other fights that night."

The major was ruddy, paunchy, threatening. He leaned toward me. "You listen to me, boy—uh—soldier. What happened out there is serious. You either tell me the truth or I'm gonna have you arrested and put under oath. You'll tell the truth then." His voice was heavy with rural South Carolina.

It wasn't a question. I looked at the ground and then glanced at Akeley. Our eyes met for a millisecond. He flushed slightly. I sensed he wasn't going to let them mistreat his nigger.

"Do you know a Corporal Joe H. Johnson in D Company, 25th Infantry?"

The blood was pounding in my temples. Half truth this time. They know something.

"Yes, sir. I got to know him when he won the machine gun competition in Huachuca."

"You seen him lately?"

"No, sir. Not since we left Huachuca." My back and scalp broke out into an itchy sweat. My God, it must have been Joe Henry.

"Did something happen to Joe Henry, sir?"

"We'll ask the questions." The major's face flushed even more.

"Something's going to happen to him," Snake Eyes said. "He opened fire on unarmed soldiers this morning. You volunteered. Why? You enlisted in the Civilian Military Training Corps. Why?"

"I went into CMTC because my dad always liked army life. I sorta wanted to become an officer in the army."

"That's why you volunteered?"

"No, sir. I believe that I should defend my country. I don't like everything, but it's my country." Snake Eyes was backing off me. I wasn't fooling Maj. Johnny Reb. There was a moment of awkward silence while they figured out how to proceed. Captain Akeley cleared his throat.

"I would like to dismiss the sergeant and speak to you all privately."

Akeley glanced at me. I rose, saluted, and left the tent. I knew what was going on in there. Akeley, from Mississippi, would say he's a good boy. Yes, from the North. Runs his mouth too much, and don't quite know his place. He's learning that the colored people still need the firm and kindly guidance of the Southern whites who know them best. Akeley would say that he was responsible for me and would vouch for me. The other two, being in the white man's club, would have to accept this. They would let me go and keep me under surveillance.

This final realization of a black man's impotence weighed against my chest. I could hardly breathe and tears were beginning to fill the emptiness. Black man will never be anything but a boy in this country. Even if you kill one of these white bastards, you're not a brave man; you're a dangerous, crazy nigger. You outsmart them, you're a sneaky, sinister nigger. I can't even raise a rebellion without the protection of a Mississippi white man.

Suddenly, I realized that this was my birthday! I was twenty and it was the worst day of my life.

"A Sunday Evening"

Peter Ota

In an excerpt from *"The Good War"*, Studs Terkel interviews Peter Ota, an American-born Japanese man who served in the American military during the war.

I think back to what happened—and sometimes I wonder: where do I come from?

He is a fifty-seven-year-old Nisei. His father had come from Okinawa in 1904, his mother from Japan. He's an accountant. His father had worked on farms and in the coal mines of Mexico. After thirty-seven years building a fruit and vegetable business, he had become a successful and respected merchant in the community. He was a leader in the Japanese Chamber of Commerce of Los Angeles.

On the evening of December 7, 1941, my father was at a wedding. He was dressed in a tuxedo. When the reception was over, the FBI agents were waiting. They rounded up at least a dozen wedding guests and took 'em to county jail.

For a few days we didn't know what happened. We heard nothing. When we found out, my mother, my sister, and myself went to jail. I can still remember waiting in the lobby. When my father walked through the door, my mother was so humiliated. She didn't say anything. She cried. He was in prisoner's clothing, with a denim jacket and a number on the back.

The shame and humiliation just broke her down. She was into Japanese culture. She was a flower arranger and used to play the *biwa*, a Japanese stringed instrument. Shame in her culture is worse than death. Right after that day she got very ill and contracted tuberculosis. She had to be sent to a sanitarium. She stayed behind when we were evacuated. She was too ill to be moved. She was there till she passed away.

My father was transferred to Missoula, Montana. We got letters from him—censored, of course—telling us he was all right. It was just my sister and myself. I was fifteen, she was twelve. In April 1942, we were evacuated to Santa Anita. At the time we didn't know where we were going, how long we'd be gone. We didn't know what to take. A toothbrush, toilet supplies, some clothes. Only what you could carry. We left with a caravan.

Santa Anita is a race track. The horse stables were converted into living quarters. My sister and I were fortunate enough to stay in a barracks. The people in the stables had to live with the stench. Everything was communal. We had absolutely no privacy. When you went to the toilet, it was communal. It was very embarrassing for women especially. The parent actually lost control of the child. I had no parents, so I did as I pleased. When I think back what happened to the Japanese family . . .

We had orders to leave Santa Anita in September of 1942. We had no idea where we were going. Just before we left, my father joined us. He was brought into camp on the back of an army state truck, he and several others who were released from Missoula. I can still picture it to this day: to come in like cattle or sheep being herded in the back of a pickup truck bed. We were near the gate and saw him come in. He saw us. It was a sad, happy moment, because we'd been separated for a year.

He never really expressed what his true inner feelings were. It just amazes me. He was never vindictive about it, never showed any anger. I can't understand that. A man who had worked so hard for what he had and lost it overnight. There is a very strong word in Japanese, *gaman*. It means to persevere. Old people instilled this into the second generation: you persevere. Take what's coming, don't react.

He had been a very outgoing person. Enthusiastic. I was very, very impressed with how he ran things and worked with people. When I saw him at Santa Anita, he was a different person.

We were put on a train, three of us and many trains of others. It was crowded. The shades were drawn. During the ride we were wondering, what are they going to do to us? We Niseis had enough confidence in our government that it wouldn't do anything drastic. My father had put all his faith in this country. This was his land.

Oh, it took days. We arrived in Amache, Colorado. That was an experience in itself. We were right near the Kansas border. It's a desolate, flat, barren area. The barracks was all there was. There were no trees, no kind of landscaping. It was like a prison camp. Coming from our environment, it was just devastating.

School in camp was a joke. Let's say it was loose. If you wanted to study, fine. If you didn't, who cared? There were some teachers who were conscientious and a lot who were not. One of our basic subjects was American history. They talked about freedom all the time. (Laughs.)

After a year, I was sent out to Utah on jobs. I worked on sugar beet farms. You had to have a contract or a job in order to leave camp. The pay was nominal. We would have a labor boss, the farmer would pay us through him. It was piecework. Maybe fifteen of us would work during the harvest season. When it was over, we went back to camp.

If you had a job waiting, you could relocate to a city that was not in the Western Defense Command. I had one in Chicago, as a stock boy in a candy factory. It paid seventy-five cents an hour. I was only in camp for a year. My sister was in until they were dismantled, about three and a half years. My father was in various camps for four years.

I went from job to job for a year. I had turned draft age, so I had to register. It's ironic. Here I am being drafted into the army, and my father and sister are in a concentration camp waiting for the war to end.

I was in the reserve, not yet inducted, in the middle of 1944, when I received a wire from my father saying that my mother was very ill. I immediately left Chicago for Amache, Colorado, to get my clearance from the Western Defense Command. It took several days. While I was waiting, my mother passed away.

Since we wanted her funeral to be at the camp where my father and sister were, I decided to go on to California and pick up her remains. At Needles, California, I was met at the train by an FBI agent. He was assigned to me. He was with me at all times during my stay there. Whether I went to sleep at night or whether I went to the bathroom, he was by my side.

As soon as we stepped off the train at the Union Station in Los Angeles, there was a shore patrol and a military police who met me. They escorted me through the station. It was one of the most . . . (He finds it difficult to talk.) I don't even know how to describe it. Any day now, I'd be serving in the same uniform as these people who were guarding me. The train stations at that time were always filled. When they marched me through, the people recognized me as being Oriental. They knew I was either an escaped prisoner or a spy. Oh, they called out names. I heard "dirty Jap" very distinctly.

After we got to the hotel, the FBI agent convinced the military that it wasn't necessary for them to stay with me. But he had to. He was disgusted with the whole situation. He knew I was in the reserve, that I was an American citizen. He could see no reason for him to be with me. But he was on assignment. We spoke personal things. His wife was having a baby; he couldn't be with her. He thought it was ridiculous.

I was in the armored division at Fort Knox. We were sent to Fort Mead for embarkation when the European war ended. They didn't know what to do with us Japanese Americans. We were in our own units. Should they send us to the Pacific side? They might not be able to tell who was the enemy and who was not. (Laughs.)

The war ended while I was at Fort McDowell on San Francisco Bay. That was the receiving point for Japanese prisoners captured in the war. I went back with a boatload of them. I didn't know how they'd react to me. I was very surprised. The professional soldiers who were captured during the early days of the war in Guadalcanal, Saipan, never believed the war ended. They would always say, when the subject came up, it was propaganda. The civilian soldiers were very different. We could get along with them. They were very young—*boheitai*, boy soldiers. We could relate to them as to children. They were scared. They had nothing to go back to. Okinawa was devastated. A lot of them lost their families.

My furloughs were spent in camp, visiting my father and sister. Going to camp was like going home for me, to see my family. We made the best of what we had. We celebrated Christmas in the American fashion. We tried to make our lives go easy.

We came back to Los Angeles at the end of the war, believing that there was no other way but to be American. We were discouraged with our Japanese culture. My feeling at the time was, I had to prove myself. I don't know why I had to prove myself. Here I am, an ex-GI, born and raised here. Why do I have to prove myself? We all had this feeling. We had to prove that we were Americans, okay?

My mother and father sent me to a Japanese school teaching the culture. My wife and I did nothing with our children in that respect. We moved to a white community near Los Angeles. It was typical American suburb living. We became more American than Americans, very conservative. My wife and I, we talk about this. We thought this was the thing we had to do: to blend into the community and become part of white America.

My children were denied a lot of the history of what happened. If you think of all those forty years of silence, I think this stems from another Japanese characteristic: when shame is put on you, you try to hide it. We were put into camps, we became victims, it was our fault. We hide it.

My oldest daughter, Cathy, in her senior year at college, wanted to write a thesis about the camp experience. She asked if we knew people she might interview. Strange thing is, many people, even now, didn't want to talk about it. Some of the people she did talk to broke down. Because this was the first time they had told this story. This is the same thing I did. When I first went into detail, it just broke me up. When it came out, I personally felt good about it. It was somethin' that was inside of me that I've wanted to say for a long time.

How do the Sansei feel about it—your daughter's generation?

Very angry. They keep saying, "Why did you go? Why didn't you fight back?" They couldn't understand it. They weren't raised in our culture. Today, I would definitely resist. It was a different situation at that time. This is what we tried to explain to our daughter. Today if this happened, I think a majority of the Japanese would resist.

When I think back to my mother and my father, what they went through quietly, it's hard to explain. (Cries.) I think of my father without ever coming up with an angry word. After all those years, having worked his whole life to build a dream—an American dream, mind you—having it all taken away, and not one vindictive word. His business was worth more than a hundred thousand. He sold it for five. When he came out of camp, with what little money he had he put a down payment on an apartment building. It was right in the middle of skid row, an old rooming house. He felt he could survive by taking in a little rent and living there. My sister worked for a family as a domestic. He was afraid for her in this area. He died a very broken man.

My wife and I, we're up on cloud nine right now. Our daughter just passed the California bar. Guess what she's doing? She works for the redress and reparations group in San Diego.* How's that?

A movement for redress of grievances has come into being on behalf of Japanese Americans who were interned during the war years.

In February 1942, President Franklin D. Roosevelt issued Executive Order 9066, which called for the exclusion of people of Japanese descent from the Pacific Coast, and their internment in "War Relocation Camps" throughout the West. Approximately 110,000 Japanese Americans—two thirds of them U.S. citizens—were forcibly relocated to remote camps such as Manzanar, in the Owens Valley of California. Manzanar was extensively photographed by the acclaimed photographer Ansel Adams in 1943.

"Entrance to Manzanar Relocation Center, Manzanar, California." (Ansel Adams, photographer; 1943; Manzanar War Relocation Center Photographs, Library of Congress)

"Mr. and Mrs. Henry J. Tsurutani and baby Bruce, Manzanar Relocation Center, California." (Ansel Adams, photographer; 1943; Manzanar War Relocation Center Photographs, Library of Congress)

"Roy Takeno reading the newspaper in front of the Manzanar Free Press offices, Manzanar Relocation Center, California." (Ansel Adams, photographer; 1943; Manzanar War Relocation Center Photographs, Library of Congress)

"Street scene, Manzanar Relocation Center." (Ansel Adams, photographer; 1943; Manzanar War Relocation Center Photographs, Library of Congress)

"Statement on Entering Prison"

David Dellinger

In an excerpt from *Home Fronts,* David Dellinger, a longtime political activist and advocate of nonviolence, issues a political statement on his status as a conscientious objector, in 1943. Dellinger was sentenced to a year in prison for his refusal to register for the draft during the war.

I. I believe that all war is evil and useless. Even a so-called war of defense is evil in that it consists of lies, hatred, self-righteousness, and the most destructive methods of violence that man can invent. These things corrupt even the most idealistic supporters of the war. They harm even the most innocent children of "enemy" countries.

Even a war fought with the highest idealism is useless in that it can produce no good result that could not be secured better in other ways. Just as it would be stupid to plant weeds and to try to harvest vegetables, so it would be stupid to encourage the lies, conscription, and murder of war, and to hope to produce democracy, freedom, and brotherhood. War is a Trojan horse from which emerge at home the enemies that destroy us.

The fact that some people sincerely believe that war will help us cannot persuade me to cooperate in their mistake. Instead it makes it all the more important to do everything possible to help free them from their error and to show them a substitute for war.

II. I believe that when anyone supports war he violates the life and teachings of Jesus.

III. I believe that the so-called United Nations and each individual resident of them bear a tremendous responsibility for this present war.

A. The rest of the world has been driven to desperation by the economic cruelty of the United States, with its Big Business Empire, and of England, with her Colonial Empire. We produced the economic, social, and psychological conditions that made war inevitable. Russia, for all her social reforms, is a bloody dictatorship that has followed a policy of selfish nationalism for years. As part of this policy she has subsidized political parties, all over the world, that have poisoned the left wing movement with dishonesty, opportunism, and violence.

B. So far as Germany and Italy are concerned, British and American politicians and industrialists supported the rise of Hitler and Mussolini. One reason they did this was to make private profits out of various business deals. A second reason was that Hitler and Mussolini were destroying the labor and socialist movements of Europe, which had the power to introduce economic and social democracy to oppressed peoples everywhere. If you find this hard to believe, let me remind you that the United States government is following a similar policy today. Of course they cannot support the two individuals, Hitler and Mussolini, but they are supporting totalitarian forces in every country—Giraud, Peyroutan, Franco, Prince Otto Habsburg, the Junkers of Germany, the land owners and business interests of Italy, the dictators of Latin America, etc. At the same time they are opposing the democratic forces of Europe—and their representatives in this country.

Even after the early honeymoon with Hitler and Mussolini, when these men began to emerge as dangerous Frankensteins, the United States and England were still ready to sell the democratic freedoms of Spain, Austria, Czechoslovakia, etc., down the river. They resisted every suggestion that we offer the hungry people of Europe the economic and social equality that would have uprooted both fascism and war.

C. So far as Asia is concerned, we introduced modern violence and robbery to the Japanese, by our rape of the orient. Later we were partners of Japan in her invasion of China. American oil, steel, and munitions were sold at huge profits for that purpose. President Roosevelt, the State Department, and politicians all conspired in this. *Every one of them is as guilty of murder as are the Japanese whom they accuse.*

We began to boycott Japan only when it began to threaten our damnable mastery of the orient, and when we needed an incident to strengthen the propaganda by which we were trying to sell the war to our own peace-loving people.

Churchill himself has admitted in Parliament that President Roosevelt committed us to war against Japan in August 1941, four months before Pearl Harbor. Shortly afterward we started issuing ultimatums and threats for *the sole purpose* of carrying out this promise—that we would wage war against Japan before the year was out.

We also began a policy of limited naval warfare. Naval officers have admitted that *before Pearl Harbor,* they were sent on secret expeditions with orders to shoot Japanese ships and aircraft—on sight and without warning. See Jeannette Rankin's speech in the House of Representatives on December 8, 1942. The same policy was pursued in the Atlantic. Rather brazen proof of this terribly policy of our government has just been given by the Navy Department in General Order No. 190, whereby the Navy, Marine Corps, and Coast Guard personnel have been ordered to wear a bronze letter A on their American defense medal service ribbon "to commemorate service on ships operating in actual or potential belligerent contact with Axis forces in the Atlantic Ocean prior to December 7, 1941."

How many Japanese ships were sunk in this way, we do not know. Nor do we know how many peace-loving Japanese reluctantly accepted the war because of our treachery. But the governments of the United States and Japan each exploited the treachery of the other, forcing war upon its own people.

D. We also went to war to avoid facing up to the failures of our selfishly organized private-ownership, private-profit system.

At home we have a system whereby the mines, factories, and other means of production are owned and operated not for the good of all but for the private profit of a few. *Such organized selfishness will not work.* It produced years of mass unemployment, depression, and unrest. But even the misery of millions did not persuade the privileged classes to give up their stranglehold on God's material gifts and to embrace the total democracy and brotherhood that alone will work. Instead, after seven desperate years of bread lines and boondoggling, they turned to the manufacture of armaments. Roosevelt himself, in an interview recorded in the *New York Times*, pointed to Nazi Germany and said that she had lots of armaments plants and no unemployment.

At the same time they played up war scares and international hatreds as an excuse for making bombs instead of bread, and as a scapegoat on which to blame the sufferings of the people.

After a time "national defense" was an insufficient excuse for slavery and injustice. The people were restless. Our privileged classes had to choose: brotherhood or war. The Axis threatened the financial and business empire of certain private interests. War offered an excellent smokescreen for profiteering, for feeling important, and for suppressing American freedom, with all its dangers to economic selfishness. Finally, the brutality of the Axis presented the idealistic mask without which neither the people nor most of their masters would have been able to face the terrible choice they made.

Very few people actually chose war. They chose selfishness and the result was war. Each of us, individually and nationally, must choose: total love or total war.

Most people are afraid to choose total love and brotherhood. It is too new, too daring. It seems to require too many sacrifices. For the privileged classes who control the normal instruments for manufacturing public opinion and making public decisions, it means abandoning certain traditional privileges which bring no real happiness—so long as they are private privileges—but which possess a superficial glitter and attractiveness. For all of us it means abandoning our pride, our self-centeredness, and whatever special privileges we have or hope to have some day.

The selfishness of all of us underlies the dishonesty of our Roosevelts and Tojos, the brutality of our Hitlers and Churchills. . . .

"Rosie"

Peggy Terry

In an excerpt from *"The Good War"*, Studs Terkel interviews a woman who went to work in a factory during the war.

She is a mountain woman who has lived in Chicago for the past twenty years. Paducah, Kentucky, is her hometown. She visits it as often as her meager purse allows.

The first work I had after the Depression was at a shell-loading plant in Viola, Kentucky. It is between Paducah and Mayfield. They were large shells: anti-aircraft, incendiaries, and tracers. We painted red on the tips of the tracers. My mother, my sister, and myself worked there. Each of us worked a different shift because we had little ones at home. We made the fabulous sum of thirty-two dollars a week. (Laughs.) To us it was just an absolute miracle. Before that, we made nothing.

You won't believe how incredibly ignorant I was. I knew vaguely that a war had started, but I had no idea what it meant.

Didn't you have a radio?

Gosh, no. That was an absolute luxury. We were just moving around, working wherever we could find work. I was eighteen. My husband was nineteen. We were living day to day. When you are involved in stayin' alive, you don't think about big things like a war. It didn't occur to us that we were making these shells to kill people. It never entered my head.

There were no women foremen where we worked. We were just a bunch of hillbilly women laughin' and talkin'. It was like a social. Now we'd have money to buy shoes and a dress and pay rent and get some food on the table. We were just happy to have work.

I worked in building number 11. I pulled a lot of gadgets on a machine. The shell slid under and powder went into it. Another lever you pulled tamped it down. Then it moved on a conveyer belt to another building where the detonator was dropped in. You did this over and over.

Tetryl was one of the ingredients and it turned us orange. Just as orange as an orange. Our hair was streaked orange. Our hands, our face, our neck just turned orange, even our eyeballs. We never questioned. None of us ever asked, What is this? Is this harmful? We simply didn't think about it. That was just one of the conditions of the job. The only thing we worried about was other women thinking we had dyed our hair. Back then it was a disgrace if you dyed your hair. We worried what people would say.

We used to laugh about it on the bus. It eventually wore off. But I seem to remember some of the women had breathing problems. The shells were painted a dark gray. When the paint didn't come out smooth, we had to take rags wet with some kind of remover and wash that paint off. The fumes from these rags—it was like breathing cleaning fluid. It burned the nose and throat. Oh, it was difficult to breathe. I remember that.

Nothing ever blew up, but I remember the building where they dropped in the detonator. These detonators are little black things about the size of a thumb. This terrible thunderstorm came and all the lights went out. Somebody knocked a box of detonators off on the floor. Here we were in the pitch dark. Somebody was screaming, "Don't move, anybody!" They were afraid you'd step on the detonator. We were down on our hands and knees crawling out of that building in the storm. (Laughs.) We were in slow motion. If we'd stepped on one . . .

Mamma was what they call terminated—fired. Mamma's mother took sick and died and Mamma asked for time off and they told her no. Mamma said, "Well, I'm gonna be with my mamma. If I have to give up my job, I will just have to." So they terminated Mamma. That's when I started gettin' nasty. I didn't take as much baloney and pushing around as I had taken. I told 'em I was gonna quit, and they told me if I quit they would blacklist me wherever I would go. They had my fingerprints and all that. I guess it was just bluff, because I did get other work.

I think of how little we knew of human rights, union rights. We knew Daddy had been a hell-raiser in the mine workers' union, but at that point it hadn't rubbed off on any of us women. Coca-Cola and Dr. Pepper were allowed in every building, but not a drop of water. You could only get a drink of water if you went to the cafeteria, which was about two city blocks away. Of course you couldn't leave your machine long enough to go get a drink. I drank Coke and Dr. Pepper and I hated 'em. I hate 'em today. We had to buy it, of course. We couldn't leave to go to the bathroom, 'cause it was way the heck over there.

We were awarded the navy E for excellence. We were just so proud of that E. It was like we were a big family, and we hugged and kissed each other. They had the navy band out there celebrating us. We were so proud of ourselves.

First time my mother ever worked at anything except in the fields—first real job Mamma ever had. It was a big break in everybody's life. Once, Mamma woke up in the middle of the night to go to the bathroom and she saw the bus going down. She said, "Oh my goodness, I've overslept." She jerked her clothes on, threw her lunch in the bag, and was out on the corner, ready to go, when

Boy Blue, our driver, said, "Honey, this is the wrong shift." Mamma wasn't supposed to be there until six in the morning. She never lived that down. She would have enjoyed telling you that.

My world was really very small. When we came from Oklahoma to Paducah, that was like a journey to the center of the earth. It was during the Depression and you did good having bus fare to get across town. The war just widened my world. Especially after I came up to Michigan.

My grandfather went up to Jackson, Michigan, after he retired from the railroad. He wrote back and told us we could make twice as much in the war plants in Jackson. We did. We made ninety dollars a week. We did some kind of testing for airplane radios.

Oh, I met all those wonderful Polacks. They were the first people I'd ever known that were any different from me. A whole new world just opened up. I learned to drink beer like crazy with 'em. They were all very union-conscious. I learned a lot of things that I didn't even know existed.

We were very patriotic and we understood that the Nazis were someone who would have to be stopped. We didn't know about concentration camps. I don't think anybody I knew did. With the Japanese, that was a whole different thing. We were just ready to wipe them out. They sure as heck didn't look like us. They were yellow little creatures that smiled when they bombed our boys. I remember someone in Paducah got up this idea of burning everything they had that was Japanese. I had this little ceramic cat and I said, "I don't care, I am not burning it." They had this big bonfire and people came and brought what they had that was made in Japan. Threw it on the bonfire. I hid my cat. It's on the shelf in my bathroom right now. (Laughs.)

In all the movies we saw, the Germans were always tall and handsome. There'd be one meanie, a little short dumpy bad Nazi. But the main characters were good-lookin' and they looked like us. The Japanese were all evil. If you can go half your life and not recognize how you're being manipulated, that is sad and kinda scary.

I do remember a nice movie, *The White Cliffs of Dover*. We all sat there with tears pouring down our face. All my life, I hated England, 'cause all my family all my life had wanted England out of Ireland. During the war, all those ill feelings just seemed to go away. It took a war.

I believe the war was the beginning of my seeing things. You just can't stay uninvolved and not knowing when such a momentous thing is happening. It's just little things that start happening and you put one piece with another. Suddenly, a puzzle begins to take shape.

My husband was a paratrooper in the war, in the 101st Airborne Division. He made twenty-six drops in France, North Africa, and Germany. I look back at the war with sadness. I wasn't smart enough to think too deeply then. We had a lotta good times and we had money and we had food on the table and the rent was paid. Which had never happened to us before. But when I look back and think of him . . .

Until the war he never drank. He never even smoked. When he came back he was an absolute drunkard. And he used to have the most awful nightmares. He'd get up in the middle of the night and start screaming. I'd just sit for hours and hold him while he just shook. We'd go to the movies, and if they'd have films with a lot of shooting in it, he'd just start to shake and have to get up and leave. He started slapping me around and slapped the kids around. He became a brute.

Some fifteen years before, Peggy had recalled her experiences during the Great Depression. She and her young husband were on the road. "We were just kids. I was fifteen and he was sixteen. . . . It was a very nice time, because when you're poor and you stay in one spot, trouble just seems to catch up with you. But when you're moving from town to town, you don't stay there long enough for trouble to catch up with you."

One of the things that bothered him most was his memory of this town he was in. He saw something move by a building and he shot.

It was a woman. He never got over that. It seems so obvious to say—wars brutalize people. It brutalized him.

The war gave a lot of people jobs. It led them to expect more than they had before. People's expectations, financially, spiritually, were raised. There was such a beautiful dream. We were gonna reach the end of the rainbow. When the war ended, the rainbow vanished. Almost immediately we went into Korea. There was no peace, which we were promised.

I remember a woman saying on the bus that she hoped the war didn't end until she got her refrigerator paid for. An old man hit her over the head with an umbrella. He said, "How dare you!" (Laughs.)

Oh, the beautiful celebrations when the war ended. They were selling cigarettes in Paducah. Up until that hour, you couldn'ta bought a pack of cigarettes for love or money. Kirchoff's Bakery was giving away free loaves of bread. Everybody was downtown in the pouring rain and we were dancing. We took off our shoes and put 'em in our purse. We were so happy.

The night my husband came home, we went out with a gang of friends and got drunk. All of us had a tattoo put on. I had a tattoo put up my leg where it wouldn't show. A heart with an arrow through it: Bill and Peggy. When I went to the hospital to have my baby—I got pregnant almost as soon as he came home—I was ashamed of the tattoo. So I put two Band-Aids across it. So the nurse just pulls 'em off, looks at the tattoo, and she says, "Oh, that's exactly in the same spot I got mine." She pulled her uniform up and showed me her tattoo. (Laughs.)

I knew the bomb dropped on Hiroshima was a big terrible thing, but I didn't know it was the horror it was. It was on working people. It wasn't anywhere near the big shots of Japan who started the war in the first place. We didn't drop it on them. Hirohito and his white horse, it never touched him. It was dropped on women and children who had nothing to say about whether their country went to war or not.

I was happy my husband would get to come home and wouldn't be sent there from Germany. Every day when the paper came out, there'd be somebody I knew with their picture. An awful lot of kids I knew, went to school and church with, were killed.

No bombs were ever dropped on us. I can't help but believe the Cold War started because we were untouched. Except for our boys that went out of the country and were killed, we came out of that war in good shape. People with more money than they'd had in years.

No, I don't think we'd have been satisfied to go back to what we had during the Depression. To be deprived of things we got used to. Materially, we're a thousand times better off. But the war turned me against religion. I was raised in the fundamentalist faith. I was taught that I was nothing. My feeling is if God created me, if God sent his only begotten son to give his life for me, then I am something. My mother died thinking she was nothing. I don't know how chaplains can call themselves men of God and prepare boys to go into battle. If the Bible says, Thou shalt not kill, it doesn't say, Except in time of war. They'll send a man to the electric chair who in a temper killed somebody. But they pin medals on our men. The more people they kill, the more medals they pin on 'em.

I was just so glad when it was over, because I wanted my husband home. I didn't understand any of the implications except that the killing was over and that's a pretty good thing to think about whether you're political or not. (Laughs.) The killing be over forever.

At the outset of World War II, the U.S. workforce included 12 million women, a quarter of the total; by 1945, this number had risen by 6 million, to nearly a third of the total. Three million women took jobs in war-related industries, including aircraft manufacturing and shipbuilding, stepping into roles traditionally limited to men. "Rosie the Riveter"—featured on propaganda posters and popular songs—quickly became a national icon, and remains a potent symbol of the economic and labor power of women.

"Women at work on a bomber, Douglas Aircraft Company, Long Beach, California." (Alfred T. Palmer, photographer; October 1943, Farm Security Administration—Office of War Information Collection, Library of Congress)

"A candid view of one of the women workers touching up the U.S. Army Air Forces insignia on the side of the fuselage of a 'Vengeance' dive bomber manufactured at Vultee's Nashville division, Tennessee." (Alfred T. Palmer, photographer; February 1943, Farm Security Administration—Office of War Information Collection, Library of Congress)

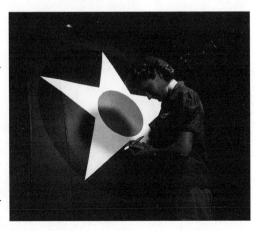

"With a woman's determination, Lorena Craig takes over a man-size job, Corpus Christi, Texas. Before she came to work at the Naval air base she was a department store girl. Now she is a cowler under civil service." (Howard R. Hollem, photographer; August 1942, Farm Security Administration—Office of War Information Collection, Library of Congress)

"We Can Do It." (Color poster by J. Howard Miller for the War Production Coordinating Committee, 1942)

"Confronting the Holocaust"

David Wyman and Hillel Kook

Historian David Wyman (from *A Race Against Death*) interviews Hillel Kook, who led the effort in the United States to
push American leaders to rescue European Jews from the
Holocaust.

WYMAN: When were you first aware that there was systematic
extermination?[1]

KOOK: When Rabbi Wise was quoted in the *Washington Post* story, in
November of 1942.[2] That morning was the most traumatic day in my
life. When I read it in the *Post*.

W: What was your reaction?

K: I ran to see [Adolf] Berle, in the State Department.[3] My first
thought was disbelief. I hoped it was not true. I ran to see Berle.
I went, I told his secretary, I'll wait until he can see me. And he saw
me. I said, is it true? And he said, yes, unfortunately. They've known
it for some time. They told Rabbi Wise he should make a statement
and they had to urge him to make a statement.[4]

W: How widely known do you think this information became to the
public in general?

K: The fact that the *Washington Post* didn't put it on the front page
speaks for itself. It was on an inside page. It *became* known, there's
no question.

w: Given a few more months, do you think the population in general was aware?

к: Oh, yes.

w: Including non-Jews, too, right across the board?

к: I don't know. I lived in Washington and New York. The press here—we ran some of those ads. But of course we didn't run them in Tallahassee.

w: Do you think that Jews were particularly well aware?

к: Yes, I would think so.

w: Do you think that people in the government were certainly aware?

к: No question about it. We tried to mobilize government counter-action. This wasn't pogroms. Here was a decision of a major European nation, a very mighty military power, to declare a war of extermination against the Jews at a time when the other major nations—the United States, England, and Russia—were fighting that nation, Germany. And my reaction was that this isn't something we can do. The only thing we can do is to get the government to act. Our whole activity was zeroed and concentrated on producing government action. In two ways—one, by lobbying, and the other by building public opinion.

In the time of the period we are talking about now, after the news came out concerning the extermination of the Jews.[5] Nothing! I wasn't *acting* as a lost fellow, we *were* lost. We were hit with this thing by shock. And we felt something ought to be done, and we knew that [the mainstream Jewish organizations] are much more powerful than we are. It wasn't a question here that we had ideas, we hadn't any ideas, we'll take anybody's ideas. When it came to questions of what should we do in Palestine we had some maybe different ideas than [the Zionist leadership]. But on this we had no preconceived notions, there was no ideology, there was nothing.

I arrived here in 1940. The American Friends of a Jewish

Palestine* was operating and had a two-room office and one secretary, but it didn't have the money to pay her. And, slowly, slowly we
started plodding along. Jabotinsky died, and then this whole thing
sort of—even we were affected by the war, the war wasn't going well.
The whole world looked very bleak.

And then we started working on the Committee for a Jewish
Army. We started early in '41. We didn't succeed in really launch-
ing the committee in a big way till late '41. It took us a whole year
to get together a few respectable names, to launch a public thing
in Washington and get someplace. Slowly we started gaining supporters, and people, and things started happening. I started going
down to Washington. One day I got a phone call from a man called
Emanuel Neumann,[6] who was then working for the Emergency
Committee for Zionist Affairs [later known as the American Zionist Emergency Council]. I'd known him briefly in Palestine, he was
an American who was in the Jewish Agency executive and one of
the Zionist parties. We met and he says, "You look familiar," and so
on. He had started hearing things from congressmen, and he started
getting questions, you know, "Is [the Committee for a Jewish Army]
okay? Is it this? Is it that?" they asked. Suddenly, we became a factor in Washington, politically. And we started meeting. He said,
"Look, you guys are young, you have energy, you are just what the
Zionist movement needs. Why can't we work together?" I said,
"Who says we can't work together?" "You're for a Jewish army," he
said, "I'm for it." I said, "Fine. Let's try and get it. We are working
for a Jewish army. If you're for it, now let's talk." And he initiated
some conversations, but nothing happened.

Dr. Neumann was then the Zionist movement's man in

*The American Friends of a Jewish Palestine was established in 1938 by a small
group of Irgun Zvai Leumi emissaries sent to the United States by Jabotinsky to
raise funds for the immigration of European Jews to Palestine in defiance of British
restrictions.

Washington. He also originated the meeting between Ben-Gurion and me at his home, in mid-1942. To try to hammer out—just he, and Ben-Gurion, and I met, and after a few minutes he left. We were supposed to meet for half an hour. We stayed there six hours. At the end of which Ben-Gurion told me I was crazy. [Laughter.]

w: It took him six hours!

k: Yes. But, it had a very profound effect on him. He knows it. There remained a kind of a contact between us. Basically, what he did in 1948 was what we tried to tell him in 1942 was to be done. We said, "Look, you have to declare independence. You can't say there *ought* to be a Jewish state." Jabotinsky and Weizmann used to debate. Jabotinsky wanted the Zionist Congress to pass a resolution that the aim of Zionism was a Jewish state. And they said that this was too extreme, this would alienate people. They were afraid to say what the purpose was. They didn't say they were against a Jewish state. But they said that the Zionist Congress shouldn't formulate it that harshly. Then Ben-Gurion came here with the aim of getting a Zionist convention—it was at the Biltmore Hotel, it's called the Biltmore Resolution—to do what Jabotinsky said should be done four years earlier. So I told him, "Look, this is a debate that is cold dishwater. It's last week's pudding." Whatever the expression is in English for such an expression. There's one in Yiddish. I said, "This isn't the issue anymore. The issue is: if we want a country, if we want independence, we have to declare it and ask for recognition. Nobody is going to do it for us." You know, like anybody else. And he thought this was crazy. That's what finally happened, obviously.

So there were—this was the first contact with Zionists. Then there started to be a series of contacts. The first big meeting was in 1942, early, when we were already sort of in full swing with the Committee for a Jewish Army, running ads which shook them. Full-page ads then were an unheard-of thing. They thought this was obscene. For political—for Jews! There were Jews on the obituary page of the *Times* or something, you know. Suddenly, an ad? So, they thought it was a disgrace.

At one point somewhat later on, there was a meeting between Roosevelt and Wise, in which Roosevelt very sharply told Wise that our work—all this yelling about the Jewish army and this thing—will bring the Arabs to an uprising. And that it would then need ten divisions from the war to overcome the Arab uprising and that this may endanger the whole war effort. And therefore, if the Zionists won't find ways to hush us up, he will have to take very stern measures against the Zionist organizations, United Palestine Appeal, and all these things. I don't know whether Roosevelt said it, that's what Wise reported. So Wise called a kind of an emergency meeting of all the Zionist pooh-bahs, all the big *machers*, as we say in Yiddish, and invited us, and we were put on the carpet, we were being given a thrashing. And Wise says that there are only half a million Jews in Palestine, and there are nearly 5 million Jews—so may the Lord help them—in this country, and what right do we have to endanger the 5 million Jews here, and this and that. So this was part of a pattern of contacting us in order to get us not to act, which continued throughout the years of the extermination.

And Wise, typical to what I call the ghetto Jewish leadership, which wasn't restricted only to the ghetto, surrendered without a word. He didn't ask Roosevelt who made the report—what report? I mean, it didn't even dawn on him to question him. To me it didn't make sense. I mean, I know the Middle East a little bit, as a student, and this figure of ten divisions is just a lot of nonsense. I mean, because the whole Lawrence business is good for a movie. Not for ten divisions then, and where are the Arabs coming using ten divisions? So we went—

W: He, after castigating your group or telling you to dampen it down—

K: We told him we wouldn't.

W: Your first ads about rescue were still in the name of the Committee for a Jewish Army, and they included the creation of a Jewish army as one of your demands. What really was the purpose in such an army?

K: To fight the Germans.

W: Because of the threat of attack on Palestine, because they were coming across North Africa?

K: No, because we felt that the Hebrew nation was a belligerent in the war. Germany was fighting—if Germany won the war, we would be obliterated, not in the sense of the Holocaust, which we didn't foresee, but Germany was more our enemy than the enemy of the British, let's say. And we felt that it was our moral duty and practical survival necessity to fight the Germans. We felt that an army—it was a purely political thing—an army should consist of the Jews of Palestine. You see, Palestine was neutral under law. A mandated territory is neutral. Jews in Palestine could volunteer, they couldn't be drafted.

W: Why wasn't that satisfactory, to volunteer for the British army? It's the same objective, it's the same force, the same enemy.

K: Well, because—for the same reason that a Frenchman doesn't want to fight in the Portuguese army. Eventually what happened is that the British agreed to establish the Palestinian units.

W: That's putting the cart before the horse. At first there was no Jewish army, and there is an enemy that needs to be defeated. Why not join the British army? Just as many Americans joined the Canadian forces before the United States got in the war.

K: Why? Because the United States could have been in the war and didn't want to.

W: And so if you wanted to fight in the war, you had to go to Canada. So you didn't have a Jewish army, so why spend your efforts on a Jewish army when you can join the British one?

K: We wanted to have a Jewish army because we felt we were a Jewish nation. We're talking about survival, as a nation, not as individuals. Also the Holocaust. I said that we wanted a Jewish army because we felt—

w: Was the thought in your mind that, come the end of the war, if we have an armed forces it's going to be very useful—and, of course, the British knew this—

k: Absolutely, absolutely. No question about it. Who do you think is the army of Israel today, or was? All the people who were in these units.

w: This was never mentioned in the publicity.

k: Well, you don't—why should you go and say that? To annoy the British? Make it difficult for them? But no—I mean, the Committee for a Jewish Army was an open, political, Zionist move, linked with the future liberation of Palestine and getting the British out of there. No question about it. But how do you advance it in time of war? You shape it down. You don't cheat. The British knew it. That's why they were against it. I think that in a practical sense, as the war became more desperate, and as the Holocaust developed, we relented. When the Holocaust came, I said, "To hell with a Jewish army."

w: That became a minor—

k: And the British—exactly, exactly. So when the time became hot enough, there was no reason not to say, "Look, we are willing to fight. We want to fight on our terms. Give us the dignity of fighting in our own name." Why should I change my name in order to go and fight the common enemy? When the war became very hot, the position of the Jews became desperate. We dropped the issue and accepted the compromise that the British offered. They did offer a compromise. So in a sense, the campaign was successful. And the compromise was Jewish Palestinian units in the British army. We said, "Fine." About 5,000 people served. Not 200,000, as we had called for.

w: Can you tell a little more about the attempts at unified action with the mainstream Zionists in the campaign for a Jewish army?[7]

k: Twice we reached an agreement [with the American Zionist leaders]. We worked out a draft agreement where we will run a committee for a Jewish army together. But their representative,

Judge [Louis] Levinthal,[8] wrote a letter saying that they wanted to postpone submission of the agreement that the subcommittee had reached. Then he said he could not bring it before the executive committee as planned, but it would be delayed. And then it petered out. I just know it died. After a little while, it became obvious to *me* that there was no bridge.

w: I got the feeling from researching the records that they felt they had to absorb your group into the Zionist movement; otherwise, they didn't feel you'd act responsibly.

k: Fundamentally, they thought we were a nuisance. They just thought, what is the best way to get rid of us, by attacking us or by trying to swallow us? At some point, they thought of trying to swallow us, by swallowing us meaning we will be a couple of guys who instead of $25 a week will get $125 a week and we will get some expenses and will be happy. They tried to make functionaries out of us. It was stupid! If ever they realized that we are not little guys who are working for their own ego and position as Jewish charity bureaucrats. They called us irresponsible. If you have some other motivation, you are irresponsible, as far as they saw it. "Responsible" means do nothing. I always asked them, by the way, to quote something irresponsible we did. It used to drive me bats. Because I really am a very cautious person; as a matter of fact I have a tendency to procrastinate because I am cautious. I check because I am an explosive person and I know it, so I recheck myself. I didn't trust my first reaction, in those days when I was working. Now when I talk, I let myself go because it's not that important.

In eight years of activity, what did we do that was irresponsible? And to hear this day after day that we were irresponsible. And they believed in it. To them, as I said, irresponsible is someone who is not a Jewish bureaucrat, who was not elected by somebody to some of their goddamned committees. They said that to run a full-page ad in *The New York Times* for the Committee for a Jewish Army was irresponsible. Within two years they were running ads in *The New York Times* about everything, even internal Jewish things—any damn parochial, Jewish thing which really doesn't belong in *The New York Times* is there. And *that's* "responsible."

w: But beyond the question of the Jewish army, after the genocide became known did you ever make overtures to the established Jewish organizations about working together for rescue? It seems to me that with what you had to offer in terms of techniques and skills and what they had to offer in terms of membership lists, organizational structure, and funding, that if you could have worked together you could have been very effective. Did you approach them, or [did] they approach you?

k: We tried. And we didn't succeed. I felt a terrible sense of frustration. In December 1942—we thought we might be able to do something about the gruesome tragedy of the Jews of Europe. That was one month after the Wise announcement, when we were groping for a way to do something. After the story in the *Washington Post*, the first thing we did was try to go to them and were flabbergasted when we couldn't move them. We said look, something has to be done—there's a fire! Something has to be done about saving the Jews. And we got involved in the same kind of tedious negotiations which weren't so terrible when we were doing it for a committee on a Jewish army. That was sort of to be expected then. I could negotiate with them in the days of the Jewish army. I could not negotiate with them for any length of time when they started with matters of rescue. There was too much of a gap.

k: Once, though, I thought I broke through, in a meeting in Proskauer's* home. But we didn't. Did you see a poem that Ben Hecht

*Joseph Proskauer (1877–1971), an attorney from Alabama, served as an appellate judge in the New York State Supreme Court from 1923 to 1930. Active in the American Jewish Committee since the early 1930s, Proskauer rose to its presidency in 1943, and continued the organization's traditional opposition to Zionism until the endorsement of the Palestine partition plan by the Truman administration, and then the United Nations, in the autumn of 1947.

wrote and Arthur Szyk[9] did a lot of designs around?[10] It appeared
finally as an ad in various newspapers.* It was written in late 1942,
because it was at the time of Christmas. It was a very sarcastic poem.
It says, "Oh, Jews, don't be bothersome, the world is busy with other
news. Burn Jews . . ." and so on. And the last stanza said, because it
was based on a story which was on the side, by Goebbels, saying that
by Christmas the job of exterminating the Jews would be finished.
And the last thing says, "Oh, world, don't be sad" or something, and
then he says, "by Christmas you will have your peace on earth without the Jews." And then we had this straight text.

You know, most of the ads had an eye-catcher to get people to
read. We had some expert advertising people helping us and they
said, "Don't write this dull copy that nobody reads. The more dramatic the situation, the more you need to do something to get somebody to read it." We did all sorts. We sometimes did straight copy.

Well, the *Times* set the ad, and there was this business of a shortage of paper, so we had to wait a little. But we had it set meanwhile.
And it leaked out. Apparently some frightened Jew read it, somebody who got frightened and thought that this will result in anti-
Semitism. "What do you mean? You are attacking Christmas. How
can you make a sneer of Christianity speaking of peace on earth

---

The advertisement appeared in modified form in The New York Times, *September
14, 1943, 12, under the title "Ballad of the Doomed Jews of Europe." The key stanzas,
the first and the last, follow:*

> *FOUR MILLION Jews waiting for death.*
> *Oh hang and burn but—quiet, Jews!*
> *Don't be bothersome; save your breath—*
> *The world is busy with other news.*
>
> *Oh World be patient—it will take*
> *Some time before the murder crews*
> *Are done. By Christmas you can make*
> *Your Peace on Earth without the Jews.*

without the Jews, and tie up Christianity with murder?" And, it got to—somehow it got to where it got. I get a telephone call from a man called Herman Shulman, who was president of the American Jewish Congress.[11] He introduced himself, I knew who he was, I didn't know him [personally]. He said that something very important has come up and he and Judge Proskauer, who was then president of the American Jewish Committee—and this was the most prestigious Jewish outfit you know. To them we couldn't even get. We tried and got to some smaller guys around in those days, some small functionaries, but we couldn't get to anybody on the top level. And he says that Judge Proskauer and he would like to see me at his earliest convenience, that Judge Proskauer was a little ill, and would I come to his home. We set an appointment for the same afternoon.

And I came there—he didn't tell me what it was about—and I thought, "Wow! Something's moving [on the rescue issue]." And they told me that they'd heard about this ad we were going to put in the *Times*, started making a long speech about how important it is not to print it. And I interrupted them, and I said, "Look, if you feel—I don't think you're right—but if you feel that this ad may do some damage, we won't print it." And they were flabbergasted because they must have heard of other meetings at which we weren't that easy to get along with. And I surprised them by saying, "Look, I understand that you think it's damaging. We won't publish it. I can assure you. We won't publish it because the subject is, unfortunately, not one, that this ad, or any one ad, is going to solve. I don't believe that this ad is going to save the Jews of Europe, so therefore, if you think it's going to hurt the Jews of America, we won't publish it. It's as simple as all that.

"But let's talk what *can* we do about saving the Jews of Europe. Now you've told me what we should not do, now let's talk about what can we do." And I sort of went on talking and Proskauer started crying, just started crying. And I really thought I got someplace, you know, he was already an older man then. Part of the thing was the contrast. He expected to find a brash, unreasonable guy—and he found a little fellow who was saying, "Look, there's a terrible situation going on, what can we do?" I mean I didn't know what to suggest. I said, "We don't know, we just do what we can. We don't know if it's good or bad. We just feel that sitting doing nothing is not the thing. So, we do. But you're a wiser man, you're an older man"—I don't remember exactly the words—"you tell me what to do. We have people, we have energy, we have mobilized a lot of people, we have writers."

At the time, we were in the middle of the rehearsals for the "We Will Never Die" pageant. Because I remember when I came and told Ben Hecht that I withheld the ad, he nearly blew his top. I went straight from there to rehearsal, I remember, the Capitol Hotel where we were rehearsing, he was rehearsing, Ed Robinson[12] and the other people who were commentators in the pageant. We decided—as it went on a little later, we sort of made it clear to them that if you don't do anything, we'll return to do the best we know how, which means publishing all sorts of ads, including this ad. We didn't do it as a threat, you know. But at the time I told Proskauer and Shulman, "It's not being published. I'm going to call the *Times* now, and I'll take it upon myself. I won't even consult with other people."

w: Did Proskauer have any answer? Did he just cry? Is that all?

k: No, no. We were talking and we decided to call a meeting of— he would call a meeting of leading organizations. I said, "We don't know how the organizations work and I realize that the American Jewish Congress is Zionist and the American Jewish Committee is non-Zionist." And I said, "Judge, whomever you feel should be called, you call as many organizations as you feel necessary. I would like to see all of them. And I'll take some people from our executive committee and we'll come, and let's sit and try and put our heads together and see what can be done." What brought him to tears was the presentation of a lost person. I mean, I didn't pretend that we had wisdom. I wasn't crusading for an idea. I was a guy yelling, "Help!" And this somehow got across because I said, "I don't know what to do." So, I just had a feeling that if we raise enough hell, we'll get the

American government to do, and anyway the more you yell it certainly can't hurt. And we talked a little bit about the importance that American Jews should know somehow, and getting radio, and doing all sorts of things that they [the Jewish leadership] had access to.

Radio, by the way, is a thing we worked like dogs on, and managed to get one broadcast, thanks to James Warburg, who was of the Warburg family, who were big Jewish philanthropists, but he was not.[13] He was a kind of black sheep, who was a nonbusiness one. He was a writer, and during the war he worked in the Office of War Information. And somehow, through somebody, I got to him and somehow penetrated and he gave us a few minutes on the radio. The energy that you had to put out! Imagine, that these guys [in the Jewish leadership] could pick up a telephone and get ten broadcasts like nothing.

Anyway, so Proskauer called a meeting—on a Sunday I think it was, at some club. And I remember that we really thought we had made a breakthrough. I had a sense of accomplishment that now things would start happening, because there was the president of B'nai B'rith, Henry Monsky,[14] and I think Abba Hillel Silver[15] was there, and also about fifteen other people, all very prominent Jewish leaders. We came there, and we spoke, and this, and that. And they wanted to hear again that we were withdrawing this ad. They were very concerned about it.[16] I think the next time I saw Judge Proskauer was, I don't know, sometime in 1946 maybe.

w: Were you able to raise the question of what can be done?

k: No. Later, we published the ad. We couldn't even get him on the phone anymore. We waited some months and published it, and published several others in between. But it didn't make sense, it didn't make sense.

w: The only issue in this meeting was the ad?

k: They wanted just to get a repeated assurance that it won't be published. We came with the suggestion that this group should immediately convene an emergency conference of Jewish organizations. And we said that we would join, that we would stop functioning as a separate organization.

w: Did they discuss that at all?

к: Yes. But they never did it. And then I sent them letters, and I tried, but they never did it.

w: You know they already had a sort of an organization going, the Joint Emergency Committee on European Jewish Affairs, which included representatives from the Zionist groups such as the American Jewish Congress, and the American Zionist organizations, and the American Jewish Committee, and the Jewish Labor Committee, and the Agudath Israel.[17] So perhaps their reaction to your suggestion was "We already have such a coordinated thing going."

к: But what we were talking about was to have a very energetic, concentrated effort on rescue. Something dedicated only to rescue. We outlined all sorts of practical suggestions there, you know. And we had this resolution in Congress already pending, and all sorts of things.

w: Now that was the group that held a mass meeting at Madison Square Garden a week before your pageant. Wise ran it. They filled the Garden, and they had a tremendous overflow, and they made the front page of the *Times*.[18] And they came up with a list of suggestions, too. One focused on the question of war trials, retributions to scare the Germans.

Beginning in late 1942, a lot of energy went into the idea of getting the government leaders—Roosevelt, Churchill, and Stalin—to threaten the Germans that they would face severe postwar punishment if they continued their atrocities against civilian populations. Several such declarations were issued, but only one, in December 1942, pointed out that the Jews were among the victims. To have the Jews specified in these declarations was one of the first things that the Jewish groups came up with, and of course your group pushed it, too. It was a psychological technique of threatening with retribution. Do you think this had any impact?

к: The fact that the Jews were not mentioned did harm to the Jews. The Germans could say, "Look, they don't really care about them." And we screamed about that. I think it would have helped. Again, on the theory that what you had to do was put a monkey wrench.

Maybe it wouldn't have affected Hitler or Himmler, but it might have affected [less highly placed Nazi leaders such as] a Kurt Becher.[19]

w: They do think it affected Horthy and the Hungarian situation finally.

к: Yeah, it may have affected a lot of people, a lot of people underneath, and had a slowing effect. The chances are it wouldn't have changed the basic thing, because these were maniacs we were dealing with. But there were thousands of people involved in the murder process, and it could have slowed the pace of the massacre.

w: Let's move to another topic.[20] How did you raise the funds needed for your work? Meetings, dinners, the pageants—?

к: Meetings, dinners, the usual. "We Will Never Die," which worried us sick in terms of financial responsibility—Billy Rose was the official producer, but he made me sign all the contracts.

w: You had to pay these people, like Billy Rose, Ben Hecht, and Moss Hart?

к: No, no, no, no. They did it free. So did the actors. The actors, we paid expenses, which were considerable, though. Say Paul Muni, we paid his hotel. And for us this was a lot of money. We had to bring them in from Hollywood; we paid them expenses. Billy Rose was a terribly stingy bastard, but he never took a penny. He was a very fabulously wealthy man, and he never gave [us] a nickel. But he did a lot of work, he did a lot of work, and very good work.

Hecht—I don't remember him contributing money, but he spent it—a lot of money on us. For a while in the beginning, you know, the only decent meals we got, he even writes about it in his book, he begins, you know, that we were hungry.* It was true. It wasn't true that day, but it was true in general principle. But he's a dramatist. I mean,

---

*"I ordered a third round of drinks for my guests [Bergson and a colleague, Jeremiah Helpern], unaware that neither had eaten that day. They kept their eyes firmly averted from the platters of fine food moving to and fro under their noses—for they were Hebrew heroes trained in self-discipline." (Ben Hecht, A Child of the Century [New York, 1954], 516.)

there was a time when the only time I ate a good meal was when Ben Hecht invited me out to the Algonquin. And I wouldn't go and tell him, "Look, invite me," but if I happened to come, there was the weekly steak sort of, you know. Ben was a very generous man. He had no sense of money, he didn't know what money was. And he knew we had no money, and everything in sight he paid and signed.

w: Did you have any big donors for the Emergency Committee?

k: No. Never. It was mostly people who clipped out those coupons in the ads and mailed them in. One of the biggest amounts of money we ever got for the Emergency Committee was through the "We Will Never Die" pageant, which was a financial success, you see, because the sell-out of the first performance in New York City more than covered the costs. And left a little bit of a profit. We weren't sure we'll sell out, you know, we didn't know what's going to happen. But then, when we did the second performance, that same night, this was all net profit.

w: And when you went to the other cities with it, then—

k: That—Washington *cost* money. We used the money we made in New York to spend the money in Washington. Washington was by invitation.

w: But you put it on in six cities, didn't you? Even out on the West Coast—in Hollywood?

k: Yes, yes, yes, yes. We put it on also in Philadelphia, Boston, and Chicago, and it covered itself in these cities.

w: What were some of the other techniques you used, both as the Committee for a Jewish Army and then as the Emergency Committee, to build support for government rescue action?

k: One area was the full-page advertisements.*

From 1942 to 1945, the Committee for a Jewish Army and the Emergency Committee to Save the Jewish People of Europe published more than seventy-five different large display advertisements, utilizing at least forty newspapers in some fifteen cities. Altogether, well over two hundred advertisements were placed.

w: What papers did you carry them in, besides *The New York Times* and the *Washington Post*, and the *New York Post?* Did you place them on the West Coast, too?

k: Yes, oh yes. We had a strong—our really effective committees were in Los Angeles, Chicago; a little weaker one in Detroit; very strong one in Philadelphia; New York, of course, which was the headquarters. And in Washington, there was a very strong Emergency Committee.

Once we ran ads in Baltimore, you see in Baltimore there was a committee. And then occasionally some other town, some people would get together, I don't even remember. I wouldn't say that we didn't appear in others, but these were fairly regular. What happened is we would run an ad either in the *Times* or in the *Washington Post* because of its political effect. If it got a good reaction, which to us was mail, in terms of contributions, we'd then scratch together the money to run it in smaller cities, with the hope that it will cover half, a third, two thirds of what it cost. Some of them did a lot more than cover themselves. But most of the times these things didn't cover themselves. The money came mostly from constant fundraising efforts, which drained us something awful. We did all sorts of things. It was a fairly sizable organization, involving many hundreds of active people.

w: If you had an ad with a good response in a pilot newspaper, say the *Washington Post* or *The New York Times*, then you would place it, say, in a Chicago paper, or a Los Angeles paper?

k: Right, right. Sometimes, though, the local committees would choose to do that—if they could scratch together the money, they put it in, anyway.

w: Do you feel that there was a conspiracy of silence on this issue in the United States press?[21] Your ads and activities helped break through the curtain of silence. But do you think this silence was intentional?

k: We used the words "conspiracy of silence," but I don't think it was an active conspiracy. It was more like a passive conspiracy. I don't think people had meetings and said, "Let's not say anything about the killing of the Jews." But the accurate phrase would be more like Ben Hecht's ballad, you know, "the world is busy with other news."

w: How much of a role did William Randolph Hearst* play in your publicity efforts?[22]

k: He was a sponsor of the Emergency Conference. And he wrote editorials in regard to the extermination of the Jews, which [were published in his] forty-some papers, which is a lot of papers. His papers sold millions of copies. The *Mirror*, in New York, was selling more than 2½ million copies a day. In terms of public opinion, it was like Nixon—everybody talks against Nixon, but the majority voted for him. So Hearst represented a large segment of what is now called middle America, what Henry Wallace called the common man. He put his name on the editorials—he very rarely wrote signed editorials—and an editorial which he signed was a signal to the whole readership that this is a cause that he's interested in. His editorials ran on the front pages, not on the editorial page. And his papers gave us a lot of coverage, which induced others to give coverage. You know how it is, if the *Journal-American* in New York or the *Mirror* started giving these things coverage, then the other papers did something.

w: Did you ever see him yourself?

k: No, no, I never saw him.

w: *The New York Times* was your best source?

m: The best source was *The New York Times*, except Sundays. Sunday was the worst day. But we did a whole page on Churchill one Sunday. When Churchill visited the country. I thought it's a brainstorm

---

William Randolph Hearst (1863–1951) was one of the most prominent figures in the American media during the 1930s and 1940s. His publishing conglomerate included twenty-eight newspapers, an array of radio stations and magazines, and film companies such as the Cosmopolitan Picture Studio. An outspoken anti-Communist as well as a sharp critic of the Roosevelt administration's New Deal policies, Hearst was immortalized as the main character in the movie Citizen Kane.

of mine that we put it in the *Sunday Times*. It had a less than medio-cre response.

w: That's interesting because this implies that working-class people who tend to read the Hearst papers were not interested, whereas people more toward an intellectual side who read *The New York Times* were the ones who were responsive.

m: Correct. The more solid people. There was *The Nation* and *The New Republic*. *The Nation* had a better circulation than *The New Republic* at that time, but we had better results from *The New Republic*. Next on the results which were satisfactory, in the sense that they covered the expenses plus, was the *New York Post*. When *PM* still appeared and we publicized in *PM*, it was less successful than *The New York Post*.

There was a time when *The New York Times* refused to publish our ads. This was a great controversy. They said that our facts may not be proven. All kinds of things. By the way, Gay Talese, in *The Kingdom and the Power*,[23] the book about *The New York Times*, tells the story that at a certain time they refused to give our ads. We argued with them. We negotiated. Talese has it in the chapter about the owners of *The New York Times* as Jews—their complexes, their problems. *The New York Times* had, and maybe still has, a censorship department in the sense that they didn't take every ad automatically, especially if it had political connotations or political contents. So, there was a fellow there and I used to argue with him—sometimes a sentence, a phrase, a word, and this and that. And we were always under pressure. We wanted the ad to go in the same day, which means tonight for tomorrow's paper. And then at a certain point, they stopped. They said we aren't going to take any more of your ads. They gave all kinds of reasons. That we make political statements without substantiating them, especially against the British.

So we thought that this is the end of the world. Without *The New York Times*—but, strangely enough, the *New York Post* picked up. And we started to give [ads to] them very often. Sometimes every week an ad. Sometimes twice a week an ad. And what's interesting, it seems that people who used to read our ads in the *Times* started to send in money in response to the ads in the *Post*, though they never did it before. Our ads were an event.

w: Did any other papers give you trouble?

m: No. All the papers around the country were after us. Tremendous. They wanted the ads first of all for the money. But not exclusively. It was also a matter of prestige.

NOTES

1. This section is from the interview of Hillel Kook by David Wyman on November 20, 1978, in New York City.

2. "2 Million Jews Slain, Rabbi Wise Asserts," November 25, 1942, 6.

3. Adolf A. Berle, Jr. (1895–1971), an attorney by profession, was a member of President Franklin Roosevelt's "Brains Trust" circle of expert advisers and a professor of corporation law at Columbia University. He served as assistant secretary of state for Latin American Affairs from 1938 to 1945. After World War II, he served briefly as U.S. ambassador to Brazil, then returned to his law practice and the Columbia faculty. He went on to become a founder and chairman of the Liberal Party and an adviser to President John F. Kennedy.

4. In fact, according to Wise's biographer, Melvin Urofsky, Wise was anxious to publicize the news and did not require urging from the State Department to do so. (*A Voice That Spoke for Justice: The Life and Times of Stephen S. Wise* [Albany, NY, 1982], 319–22.) According to Wise's account (cited in David S. Wyman, *The Abandonment of the Jews: America and the Holocaust 1941–1945* [New York, 1984], 51), Undersecretary of State Sumner Welles confirmed the authenticity of the genocide reports during Wise's November 24, 1942, meeting with him, and Welles then withdrew his earlier request to Wise to refrain from publicizing the information. According to Wise, Welles said, "For reasons you will understand, I cannot give these [reports] to the press, but there is no reason why you should not. It might even help if you did."

5. This section begins the main interview of Hillel Kook by David Wyman, conducted on April 13–15, 1973, in Amherst, Massachusetts.

6. Emanuel Neumann (1893–1980) worked for American Zionist organizations throughout his career. He served as education director of the Zionist Organization of America (1918–1920), national director of the U.S. wing

of the Keren Hayesod (1921–25), chairman of the executive committee of the United Palestine Appeal (1925–27), and president of the Jewish National Fund (1928–1930). After spending the 1930s in Jerusalem as the director of the Jewish Agency's Economic Department and in related positions, Neumann returned to the United States in 1939 as director of public relations for the Emergency Committee for Zionist Affairs, and later played a key role in elevating Abba Hillel Silver to the leadership of the American Zionist movement. Neumann was elected national president of the ZOA in 1947.

7. The section that follows is from the interview of Hillel Kook by David Wyman on May 5, 1973, in New York City.

8. Louis E. Levinthal (1892–1976), a judge of the Court of Common Pleas in Philadelphia from 1937 to 1959, served as president of the Zionist Organization of America (1941–43), chairman of the executive committee of the Emergency Committee for Zionist Affairs (1941–43), and held other positions in the Zionist movement.

9. Arthur Szyk (1894–1951), a Polish-born illustrator and miniaturist, so impressed British officials with his anti-Nazi caricatures that they sent him to the United States in 1940 to help sway American public opinion to support U.S. military intervention against Hitler. He became the editorial cartoonist for the *New York Post* and contributed to many other publications. Szyk joined the Committee for a Jewish Army in 1941 and was subsequently active in Bergson's other groups as well. His dramatic illustrations frequently adorned the Bergson group's newspaper advertisements.

10. The section that follows is from the interview of Hillel Kook by David Wyman on April 13–15, 1973.

11. Herman Shulman (1897–1945), a prominent New York attorney, was also active in the Zionist Organization of America and the American Zionist Emergency Council, of which he served as vice chairman during the 1940s.

12. Edward G. Robinson (1893–1973), a prominent movie actor in the 1930s and 1940s, is best known for his role as a mobster in *Little Caesar* (1931).

13. During his stint with the Office of War Information, James Warburg (1896–1969) repeatedly became embroiled in controversy. After the OWI took part in a diversionary scheme to aid the Allied invasion of North Africa, Warburg was horrified by the Allies' initial decision to leave in place the anti-Jewish laws from the previous Vichy regime, and "circulated strong internal denunciations of the pact" that made waves in his

department. The following year, Warburg and his colleagues, in London, broadcast sharp criticism of Mussolini's pro-Axis successors, but the Roosevelt administration "wanted to negotiate with these Mussolini sympathizers and repudiated the London broadcasts." Warburg chose to resign. (Ron Chernow, *The Warburgs* [New York, 1993], 520–21.)

14. Henry Monsky (1890–1947), an attorney from Nebraska, became president of the Jewish social service organization B'nai B'rith in 1938, and was reelected in 1941. He was a prime moving force behind the convening of the 1943 American Jewish Conference, which sought to establish a unified American Jewry to address issues such as "the rights and status of Jews in the post-war world" and "implementation of the rights of the Jewish people with respect to Palestine." (Alexander Kohanski [ed.], *The American Jewish Conference: Its Organization and Proceedings of the First Session, August 29-September 2, 1943* [New York, 1944], 325, 332–33.)

15. Abba Hillel Silver (1893–1963) first rose to prominence during the 1930s as leader of the large Cleveland district of the Zionist Organization of America, organizing boycotts of products from Nazi Germany and protests against British policy in Palestine. Silver's growing prominence in the American Zionist movement in the early 1940s coincided with a mood of frustration in the Jewish community stemming from the apathetic Allied response to Nazi genocide and the British refusal to open Palestine to Jewish refugees. Silver both symbolized American Jewish militancy and helped promote it. His speech at the August 1943 American Jewish Conference, calling for Jewish statehood, elicited waves of thunderous applause and catapulted him to cochairmanship of the American Zionist Emergency Council, in effect usurping the leadership role of AZEC chairman Stephen Wise. Under Silver's leadership, American Zionists intensified their lobbying in Washington on behalf of the Zionist cause and mobilized grass roots activists to deluge Capitol Hill with calls and letters urging U.S. support for the creation of a Jewish national home in Palestine. Silver's efforts helped bring about the inclusion of pro-Zionist planks in the election platforms of the Republican and Democratic parties in 1944, setting the precedent for future competition between the two parties for Jewish support. Silver did not focus on the issue of rescuing Jews from Hitler, maintaining that the establishment of a Jewish state in Palestine was the answer to the persecution of European Jewry.

16. In a column on March 26, 1943, David Deutsch, the political gossip columnist for the Independent Jewish Press Service, wondered aloud "if

there is any truth in the story that the newly created, super-duper Joint Emergency Committee on European Jewish Affairs squelched one of Ben Hecht's brain-children that was to see the light of day in one of those eye-catching full page ads. Well, the inside dope is that Mr. Hecht is supposed to have penned a poem saying that there's going to be a very happy Christmas this year because by December there wouldn't be any Jews left for the Christian world to spit at. Those who are in the know say that the piece would have to be printed on asbestos, it was so hot. Anyhow, the new committee is said to have gotten after the Committee on Stateless Jews or more appropriately the Committee on Meeting Your Customers through Morning Advertising, and hushed the whole thing up. Yep, Mr. Hecht, the bad boy, was given an ice-cold shower." (David Deutsch, "Heard in the Lobbies," Independent Jewish Press Service, March 26, 1943, 1-E.)

17. In addition to the AJCongress, the AJCommittee, the Jewish Labor Committee, and Agudath Israel, the Joint Emergency Committee on European Jewish Affairs included representatives from the American Emergency Committee for Zionist Affairs (later known as the American Zionist Emergency Council), the Synagogue Council of America, the Union of Orthodox Rabbis, and B'nai B'rith.

18. According to *The New York Times*, there was "an audience of 21,000 that filled the huge auditorium, while several thousand others were unable to get in." ("Save Doomed Jews, Huge Rally Pleas," *NYT*, March 2, 1943, 1.)

19. Kurt Becher served in the SS Death's Head Equestrian Unit 1, which carried out the mass murder of Jews in Poland and western Russia from 1941 to 1943, for which he was promoted to the rank of SS-Obersturmbannführer (SS Major). Becher served as an aide to Adolf Eichmann during the Nazi occupation of Hungary and conducted negotiations with local Jewish leaders for the release of small numbers of Jews in exchange for bribes. He also negotiated with Jewish leaders and representatives of the War Refugee Board concerning a failed proposal to provide 10,000 Allied trucks and supplies to the Nazis in order to halt the deportations of the Jews. After the war, he prospered as a private businessman and escaped prosecution as a war criminal due to the intervention of one of the Hungarian Jewish leaders from whom he had accepted bribes, Rudolf Kastner.

20. The section that follows is from the interview of Hillel Kook by David Wyman on April 13–15, 1973.

21. This paragraph and the one that follows it are from the interview of Hillel Kook by David Wyman on April 13–15, 1973.

22. The section that follows is from the interview of Hillel Kook by David Wyman on April 13–15, 1973.

23. New York: World Publishing Company, 1969. For a more detailed examination of editorial policies at *The New York Times* regarding coverage of the Holocaust, see Laurel Leff, "A Tragic 'Fight in the Family': *The New York Times*, Reform Judaism and the Holocaust," *American Jewish History* 88 (March 2000), 4–51.

In the early years of the war, Theodore Seuss Geisel (known to millions as the children's book author Dr. Seuss) sketched over 400 wartime political cartoons for PM Magazine.

February 12, 1942

June 2, 1942

Beware the Vendor of Breakable Toys!

October 14, 1942

Don't Lean on It Too Hard, Pal!

December 3, 1942

Part IV

The Pacific War

At its high water mark, the Empire of Japan occupied nearly all of East Asia, from Manchuria in the north, to the Solomon Islands in the South Pacific—an expanse encompassing more than 500 million people. Over the course of the Imperial Japanese Army's conquest of Asia, between 1937 and 1945, over 24 million people were killed.

Japanese ambitions foundered under the combined pressures of pushback by Chinese nationalists on the mainland and by a massive Allied counteroffensive beginning in 1942. The island campaigns in the South Pacific saw some of the most vicious fighting in the history of warfare, tinged with racial animosities on both sides of the conflict.

As in the European war, strategic bombing was the scourge of civilian populations. Japanese bombing raids against Chinese cities claimed over a quarter million lives. Beginning in 1944, American long-range B-29 bombers targeted the Japanese home islands directly; on the night of March 15, 1945, the firebombing of Tokyo killed an estimated 100,000 Japanese, and left over a million homeless.

On August 6, 1945, the Japanese city of Hiroshima was obliterated by an American atomic bomb dropped by the B-29 bomber Enola Gay; on August 9, a second atomic bomb destroyed Nagasaki. Over 240,000 people were killed in the atomic attacks. On August 15, a radio broadcast by Emperor Hirohito declared Japan's capitulation.

"The Slaughter of an Army"

Osawa Masatsugu

Interviewed by Haruko Taya Cook and Theodore F. Cook in
Japan at War, Osawa Masatsugu relates his experiences as a
soldier in the Japanese Imperial Army in New Guinea, in 1943.

A fter the main force had passed over the gorge, they blew up the
suspension bridge. The thousands who trailed behind were left
to die. We were at the end of the line. Soldiers who had struggled
along before us littered the sides of the trail. It was a dreadful sight.
Some were already skeletons—it was so hot that they soon rotted—
or their bodies were swollen and purple. What little they wore was
removed by those who had less. Wearable boots were instantly
taken, so most of the dead lay barefoot. The worms crawling over the
more recently dead gave them a silver sheen. The whole mountain
range was wreathed in the stench of death. That was what it was like.

Our own forces blew up the bridge before we could cross it! We
marched for another month because we were one day late. We'd
already been marching for nearly two months by then, ever since
the many battles at Finschhafen, and we'd almost gotten through
the mountains to the coast. It was about the tenth day of February
1944. Behind me there were more thousands, completely dispersed,
scattered. Many had gone mad. I couldn't get over the fact that,

165

delirious as they were, they still continued to march in the same direction. Nobody, no matter how insane, walked the wrong way. The dead bodies became road markers. They beckoned to us: "This is the way. Just follow us corpses and you'll get there." That was true until we came to the gorge where the bridge had been. Now, we had to find the way for ourselves.

New Guinea was green, full of greenness, all year long. If it had been any other color, you couldn't have stood it. The green provided some relief, but it was a desert of green. The advance units had quickly eaten all available food. The rest of the column had to survive on what little was left after they'd passed. The soldiers who fell by the side of the mountain trail increased rapidly, so mixed together that you ceased to be able to distinguish their units. When we left Finschhafen, we had already passed the limits of our energy, and yet we had to crawl along the very tops of ridges and cross mountain ranges. It was a death march for us.

It had rained for more than half a year straight. Our guns rusted. Iron just rotted away. Wounds wouldn't heal. Marching in the rain was horrible. Drops fell from my cap into my mouth mixing with my sweat. You slipped and fell, got up, went sprawling, stood up, like an army of marching mud dolls. It went on without end, just trudging through the muddy water, following the legs of somebody in front of you.

As you marched, you lost comrades from your unit. Usually, you just flopped down by the road, rested together, then moved on. But sometimes the one you were with would say, "I'll just rest a little longer." You'd lose the will to stand up if you sat too long. "Let's get going. Come on!" I said to one. He was sitting at the edge of a cliff. He only lifted his glasses and wiped his face. He looked utterly exhausted. I never saw him again.

The worst was the jungle at night. Even if you attached a white cloth to your pack, it couldn't be seen. You'd have to follow the person in front of you by pushing lightly up against his pack. You had to keep your mind focused only on that. Sometimes you'd move swiftly. At other times you slowed to nothing at all. Then you'd shout, "Get going!" and find yourself pushing against a tree. If you tried to rush, you'd stumble, as if your feet were grabbed or clutched at by something. You weren't supposed to call out. The enemy might hear. Each step, you had no way of knowing if there was going to be ground under your foot when it next came down.

At times the rain was heavy in the mountains, not like in Japan. It was more like a waterfall. You'd have to cover your nose or it would choke you. A valley stream could turn into a big river instantly. If you got caught there washing your face, away you went. People could die of drowning while crossing the mountains. I climbed mountains four thousand meters high. Dark black clouds swirled around us. I had the feeling the heavens were glowering down at me. Beyond the clouds, you could see stars even in daylight. It was like being in the eye of a typhoon, suddenly seeing those stars shining behind the dark clouds. It was a weird experience.

For a time after the bridge was blown up, military police, the Kempei, were stationed here and there on the trail, ostensibly to protect the security of villages along the way, and to direct stragglers. Soldiers often grumbled about them. One day I encountered a Kempei. He demanded that I salute him, even though he was a non-com. "I'm a sergeant too," I insisted, "even though I don't have any stripes." "You must salute the Kempei forces!" was his only response. We didn't even salute officers in those conditions. "You're alone?" he asked. I replied that I had a companion, but he was a little behind. "Why didn't you kill him, then?" he demanded. "You can't get out of these mountains if you wait for stragglers. It's all right to kill them. One or two of you doesn't mean anything." He looked two or three years younger than me. The dark shadow of the Kempei disappeared from the mountains about half a month after the bridge went down.

In the army, anyone over thirty was an old man. Twenty-six or twenty-seven, that was your peak. The young soldiers, serving for the first time, didn't know how to pace themselves and died quickly, though there were many strong men, fishermen and farmers, among them. If you were older, you knew what you could do and what you couldn't. I was in what was called the regimental "labor company," but it was really a special unit organized for all kinds of difficult missions. We blew up enemy tanks with saucer-shaped mines. We'd approach moving tanks from their blind side and attach the charge directly to their hull. We'd trap them in tank pits. We were sometimes called the Special Attack Raiders. The heaviest casualties were in our labor unit. We were like a small engineering unit, building bridges and destroying enemy strongpoints, but we took pride in being like tiger cubs, the most valuable unit in the division. Our primary weapon was a flame-thrower.

One thing that surprised me when I went into the military was that the majority of the long-service soldiers had only gotten through elementary school. Many of the conscripts were well educated, many beyond middle school. You could recognize conscripts by their glasses. Regular soldiers often said, "draftees have glib tongues, but are useless in action." When I was a corporal, I once got into a fistfight with a sergeant for saying that there wasn't any difference between a regular soldier and a conscript when both are on the same battlefield risking their lives.

I turned down the chance to become an officer candidate. When they told me I had permission to apply, I said "I don't like the army. If I liked the military I'd have gone to the military academy in the first place." They beat me mercilessly for my impudence that time, I can tell you. You see, I didn't want to kill subordinates with my orders. I could watch out for myself, but I didn't want to determine what others should do. Eventually I reached the rank of sergeant, but it didn't mean much in New Guinea. Nobody ever seemed to rank below me, since reinforcements never reached us. I was always near the bottom.

I heard later that our high command considered the battle at Finschhafen a turning point of the Pacific War. It seems they had an expectation that a victory there could have reversed the tide of war. In fact, we did rout the enemy easily—at first. I was amazed how weak the Australian soldiers seemed. Their infantrymen ran before us when we attacked. The next day, though, their artillery and airplanes bombarded us from all sides. Only when we were totally exhausted did their infantry return to mop up at their leisure. Our side had no fighting capability left.

The bigger the scale of the battle, the less we riflemen had to do with it. Cannons and machine guns dominated then. As you can imagine, in infantry battles, machine guns were the stars. Five machine guns blaze away, spewing out six hundred rounds a minute. The bullets just come *"Ba-ba-ba-ba, dah-dah-dah-dah!"* You want to dig into the earth even just five or ten centimeters more. You can't raise your head. You know how well they know your position by the height of their fire. When the bullets come low you can't move. Your back is heated by the bullets. You can't fire your single-shot, bolt-action Type-38 infantry rifle. You'd feel too absurd. It's like a kind of symphony coming from both sides. You'd get intoxicated by it. An hour of firing like that and my whole way of looking at the world around me was different. I was transformed, along with Nature itself.

I came to feel the Australian military was very strong indeed. They didn't want to have infantry battles. They wanted to leave the fighting to mechanized power. The Japanese military only had infantry. Our artillery had almost no ammunition. If we fired even one shell, hundreds came back at us. "Please don't fire at them," we'd pray to our guns from our trenches. I had a sense then that one day war would be fought without humans. Just airplanes and artillery. War in which human beings actually shot at each other, where we could see each other's faces, that was over. What were we infantrymen there for? Only, it often seemed to me, to increase the number of victims.

The "enemy"? I often wondered what that meant. We didn't hate the enemy. We seemed to fight them only because they showed up. I sometimes wondered why either side was there. It was like a plot by both sides to fight in this place. In China, at least, when our soldiers were killed I sensed they had been killed by a real enemy. There, two sides, similarly armed, grappled fiercely with each other, man-to-man.

In New Guinea, we didn't know what was killing us. Who killed that one? Was it death from insanity? A suicide? A mercy killing? Maybe he just couldn't endure the pain of living. I remember that war as mainly one of suicides and mercy killings. Once, as I was trudging along, a soldier by the road caught my eye. He'd lost his voice. He just pointed at my rifle and with a bent finger signaled that he wanted me to pull the trigger. I couldn't. My mind was still mired in some kind of lukewarm sentimentalism. I knew he had no hope, but I couldn't shoot him. Another time, I saw a man kill his younger brother. Love is such a cruel thing. That's what I felt then. The younger brother had gone insane, although he was the physically stronger of the two. They were in different units, and met by chance in a shack in the mountains. The younger brother was cackling madly when we came upon him. The elder one slapped him across the face and shook him, calling out his name. He just kept laughing. Finally, the elder brother shot him dead. I didn't even raise my voice. The brother and I dug a grave for him.

I knew an army doctor, about thirty-five years old, who volunteered to shoot all those who knew they couldn't survive. This I consider "sacred murder." Often subordinates asked their superiors to kill them when the main force was about to depart. If you were left behind, that was the end. A man who had the strength left to pull the pin could always blow himself up, so everyone tried to keep one hand grenade until the last moment. Even those who tossed away their rifles never threw away their last grenade.

My three years in New Guinea were a succession of such horrors. Everything was beyond my control. Planes roared directly overhead. We could smell their thirst for blood. No matter how many flew over, you knew the one that was after you. Once, I was just aiming my rifle when an enemy bullet actually got stuck in my barrel. If it had been a touch off line, the umpire's call would have been "You're out!" A bullet went through a man's helmet, spun around inside and exited through the same hole. Around his head was inscribed a bald line where the bullet had gone. How can you explain something like that? You move your body just a little and immediately the place where you've been lying is hit directly. Luck? Accident? That just won't do it. I was forced to learn the limits of human intelligence. Things you'd think would logically be best for you often proved to be the worst. "If you're going to die anyway, die gloriously," I'd think. I often volunteered for special missions. Yet again and again I'd come back and find it was the main unit that had been wiped out while I was off on a dangerous assignment. I felt something was controlling us.

I never really killed anyone directly. I shot my rifle, so I might have hit somebody, but I never ran anyone through with my bayonet. In China, soldiers were forced to practice on prisoners, slashing and stabbing, as soon as they arrived for training. "Stab him!" they'd order, indicating an unresisting prisoner. I didn't move. I just stood there. The platoon leader became enraged, but I just looked away, ignoring the order. I was beaten. I was the only one who didn't do it. The platoon leader showed them how, with vigor. "This is how you stab a person!" he said. He hit the man's skull and knocked him into a pit. "Now stab him!" They all rushed over and did it. I'm not saying I determined it good or bad through reason. I just couldn't take the thought of how it would feel, running a man through with my bayonet.

The New Guineans seemed immaculate. To get help from the natives in the mountains was the only means left to us. I was so happy to see that they accepted words without twisting them all around. We could communicate directly. When I first caught a glimpse of black people, I thought we'd never be able to communicate, but one of them spoke Pidgin English. That saved me. Because of Pidgin, I was not afraid. I understood German, French, and English, but I was amazed how useful a few simple words could be. I was impressed by how beautiful human beings could be, too. An old native once left a mixture of roots and water and a little salt by my head when I'd collapsed flat on my back in the trail. And a village headman went himself to tell other Japanese two kilometers away that I had fallen ill, even though his people thought I was already dead.

I think the natives and the Japanese got along well. They'd dance in a circle when the moon was full. Those of us who were from farming or fishing villages would casually join in and dance, too, as if they were dancing in the Japanese countryside. They'd borrow drums and do it pretty well. The natives seemed really pleased by this. The whites never approached them; they merely frightened them with their guns. With the Japanese, they shared living. Sometimes I wonder why they cooperated with an army that was disintegrating. The Australians would win them over with goods, things like canned corned beef. We never had anything to return to them. All we could say was, "Thank you." Yet their kindness lasted to the very end of the war. Some village chiefs were executed after the war because they provided us with food. They were accused of "hostile action" by the Allies. The enemy organized them to work as irregular guerrillas against us. Indeed, the thing I most regret about New Guinea is the incidents I learned of later where New Guineans were killed by Japanese. It makes me despondent to think that we could have killed people like that chief who saved me.

In the world we lived in on New Guinea, you had no use for the language or knowledge you had accumulated before you went there. Literature, which I'd studied at Keijō Imperial University, meant nothing. I sensed that the extremes of existence could be reduced to the human stomach. Lack of protein, in particular, fostered a kind of madness in us. We ate anything. Flying insects, worms in rotten palm trees. We fought over the distribution of those worms. If you managed to knock down a lizard with a stick, you'd pop it into your mouth while its tail was still wriggling. Yet, under these conditions, a soldier offered me his final rice and a soldier I met for the first time gave me half of a taro root he'd dug up.

We had other fears on New Guinea. Near the end we were told

not to go out alone to get water, even in daytime. We could trust the men we knew, but there were rumors that you could never be sure what would happen if another of our own soldiers came upon you. We took precautions against attack. I once saw a soldier's body with the thigh flesh gouged out, lying by the path. The stories I heard made me shiver and left me chilled to the bone. Not all the men in New Guinea were cannibals, but it wasn't just once or twice. I saw this kind of thing. One time, when we were rushing along a mountain trail, we were stopped by four or five soldiers from another unit. They told us they had meat from a big snake that they were willing to share with us. Their almost sneering faces unnerved me. Maybe we were thinking too much, but my companion and I didn't stop. "Thank you, maybe next time," we said, and left. I knew that if it were really snake, they'd never have shared it. They were trying to pull us in to share their guilt. We never talked about it afterwards, but when we reached the coast other soldiers warned us that there were demons in the jungle. Maybe this was just wild fear, but I can still visualize it clearly.

I didn't really have a future while I was trudging along in those mountains. There was no tomorrow, no next day. All I could think about was falling asleep, or following pleasant memories back into the past. Still, when a staff officer showed up, gathered maybe fifteen of us together, and told us to prepare for our final battle and issued us our final rations, I felt that the future had been foreclosed. I was now completely uncoupled from anything to come, in a closed universe. I thought if I could just drag myself a few steps further, I might actually grasp the situation a little better, know where I was, but I couldn't even climb the slightest incline without crawling on my hands and knees. Near the end, everything was called *gyokusai*. In the end, I never did it, but whole regiments were used up in those attacks, protecting us as we trudged through the mountains on our fighting withdrawal. This can be interpreted as a comradeship of which we were unaware.

Human beings can be divided into two extremes. I collapsed

from fever many times. Sometimes a soldier who happened to pass by carried me on his back to the next village. One time a soldier I didn't know told me he had two *gō*, just a handful, of rice in his pack. "It's no good to me now," he said. "You take it." Some people are like that. They become extraordinarily lucid in the face of death. I was deeply moved, in a sense, but I couldn't say, "All right, I'll take it." After all, each of us kept that two *gō* of rice for the time of our own death, so we could say, "Now I'll eat my last meal."

Another time, when we were climbing from Kali into the mountains, I was hailed by a soldier unable to move. He asked me to cook some rice porridge for him with the rice in his mess kit. I got water but asked one of our men to make it for him, since I was such a bad cook. By the time the rice was ready, darkness had descended in the jungle. At last somebody guided me back to where he was. "Your porridge is ready!" I said as I shook him by the shoulder. He simply fell over. Already dead. I wonder what on earth he must have been thinking while that rice porridge was cooking. Maybe "That guy ran away with my last rice!" I did my best and it was no good. I felt wretched. The soldier who'd guided me there opened the dead man's mouth and put some of the porridge in. All he kept muttering was "What a pity, what a pity." I saw the two extremes of humanity. I don't know what divides men that way. There's something murky and filthy in human beings. If you've seen this, you might find yourself at one or the other of the poles.

One day natives brought in a soldier on a stretcher. I couldn't tell who he was at first, but he was from our special unit. He told us his name. We'd last seen him when we were going over the ridge line more than a year earlier. On the very day they carried him in, he was shot as a deserter. The man who shot him still regrets doing it. But if you were ordered to do it, you had to. If they had gone strictly by rank, it would have been my job. I was officer of the day, so in one way, I'm the one most responsible, but the warrant officer didn't pick me. I'm grateful for that and I feel guilt and responsibility toward Yoshimura, my friend, who had to shoot him. "Forgive me, Nagayama," Yoshimura said twice in Osaka dialect, and then shot him. This took place after the end of the war, but just before we became prisoners.

I understand there were many such deaths by execution. For example, you'd get an order to "take the message and report back in three days no matter how difficult." You might have to travel a distance as far as from Osaka to Kobe in that time. But malaria was like a time bomb. If it went off you just collapsed and couldn't move. That happened to me. So a week later, you return and you're charged as a deserter. Even many officers were ordered to kill themselves for the crime of desertion. They'd go out on scouting missions, find themselves unable to get back in time, and so leave death poems behind. What a bitter feeling they must have had before being shot. The military was a place where only results were weighed, not reasons.

We didn't know anything about the war situation outside our bit of jungle. One day at the enemy camp we saw two flags go up, the Union Jack and the Japanese flag. We heard *"Banzai! Banzai!"* in Japanese. We'd never seen anything like this before. We then had three days of silence. Planes flew over and dropped leaflets proclaiming "Peace has come to the Orient." Even the regimental commander didn't know about the end of the war. This must have been about August 15, but even that I don't know exactly. It would be a lie if I said I felt sad, or happy. I can't analyze my feelings at that time. I just felt, "Well, so it's over."

Our Seventy-Ninth Regiment had sailed from Pusan, Korea, on New Year's Day 1943 with 4,320 men. Including reinforcements, 7,000 men in all were assigned to our unit. Only 67 survived. My own company broke camp in Pusan with 261 men. I was the only one who boarded a transport ship bound for Japan and home after the war. I was told that of about 170,000 officers and soldiers in eastern New Guinea, 160,000 died. When we were imprisoned as POWs on Mushu Island, after the war had officially ended, a dozen or so men died every day. The island was all coral, so we couldn't dig graves for them. We didn't have the strength, anyway. They had to hasten our repatriation because they couldn't keep us there any longer. We were shells of men, completely burned out. Even on the way back to Japan, the transport had to stop several times to commit the latest dead to the sea. They were only one step away from home.

It's such a long time ago, so it's probably all right to put all this down about individuals, but I often wonder what the family members of the deceased will feel. You can't call how their relation died "glorious," and of course they'd like to believe that if they had to die, at least they died accomplishing a soldier's duty, not in a ditch by the trail, through madness, by their own hand, or eaten by their fellow soldiers. Relatives of those whose deaths I can confirm with the evidence of my own eyes still ask me, "Isn't there any chance he could have survived?" When I was being held as a POW, even I thought that one day soldiers might begin to pour out of the jungle. But it didn't happen.

All battlefields are wretched places. New Guinea was ghastly. There was a saying during the war: "Burma is hell; from New Guinea no one returns alive." Former company commander Captain Katada told me after the war that when his ship stopped in Korea, he went as far as my parents' home, intending to tell them about me. He paced up and down in front of it, but couldn't bring himself to let them know where I was, so he never went in. I guess people at home already realized that there would be no return from New Guinea.

"Tales of the Pacific"

E.B. (Sledgehammer) Sledge

Studs Terkel interviews E.B. (Sledgehammer) Sledge in *"The Good War"* about the American experience of war in the Pacific.

Half-hidden in the hilly greenery, toward the end of a winding country road, is the house he himself helped build. It is on the campus of the University of Montevallo, a forty-five-minute drive from Birmingham, Alabama.

On the wall near the fireplace—comforting on this unseasonably cool day—is a plaque with the familiar Guadalcanal patch: "Presented to Eugene B. Sledge. We, the men of K Co., 3rd Bn., 5th Reg., 1st Marine Div., do hereby proudly bestow this testimonial in expression of our great admiration and heartfelt appreciation to one extraordinary marine, who had honored his comrades in arms by unveiling to the world its exploits and heroism in his authorship of With the Old Breed at Peleliu and Okinawa. *God love you, Sledgehammer. 1982." It is his remarkable memoir that led me to him.*

Small-boned, slim, gentle in demeanor, he is a professor of biology at the university. "My main interest is ornithology. I've been a bird-watcher since I was a kid in Mobile. Do you see irony in that? Interested in birds, nature, a combat marine in the front lines? People think of bird-watchers as not macho."

There was nothing macho about the war at all. We were a bunch of scared kids who had to do a job. People tell me I don't act like an ex-marine. How is an ex-marine supposed to act? They have some Hollywood stereoptype in mind. No, I don't look like John Wayne. We were in it to get it over with, so we could go back home and do what we wanted to do with our lives.

I was nineteen, a replacement in June of 1944. Eighty percent of the division in the Guadalcanal campaign was less than twenty-one years of age. We were much younger than the general army units.

To me, there were two different wars. There was the war of the guy on the front lines. You don't come off until you are wounded or killed. Or, if lucky, relieved. Then there was the support personnel. In the Pacific, for every rifleman on the front lines there were nineteen people in the back. Their view of the war was different than mine. The man up front puts his life on the line day after day after day to the point of utter hopelessness.

The only thing that kept you going was your faith in your buddies. It wasn't just a case of friendship. I never heard of self-inflicted wounds out there. Fellows from other services said they saw this in Europe. Oh, there were plenty of times when I wished I had a million-dollar wound. (Laughs softly.) Like maybe shootin' a toe off. What was worse than death was the indignation of your buddies. You couldn't let 'em down. It was stronger than flag and country.

With the Japanese, the battle was all night long. Infiltratin' the lines, slippin' up and throwin' in grenades. Or runnin' in with a bay-onet or saber. They were active all night. Your buddy would try to get a little catnap and you'd stay on watch. Then you'd switch off. It went on, day in and day out. A matter of simple survival. The only way you could get it over with was to kill them off before they killed you. The war I knew was totally savage.

The Japanese fought by a code they thought was right: *bushido*. The code of the warrior: no surrender. You don't really comprehend it until you get out there and fight people who are faced with an absolutely hopeless situation and will not give up. If you tried to help one of the Japanese, he'd usually detonate a grenade and kill himself as well as you. To be captured was a disgrace. To us, it was impossible, too, because we knew what happened in Bataan.

Toward the end of the Okinawa campaign, we found this emaciatated Japanese in the bunk of what may have been a field hospital. We were on a patrol. There had been torrential rains for two weeks. The foxholes were filled with water. This Jap didn't have but a G-string on him. About ninety pounds. Pitiful. This buddy of mine picked him up and carried him out. Laid him out in the mud. There was no other place to put him.

We were sittin' on our helmets waitin' for the medical corpsman to check him out. He was very docile. We figured he couldn't get up. Suddenly he pulled a Japanese grenade out of his G-string. He jerked the pin out and hit it on his fist to pop open the cap. He was gonna make hamburger of me and my buddy and himself. I yelled, "Look out!" So my buddy said, "You son of a bitch, if that's how you feel about it—." He pulled out his .45 and shot him right between the eyes.

This is what we were up against. I don't like violence, but there are times when you can't help it. I don't like to watch television shows with violence in them. I hate to see anything afraid. But I was afraid so much, day after day, that I got tired of being scared. I've seen guys go through three campaigns and get killed on Okinawa on the last day. You knew all you had was that particular moment you were living.

I got so tired of seein' guys get hit and banged up, the more I felt like takin' it out on the Japanese. The feeling grew and grew, and you became more callous. Have you ever read the poem by Wilfred Owen? The World War One poet? "Insensibility." (He shuts his eyes as he recalls snatches of the poem and interpolates) "Happy are the men who yet before they are killed/Can let their veins run cold. . . . And some cease feeling/Even themselves or for themselves/Dullness best solves/The tease and doubt of shelling." You see, the man who can go through combat and not be bothered by the deaths of others and escape what Owen calls "Chance's strange arithmetic"—he's the fortunate one. He doesn't suffer as much as the one who is sensitive to the deaths of his comrades. Owen says you can't compare this man to the old man at home, who is just callous and hardened to everything and has no compassion. The young man on the front line develops this insensitivity because it is the only way he can cope.

You developed an attitude of no mercy because they had no mercy on us. It was a no-quarter, savage kind of thing. At Peleliu, it was the first time I was close enough to see one of their faces. This Jap had been hit. One of my buddies was field-stripping him for souvenirs. I must admit it really bothered me, the guys dragging him around like a carcass. I was just horrified. This guy had been a human being. It didn't take me long to overcome that feeling. A lot of my buddies hit, the fatigue, the stress. After a while, the veneer of civilization wore pretty thin.

This hatred toward the Japanese was just a natural feeling that developed elementally. Our attitude toward the Japanese was different than the one we had toward the Germans. My brother who was with the Second Infantry Division in the Battle of the Bulge, wounded three times, said when things were hopeless for the Germans, they surrendered. I have heard many guys who fought in Europe who said the Germans were damn good soldiers. We hated the hell of having to fight 'em. When they surrendered, they were guys just like us. With the Japanese, it was not that way. At Peleliu, my company took two prisoners. At Okinawa, we took about five. We had orders not to kill the wounded, to try to take prisoners. If they surrendered, they'd give you information. But the feeling was strong . . . Some guys you meet say they didn't kill any wounded. They weren't up there living like animals, savages.

Our drill instructor at boot camp would tell us, "You're not going to Europe, you're going to the Pacific. Don't hesitate to fight the Japs dirty. Most Americans, from the time they're kids, are taught not to hit below the belt. It's not sportsmanlike. Well, nobody has taught the Japs that, and war ain't sport. Kick him in the balls before he kicks you in yours."

I've seen guys shoot Japanese wounded when it really was not necessary and knock gold teeth out of their mouths. Most of them had gold teeth. I remember one time at Peleliu, I thought I'd collect gold teeth. One of my buddies carried a bunch of 'em in a sock. What you did is you took your K-bar (he displays a seven-inch knife), a fighting knife. We all had one because they'd creep into your foxhole at night. We were on Half Moon Hill in Okinawa about ten days. It happened every night.

The way you extracted gold teeth was by putting the tip of the blade on the tooth of the dead Japanese—I've seen guys do it to wounded ones—and hit the hilt of the knife to knock the tooth loose. How could American boys do this? If you're reduced to savagery by a situation, anything's possible. When Lindbergh made a trip to the Philippines, he was horrified at the way American GIs talked about the Japanese. It was so savage. We *were* savages.

When I leaned to make the extraction, as the troops used to say, this navy medic, Doc Castle, God bless his soul, said, "Sledgehammer, what are you doing?" I says, "Doc, I'm gonna get me some gold teeth." He said, (very softly) "You don't want to do that." I said, "All the other guys are doin' it." He says, "What would your folks think?" I said, "Gosh, my dad is a medical doctor back in Mobile, he might think it's interesting." He said, "Well, you might get germs." I said, "I hadn't thought of that, doc." In retrospect, I realized Ken Castle wasn't worried about germs. He just didn't want me to take another step toward abandoning all concepts of decency.

I saw this Jap machine-gunner squattin' on the ground. One of our Browning automatic riflemen had killed him. Took the top of his skull off. It rained all that night. This Jap gunner didn't fall over for some reason. He was just sitting upright in front of the machine gun. His arms were down at his sides. His eyes were wide open. It had rained all night and the rain had collected inside of his skull. We were just sittin' around on our helmets, waiting to be relieved. I noticed this buddy of mine just flippin' chunks of coral into the skull about three feet away. Every time he'd get one in there, it'd splash. It reminded me of a child throwin' pebbles into a puddle. It was just so unreal. There was nothing malicious in his action. This was just a mild-mannered kid who was now a twentieth-century savage.

Once on another patrol, on Okinawa, I saw Mac take great pains to position himself and his carbine near a Japanese corpse. After getting just the right angle, Mac took careful aim and squeezed off a couple of rounds. The dead Japanese lay on his back with his trousers pulled down to his knees. Mac was trying very carefully to blast off the head of the corpse's penis. He succeeded. As he exulted over his aim, I turned away in disgust. Mac was a decent, clean-cut man.

We had broken through the Japanese lines at Okinawa. I had a Thompson submachine gun and went in to check this little grass-thatched hut. An old woman was sitting just inside the door. She held out her hands. There was an hourglass figure tattooed on it to show she was Okinawan. She said, "No Nipponese." She opened her kimono and pointed to this terrible wound in her lower abdomen. You could see gangrene had set in. She didn't have a chance to survive and was obviously in great pain. She probably had caught it in an exchange of artillery fire or an air strike.

She very gently reached around, got the muzzle of my tommy gun, and moved it around to her forehead. She motioned with her other hand for me to pull the trigger. I jerked it away and called the medical corpsman: "There's an old gook woman, got a bad wound." This is what we called the natives in the Pacific. "Hey, doc, can you do anything?"

He put a dressing on it and called someone in the rear to evacuate the old woman. We started moving out when we heard a rifle shot ring out. The corpsman and I went into a crouch. That was an M-1, wasn't it? We knew it was an American rifle. We looked back toward the hut and thought maybe there was a sniper in there and the old woman was acting as a front for him. Well, here comes one of the guys in the company, walking out, checking the safety on his rifle. I said, "Was there a Nip in that hut?" He said, "Naw, it was just an old gook woman. She wanted to be put out of her misery and join her ancestors, I guess. So I obliged her."

I just blew my top: "You son of bitch. They didn't send us out here to kill old women." He started all these excuses. By that time, a sergeant came over and we told him. We moved on. I don't know what was ever done about it. He was a nice guy, like the boy next door. He wasn't just a hot-headed crazy kid. He wanted to join the best. Why one individual would act differently from another, I'll never know.

We had all become hardened. We were out there, human beings, the most highly developed form of life on earth, fighting each other like wild animals. We were under constant mortar fire. Our wounded had to be carried two miles through the mud. The dead couldn't be removed. Dead Japs all around. We'd throw mud over 'em and shells would come, blow it off, and blow them apart. The maggots were in the mud like in some corruption or compost pile.

Did you ever get to know a Japanese soldier?

One of the few we captured at Okinawa was a Yale graduate. He spoke perfect English, but we never said anything to him. I must be perfectly honest with you, I still have a great deal of feeling about them. The way they fought. The Germans are constantly getting thrown in their face the horrors of nazism. But who reminds the Japanese of what they did to China or what they did to the Filipinos? Periodically, we remember Bataan.

It always struck me as ironic, the Japanese code of behavior. Flower arranging, music, striving for perfection. And the art of the warrior. Very often, we'd get a photograph off a dead Japanese. Here would be this soldier, sitting in a studio, with a screen behind and a table with a little flower on it. Often he'd be holding a rifle, yet there was always that little vase of flowers.

We all had different kinds of mania. To me, the most horrible thing was to be under shellfire. You're absolutely helpless. The damn thing comes in like a freight train and there's a terrific crash. The ground shakes and all this shrapnel rippin' through the air.

I remember one afternoon on Half Moon Hill. The foxhole next to me had two boys in it. The next one to that had three. It was fairly quiet. We heard the shell come screeching over. They were firing it at us like a rifle. The shell passed no more than a foot over my head. Two foxholes down, a guy was sitting on his helmet drinking C-ration hot chocolate. It exploded in his foxhole. I saw this guy, Bill Leyden, go straight up in the air. The other two kids fell over backwards. Dead, of course. The two in the hole next to me were killed instantly.

Leyden was the only one who survived. Would you believe he gets only partial disability for shrapnel wounds? His record says nothing about concussion. He has seizures regularly. He was blown up in the air! If you don't call that concussion . . . The medics were too busy saving lives to fill out records.

Another kid got his leg blown off. He had been a lumberjack, about twenty-one. He was always telling me how good spruce Christmas trees smelled. He said, "Sledgehammer, you think I'm gonna lose my leg?" If you don't think that just tore my guts out . . . My God, there was his field shoe on the stretcher with this stump of his ankle stickin' out. The stretcher bearers just looked at each other and covered him with his poncho. He was dead.

It was raining like hell. We were knee-deep in mud. And I thought, What in the hell are we doin' on this nasty, stinkin' muddy ridge? What is this all about? You know what I mean? Wasted lives on a muddy slope.

People talk about Iwo Jima as the most glorious amphibious operation in history. I've had Iwo veterans tell me it was more similar to Peleliu than any other battle they read about. What in the hell was glorious about it?

POSTSCRIPT: *During the next day's drive to the airport, he reflected further:* "My parents taught me the value of history. Both my grandfathers were in the Confederate Army. They didn't talk about the glory of war. They talked about how terrible it was.

"During my third day overseas, I thought I should write all this down for my family. In all my reading about the Civil War, I never read about how the troops felt and what it was like from day to day. We knew how the generals felt and what they ate.

"We were told diaries were forbidden, because if we were killed or captured, any diary might give the Japanese information. So I kept little notes, which I slipped into the pages of my Gideon's New Testament. I kept it in a rubber bag I got off a dead Jap. I committed the casualties to memory. We had more than a hundred percent in Okinawa and almost that many at Peleliu.

"Any time we made an attack, I recited the Twenty-third Psalm. Snafu Shelton says, 'I don't know what it is that got us through. I was doin' a hell of a lot of cussin' and Sledgehammer was doin' a hell of a lot of prayin'. One of those might have done it.' Some of the survivors never knew I was keepin' notes: 'We just thought you were awfully pious.' Some of the guys were very religious. But some of 'em, after a while, got so fatalistic they figured it was nothing but dumb chance anyway."

"An American Revolutionary"

Nelson Peery

In an excerpt from his memoir *Black Fire,* Nelson Peery relates his experiences as an African American soldier in the fight against Japan.

One by one the white regiments pulled out for the invasion of Sansapore and Morotai. We were left behind to finish the job of mopping up what resistance remained. We were also given the responsibility of securing the island from the Japanese army corps that had been bypassed, bombed to pieces, and starved out at the once formidable base across the bay at Manokwari, New Guinea.

As the patrolling subsided, we set about improving our quarters and strengthening the defenses, and returned to close-order drills. A base postal unit and base hospital were moved to the island to service the anticipated invasion of the Philippines. As the WACs and nurses moved in, it became like a state-side garrison—at least for the white officers.

The Japanese airstrip was too small for U.S. Army aircraft. A new one was built a quarter of a mile away. We converted the old strip into a movie theater by laying out rows of coconut logs as seats. When the movies started, the Japanese stragglers would creep out of their hiding places to sit on the cliff overlooking the theater and enjoy the movie. Some kind of unspoken truce evolved. They wouldn't shoot into the theater, and we wouldn't attempt to ambush them.

I never went to the movies. Along with most of the infantrymen, I had a deep-seated fear of airstrips—they were the nerve centers and magnets for combat. We weren't missed. The white men and women soldiers filled the place every night.

Hollywood saluted the various infantry divisions in the Pacific by having a world premiere showing on their island. Our turn came. The world premier showing of the movie *Rhapsody in Blue* would be in honor of the black infantrymen of the Ninety-third Division. Headquarters made quite a to-do about the honor. Work details manicured the area and prepared for the night as if we were at Hollywood and Vine. Rumor had it that Dinah Shore was going to open the movie with her hit song, "I'll Walk Alone." We all thought a voice like that had to have some Negro blood in it. We liked her.

Time came to take the half-mile walk to the theater. I decided not to go, then, as it began to darken, I reconsidered. Apprehensive but not wanting to miss the event, I started down the dirt road. The floodlights were on at the theater and landing lights had just been turned on at the airstrip. A hundred yards from the theater, I instinctively jumped to the side of the road and looked upward as two incoming planes roared by. The first was an American C54 transport. Slightly above and behind the transport was the unmistakable outline of a Japanese "Betty" bomber.

At first I ran toward the airport screaming, "Japs—Japs!" The service troops, scattered along the road to the theater, unaware of the imminent catastrophe, moved away from me as if I were crazy. Then I realized how useless it was. I stood watching the drama. The Betty cut her motors and glided in fifty feet above the transport. The closeness of the planes confused the radar and cutting the motors silenced the approach. The transport touched down; the Betty glided over it, dropping two fragmentation bombs. Bodies, seats, and debris blasted up as the plane disintegrated. The Betty gunned its motors, destroyed the control tower with machine gun fire, and turned sharply, passing over the theater. Two "daisy cutter" antipersonnel bombs and machine gun fire raked the theater. Utter pandemonium took over as the Betty disappeared into the night in the direction of Manokwari.

Shore batteries, informed we were under naval attack, shook the island with their heavy guns firing at predetermined positions. The field artillery opened up on targets in the hills. The anti-aircraft artillery gouged flaming holes in the darkness of the sky. Everyone thought everything else was attacking him. A platoon of tanks churned onto the road, blocking the ambulances screaming toward the theater. A 6×6 truck carrying latecomers to the theater stalled lengthwise across the road as it tried to turn around. A commandeered tank pulled it away. Everywhere soldiers were running from the area. Inside the theater was a scene of carnage—nearly three hundred people dead and wounded from the ten-second attack.

I made it back to the company area and spent the night in my foxhole.

The next morning the regimental commander called the reconnaissance men together. When he passed out the shot glasses of whiskey, we knew we were in trouble.

"Men." The uniform hadn't changed him. The white man boss always puts on an air of friendly equality when he wants something difficult or dangerous done.

"The general has determined the air raid last night was directed by radio. The Japanese up in those hills must still have an operational radio. We have been assigned to find and destroy it."

We all knew better. The Japanese had patched that plane together out of the scrap left from the bombings and hit it lucky. The general was under sharp criticism from corps headquarters. It sounded better if there was an organized force to deal with, rather than a lucky punch. We were going to pay the price for someone's fuckup.

A World War II infantryman can never forget the sound of a Japanese rifle. Unlike our M1s, with their husky, semiautomatic bam-bam-bam!, the Japanese .25 has a sharp, cracking pow! It is followed by a pause while the bolt is pulled back, the spent cartridge ejected, another round shoved into the firing chamber, and then another pow!

The point man had passed the banyan tree and looked back, signaling that it was safe to move forward. The men stepped from their hiding places—Jeff, Bunk, Brad, and then Lonnie.

It wasn't like the movies. There was nothing dramatic. The pow! ripped the eerie silence and ricocheted into the jungle. The earth paused as each set of eyes darted into the underbrush and up into the banyan tree. The sound seemed to have come from all around us. Then I saw Lonnie. He took one step back and sat down, feet apart, rifle held firmly in his right hand. Slowly he leaned forward until, yogalike, his face pressed against the ground between his ankles. There was no scream. There was no blood. The bullet that hit the center of his heart ended his life before the brain could react.

Our years of training beat back the terror of death in the jungle. We fanned outward, firing a few shots at likely hiding places. Big Joe, kneeling behind a scrub bush, squinted into the tree, his teeth clamped tightly upon the cigar stump. He raised the B.A.R. as if it were a carbine and squeezed the trigger. The clip of shots tore into the tree, sending the leaves floating downward in peaceful incongruity.

We all heard the gurgling moan. The Japanese soldier fell the fifteen feet to the ground, his chest torn by bullets. A rifle fell and we could see another dead soldier dangling from the tree, his leg stuck between two branches, the blood running from the rips and tears in his body.

Then we saw the third soldier. The wet red splotch on his shirt widened as he struggled for balance. Looking down at the six rifles pointed at him, he pushed his rifle away. It fell to the ground. Weak and unsteady, he slithered and inched along the huge branch. The rifles were lowered. The men were pulling for him to make it. Somehow, we didn't connect this man to Lonnie's death. Reaching the trunk, he leaned to grasp the next-lower limb. Pain was etched in his face as, branch by branch, he half crawled, half fell toward the ground. Five feet from the ground he attempted to hold on to the trunk and find his footing on the huge, twisted roots. Too far gone, too weak for the effort, he fell. He rolled over onto his back, eyes half closed with pain and death.

I was nearest and stepped over to him. My mind focused on the stories of wounded or supposedly dead Japanese soldiers using the last grenade to kill themselves and anyone near. I thought of the slogan—"If they don't stink—stick 'em." Half afraid, half compassionate, I lowered the barrel of my rifle, the bayonet tip inches from his chest. He couldn't have been more than twenty-three. His mouth moved slightly. He closed his eyes, thin lips clamped between his teeth. Suddenly he moved as if to turn over. Instinctively, I lunged against the rifle. The bayonet point disappeared into his body. Kill the bastard—kill him—kill him! The weight of my body pinned him back to the ground. The mouth opened and gasped. The eyes opened and glared at me. The body relaxed, the death stare fixed into the branches of the banyan tree. I answered him, "You made me do it, you motherfuckin' Jap bastard—you made me do it."

I felt Brad's arm around me—I was still pushing against the rifle. Together we pulled the bayonet from his rib cage and wiped it clean on his pants.

"I think he had a grenade," I said almost defensively.

We rolled him over. When he fell, a stick had punctured his body. That caused the look of pain and biting the lips. That's why he tried to roll over. Brad knew what I was thinking.

"He'd a' died anyway, man. We couldn't a' taken him back. We got to find that transmitter."

We spread out the poncho and laid Lonnie on it. Red, the medic, closed his bulging, staring, sightless eyes. Three minutes before he had whispered to me. It was hard to believe he was dead. None of us had done this before, and we mechanically followed the instructions from the medic. Lonnie was securely tied into the poncho. A pole was cut and the body tied to it. Jeff and Bunk hoisted the pole to their shoulders and, with Lee acting as guard, they started back to camp.

Harold put a bullet into each corpse to make sure. Big Joe shoved a fresh clip into the B.A.R. Brad moved up to become the point, and the patrol moved out.

"One World or None"

Niels Bohr and J.R. Oppenheimer

An excerpt from public statements by leading atomic scientists, warning of the dangers of nuclear weapons.

NIELS BOHR[*]

The possibility of releasing vast amounts of energy through atomic disintegration, which means a veritable revolution of human resources, cannot but raise in the mind of everyone the question of where the advance of physical science is leading civilization. While the increasing mastery of the forces of nature has contributed so prolifically to human welfare and holds out even greater promises, it is evident that the formidable power of destruction that has come within reach of man may become a mortal menace unless human society can adjust itself to the exigencies of the situation. Civilization is presented with a challenge more serious perhaps than ever before, and the fate of humanity will depend on its ability to unite

---

[*]*NIELS BOHR, whose nuclear research did much to create the atomic age and won him the Nobel Prize in 1922 at the age of 37, escaped from the Nazis in his native Denmark in 1943. Coming to America, he played a major part in the development of the uranium project.*

in averting common dangers and jointly to reap the benefit from the immense opportunities which the progress of science offers.

In its origin science is inseparable from the collecting and ordering of experience, gained in the struggle for existence, which enabled our ancestors to raise mankind to its present position among the other living beings that inhabit our earth. Even in highly organized communities where, within the distribution of labor, scientific study has become an occupation by itself, the progress of science and the advance of civilization have remained most intimately interwoven. Of course, practical needs are still an impetus to scientific research, but it need hardly be stressed how often technical developments of the greatest importance for civilization have originated from studies aimed only at augmenting our knowledge and deepening our understanding. Such endeavors know no national borders, and where one scientist has left the trail another has taken it up, often in a distant part of the world. For scientists have long considered themselves a brotherhood working in the service of common human ideals.

In no domain of science have these lessons received stronger emphasis than in the exploration of the atom, which just now is bearing consequences of such overwhelming practical implications. As is well known, the roots of the idea of atoms as the ultimate constituents of matter go back to ancient thinkers searching for a foundation to explain the regularity which, in spite of all variability, is ever more clearly revealed by the study of natural phenomena. After the Renaissance, when science entered so fertile a period, atomic theory gradually became of the greatest importance for the physical and chemical sciences, although until half a century ago it was generally accepted that, owing to the coarseness of our senses, any direct proof of the existence of atoms would always remain beyond human scope. Aided, however, by the refined tools of modern technique, the development of the art of experimentation has removed such limitation and even yielded detailed information about the interior structure of atoms.

In particular, the discovery that almost the entire mass of the atom is concentrated in a central nucleus proved to have the most far-reaching consequences. Not only did it become evident that the remarkable stability of the chemical elements is due to the immutability of the atomic nucleus when exposed to ordinary physical agencies, but a novel field of research was opened up by the study of the special conditions under which disintegrations of the nuclei themselves may be brought about. Such processes, whereby the very elements are transformed, were found to differ fundamentally in character and violence from chemical reactions, and their investigation led to a rapid succession of important discoveries through which ultimately the possibility of a large-scale release of atomic energy came into sight. This progress was achieved in the course of a few decades and was due not least to most effective international cooperation. The world community of physicists was, so to speak, welded into a single team, rendering it more difficult than ever to disentangle the contributions of individual workers.

The grim realities being revealed to the world these days will no doubt, in the minds of many, revive the terrifying prospects forecast in fiction. With all due admiration for such imagination, it is, however, most essential to appreciate the contrast between these fantasies and the actual situation confronting us. Far from offering any easy means to bring destruction forth, as it were by witchcraft, scientific insight has made it evident that use of nuclear disintegration for devastating explosions demands most elaborate preparations, involving a profound change in the atomic composition of the materials found on earth. The astounding achievement of producing an enormous display of power on the basis of experience gained by the study of minute effects, perceptible only by the most delicate instruments, has in fact, besides a most intensive research effort, required an immense engineering enterprise, strikingly illuminating the potentialities of modern industrial development.

Indeed, not only have we left the time far behind where each man, for self-protection, could pick up the nearest stone, but we have even reached the stage where the degree of security offered to the citizens of a nation by collective defense measures is entirely insufficient. Against the new destructive powers no defense may be possible, and the issue centers on worldwide cooperation to prevent any use of the new sources of energy that does not serve mankind as a whole. The possibility of international regulation for this purpose should be ensured by the very magnitude and the peculiar character of the efforts that will be indispensable for the production of the formidable new weapon. It is obvious, however, that no control can be effective without free access to full scientific information and the granting of the opportunity of international supervision of all undertakings that, unless regulated, might become a source of disaster.

Such measures will, of course, demand the abolition of barriers hitherto considered necessary to safeguard national interests but now standing in the way of common security against unprecedented dangers. Certainly the handling of the precarious situation will demand the goodwill of all nations, but it must be recognized that we are dealing with what is potentially a deadly challenge to civilization itself. A better background for meeting such a situation could hardly be imagined than the earnest desire to seek a firm foundation for world security, so unanimously expressed by all those nations which only through united efforts have been able to defend elementary human rights. The extent of the contribution that agreement on this vital matter would make to the removal of obstacles to mutual confidence, and to the promotion of a harmonious relationship between nations, can hardly be exaggerated.

In the great task lying ahead, which places on our generation the gravest responsibility toward posterity, scientists all over the world may offer most valuable services. Not only do the bonds created through scientific intercourse form some of the firmest ties between individuals from different nations, but the whole scientific community will surely join in a vigorous effort to induce in wider circles an adequate appreciation of what is at stake and to appeal to humanity at large to heed the warning that has been sounded. It need not be added that every scientist who has taken part in laying the foundation for the new development or who has been called upon to participate in work that might have proved decisive in the struggle to preserve a state of civilization where human culture can freely develop is prepared to assist, in any way open to him, in bringing about an outcome of the present crisis of humanity that is worthy of the ideals for which science through the ages has stood.

J.R. OPPENHEIMER[*]

"The release of atomic energy constitutes a new force too revolutionary to consider in the framework of old ideas. . . ." President Harry S. Truman, in his message to Congress on Atomic Energy, October 3, 1945.

In these brave words the President of the United States has given expression to a conviction deep and prevalent among those who have been thinking of what atomic weapons might mean to the world. It is the conviction that these weapons call for and by their existence will help to create radical and profound changes in the politics of the world. These words of the President have often been quoted and for the most part by men who believed in their validity. What is the technical basis for this belief? Why should a development that appeared in this past war to be merely an extension and consummation of the techniques of strategic bombing be so radical a thing in its implications?

Certainly atomic weapons appeared with dramatic elements of novelty; certainly they do embody, as new sources of energy, very real changes in the ability of man to tap and to control such sources, very real differences in the kind of physical situation we can realize on earth. These Promethean qualities of drama and of novelty, that touch so deeply the sentiments with which man regards the natural

---

[*]*J.R. OPPENHEIMER before the war was professor of physics at the University of California and there led the most important school for theoretical physics in the United States. During the war he was in charge of the Los Alamos, New Mexico, laboratory.*

world and his place in it, have no doubt added to the interest with which atomic weapons have been regarded. Such qualities may even play a most valuable part in preparing men to take with necessary seriousness the grave problems put to them by these technical advances. But the truly radical character of atomic weapons lies neither in the suddenness with which they emerged from the laboratories and the secret industries, nor in the fact that they exploit an energy qualitatively different in origin from all earlier sources. It lies in their vastly greater powers of destruction, in the vastly reduced effort needed for such destruction. And it lies no less in the consequent necessity for new and more effective methods by which mankind may control the use of its new powers.

Nothing can be effectively new in touching the course of men's lives that is not also old. Nothing can be effectively revolutionary that is not deeply rooted in human experience. If, as I believe, the release of atomic energy is in fact revolutionary, it is surely not because its promise of rapid technological change, its realization of fantastic powers of destruction, have no analogue in our late history. It is precisely because that history has so well prepared us to understand what these things may mean.

Perhaps it may add to clarity to speak briefly of these three elements of novelty: 1. atomic weapons as a new source of energy, 2. atomic weapons as a new expression of the role of fundamental science, and 3. atomic weapons as a new power of destruction.

1. The energy we derive from coal and wood and oil came originally from sunlight, which, through the mechanisms of photosynthesis, stored this energy in organic matter. When these fuels are burned, they return more or less to the simple stable products from which, by sunlight, the organic matter was built up. The energy derived from waterpower also comes from sunlight, which raises water by evaporation, so that we may exploit the energy of its fall. The energy necessary to life itself comes from the same organic matter, created by

sunlight out of water and carbon dioxide. Of all the sources of energy used on earth, only tidal power would appear not to be a direct exploitation of the energy radiated by the sun.

Solar energy is nuclear energy. Deep in the interior of the sun, where matter is very hot and fairly dense, the nuclei of hydrogen are slowly reacting to form helium, reacting not directly with each other but by a complex series of collisions with carbon and nitrogen. These reactions, which proceed slowly even at the high temperatures that obtain in the center of the sun, are made possible at all only because those temperatures, of some twenty million degrees, are maintained. The reason they are maintained is that the enormous gravitational forces of the sun's mass keep the material from expanding and cooling. No proposals have ever been made for realizing such conditions on earth or for deriving energy on earth in a controlled and large-scale way from the conversion of hydrogen to helium and heavier nuclei.

The nuclear energy released in atomic weapons and in controlled nuclear reactors has a very different source, which would appear to us now as rather accidental. The nuclei of the very heavy elements are less stable than those of elements like iron, of moderate atomic weight. For reasons we do not understand, there are such heavy unstable elements on earth. As was discovered just before the war, the heaviest of the elements do not need to be very highly excited to split into two lighter nuclei. It is surely an accident, by all we now know, that there are elements heavier than lead in the world, and for lead no practical method of inducing fission would seem to exist. But for uranium the simple capture of a neutron is sufficient to cause fission. And in certain materials—notably U-235 and plutonium—enough neutrons are produced by such fission, with a great enough chance that under proper circumstances they can cause other fissions in other nuclei, so that the fission reaction will build up in a diverging chain of successive reactions, and a good part of the energy latent in the material actually will be released.

To our knowledge such things do not happen except in the atomic weapons we have made and used and, in a somewhat more complex form, in the great reactors or piles. They do not, to our knowledge, happen in any other part of the universe. To make them happen involves specific human intervention in the physical world.

The interior of an exploding fission bomb is, so far as we know, a place without parallel elsewhere. It is hotter than the center of the sun; it is filled with matter that does not normally occur in nature and with radiations—neutrons, gamma rays, fission fragments, electrons—of an intensity without precedent in human experience. The pressures are a thousand billion times atmospheric pressure. In the crudest, simplest sense, it is quite true that in atomic weapons man has created novelty.

2. It would appear to be without parallel in human history that basic knowledge about the nature of the physical world should have been applied so rapidly to changing, in an important way, the physical conditions of man's life. In 1938, it was not known that fission could occur. Neither the existence nor the properties nor the methods of making plutonium had been thought of—to the best of my knowledge—by anyone. The subsequent rapid development was made possible only by the extremities of the war and the great courage of the governments of the United States and Britain, by an advanced technology and a united people. Nevertheless it made very special demands of the scientists, who have played a more intimate, deliberate, and conscious part in altering the conditions of human life than ever before in our history.

The obvious consequence of this intimate participation of scientists is a quite new sense of responsibility and concern for what they have done and for what may come of it. This book* itself is an expression of that sense of concern. A more subtle aspect of it, not frequently recognized but perhaps in the long term more relevant

*One World or None, *originally published in 1946. Reprinted by the New Press, New York, 2007.*

and more constructive, is this: scientists are, not by the nature of what they find but by the way in which they find it, humanists; science, by its methods, its values, and the nature of the objectivity it seeks, is universally human. It is therefore natural for scientists to look at the new world of atomic energy and atomic weapons in a very broad light. And in this light the community of experience, of effort, and of values that prevails among scientists of different nations is comparable in significance with the community of interest existing for the men and the women of one nation. It is natural that they should supplement the fraternity of the peoples of one country with the fraternity of men of learning everywhere, with the value that these men put upon knowledge, and with the attempt—which is their heritage—to transcend the accidents of personal or national history in discovering more of the nature of the physical world.

The injection of the spirit of the scientist into this problem of atomic weapons, in which it has been clear from the first that purely national ideas of welfare and security would doubtless prove inadequate, has been recognized, if not clearly understood, by statesmen as well as by scientists. The emphasis that has been given—in the statements of the President and in the agreed declaration of the heads of state of Britain, Canada, and the United States—to the importance of the reestablishment of the international fraternity and freedom of science is an evidence of this recognition. It should not be thought that this recognition implies either that collaboration in science will constitute a solution to the problems of the relations of nations, nor that scientists themselves can play any disproportionate part in achieving that solution. It is rather a recognition that in these problems a common approach, in which national interests can play only a limitedly constructive part, will be necessary if a solution is to be found at all. Such an approach has been characteristic of science in the past. In its application to the problems of international relations there is novelty.

• • •

3. In this past war it cost the United States about $10 a pound to deliver explosives to an enemy target. Fifty thousand tons of explosive would thus cost a billion dollars to deliver. Although no precise estimates of the costs of making an atomic bomb equivalent to 50,000 tons of ordinary explosive in energy release can now be given, it seems certain that such costs might be several hundred times less, possibly a thousand times less. Ton for equivalent ton, atomic explosives are vastly cheaper than ordinary explosives. Before conclusions can be drawn from this fact, a number of points must be looked at. But it will turn out that the immediate conclusion is right: atomic explosives vastly increase the power of destruction per dollar spent, per man-hour invested; they profoundly upset the precarious balance between the effort necessary to destroy and the extent of the destruction.

The area destroyed by explosive is a better guide to its destructive power than the energy of the explosion. For an atomic bomb the area destroyed by blast increases with the two-thirds power, not proportionately to the energy release. So far as blast is concerned, an atomic bomb is perhaps five times less effective than the same equivalent tonnage delivered in blockbusters or smaller missiles would be. But in the strikes against Hiroshima and Nagasaki the effects, especially the antipersonnel effects, of heat were comparable to the blast effects. These effects increase proportionately in the area affected with the energy release of the weapon and thus become of greater importance as the power of the weapon is increased.

In this connection it is clearly relevant to ask what technical developments the future might have in store for the infant atomic-weapon industry. No suggestions are known to me that would greatly reduce the unit size of the weapons while keeping down the cost per unit of area devastated or reducing it still further. On the other hand proposals that appear sound have been investigated in a preliminary way, and it turns out that they would reduce the cost of destruction per square mile probably by a factor of ten or more, but they would involve a great increase in the unit power of the weapons. Such weapons would clearly be limited in application to the destruction of very major targets, such as greater New York.

A word may be in order concerning the specific effect of the nuclear radiations—neutrons and gamma rays—produced by the explosion. The novel character of these effects, and the fact that lethal effects kept appearing many weeks after the strikes, attracted much attention. But these radiations accounted, in Hiroshima and Nagasaki, for a quite small fraction of the casualties. It is probable that this would be true of future atomic weapons as well, but it is not certain.

No discussion of the economics of atomic destruction can be complete without some mention of possible countermeasures. One such countermeasure, which might have the effect of increasing the cost of destruction by eliminating targets large enough for the more powerful weapons, is the dispersal of cities and industry. More difficult to evaluate is the effect of greatly improved methods of interception on the carrier of the atomic weapon. It may be said here that the present situation hardly warrants the belief that techniques of interception will greatly alter the cost of atomic destruction.

Although it would seem virtually certain that atomic weapons could be used effectively against combat personnel, against fortifications at least of certain types, and against naval craft, their disproportionate power of destruction is greatest in strategic bombardment: in destroying centers of population, and population itself, and in destroying industry. Since the United States and Britain in this past war were willing to engage in mass demolition and incendiary raids against civilian centers and did in fact use atomic weapons against primarily civilian targets, there would seem little valid hope that such use would not be made in any future major war.

The many factors discussed here, and others that cannot be discussed here, clearly make it inappropriate and impossible to give a precise figure for the probable cost and thus the probable effort involved in atomic destruction. Clearly, too, such costs would in the first instance depend on the technical and military policies of nations engaging in atomic armament. But none of these uncertainties can becloud the fact that it will cost enormously less to destroy a square mile with atomic weapons than with any weapons hitherto known to warfare. My own estimate is that the advent of such weapons will reduce the cost, certainly by more than a factor of ten, more probably by a factor of a hundred. In this respect only biological warfare would seem to offer competition for the evil that a dollar can do.

It would thus seem that the power of destruction that has come into men's hands has in fact been qualitatively altered by atomic weapons. In particular it is clear that the reluctance of peoples and of many governments to divert a large part of their wealth and effort to preparations for war can no longer be counted on at all to insure the absence of such preparations. It would seem that the conscious acquisition of these new powers of destruction calls for the equally conscious determination that they must not be used and that all necessary steps be taken to insure that they will not be used. Such steps, once taken, would provide machinery adequate for the avoidance of international war.

The situation, in fact, bears some analogy to one that has recently, without technical foundation, been imagined. It has been suggested that some future atomic weapon might initiate nuclear reactions that would destroy the earth itself or render it unsuitable for the continuance of life. By all we now know, and it is not inconsiderable, such fears are groundless. An atomic weapon will not, by what we know, destroy physically the men or the nation using it. Yet it seems to me that an awareness of the consequences of atomic warfare to all peoples of the earth, to aggressor and defender alike, can hardly be a less cogent argument for preventing such warfare than the possibilities outlined above. For the dangers to mankind are in some ways quite as grave, and the inadequacy of any compensating national advantage is, to me at least, quite as evident.

The vastly increased powers of destruction that atomic weapons give us have brought with them a profound change in the balance between national and international interests. The common interest of all in the prevention of atomic warfare would seem immensely to overshadow any purely national interest, whether of welfare or of security. At the same time it would seem of most doubtful value in any long term to rely on purely national methods of defense for insuring security. The true security of this nation, as of any other, will be found, if at all, only in the collective efforts of all.

It is even now clear that such efforts will not be successful if they are made only as a supplement, or secondary insurance, to a national defense. In fact it is clear that such collective efforts will require, and do today require, a very real renunciation of the steps by which in the past national security has been sought. It is clear that in a very real sense the past patterns of national security are inconsistent with the attainment of security on the only level where it can now, in the atomic age, be effective. It may be that in times to come it will be by this that atomic weapons are most remembered. It is in this that they will come to seem "too revolutionary to consider in the framework of old ideas."

"The Atomic Bomb"

Philip Morrison

In an excerpt from *"The Good War"*, Studs Terkel talks with Philip Morrison, a nuclear physicist who worked on the Manhattan Project, the U.S government program that developed the atomic bomb.

The folklore of the day is, the physicists were approached by the army. The army said, We will make you rich and famous. We'll give you the wonderful opportunity to make the world's greatest explosion and all you have to forget is, it's going to make a bomb to kill very many people. A Faustian bargain.

That was not the idea at all. It's a complete misapprehension. *We* went to the army. I mean the scientific profession, Einstein, the pacifist, at its head. We beat on the doors and said, We must be allowed to make this weaponry or we're going to lose the war. Once we did that, we didn't stop. I didn't work a forty-hour week. I worked a seventy-hour week. At night, I sat and I thought. I woke up in the morning and I thought. All my friends did the same thing. What can we do about this war? Physicists invented the bomb.

His office at the Massachusetts Institute of Technology reflects his incredible multi-interests and impulses. There are jagged mountains of books, journals, and dissertations formed higgledy-piggledy on the floor, at the window, on his desk. He will undoubtedly write critiques of some, comment on others; subjects including and beyond theoretical physics, from which he "strayed about twenty years ago," to astronomy, with which he is currently concerned. "I'm really an astronomer today."

During the war, I was a nuclear physicist. Actually, I was an engineer. We made weapons.

Before the war, in Berkeley, California, I was listening to the speeches in Nuremberg, in the middle of the night. Hitler was speaking on the radio. I was a student of Oppenheimer. My friends were in Spain: the Spanish Civil War seemed even more real to me than World War Two. I know more people who were killed in Spain than were killed in World War Two. We felt it was a prelude to the war in Europe. Had the Spanish Civil War been stopped, had the German and Italian aid to Franco been beaten back, the world war might have been aborted. Or so we thought.

The whole thing really began for us in late December '38, right after Munich. That first paper arrived in German, by Hahn and Strassmann. This queer paper showed that uranium could be changed into barium. Before we could understand it very well, we heard rumors from Sweden that Robert Frisch and Lise Meitner had understood it. Frisch told me this story himself. She was his aunt. They went for a walk in the woods. They sat down on a log. He drew a little something, and she said, "I think of it this way." She drew a little something. They couldn't understand each other's drawings. Then they realized at once, together, that they were exactly the same drawing, seen from two different points of view. The uranium atom was splitting in half. Three days later, they gave it the name: fission. By the middle of January, it was clear to everybody.

We, Oppenheimer's students, drew on the boards all kinds of fantastic designs of atomic bombs. We didn't know much about it. A year later, I wrote an article, but they didn't print it. Nobody seemed interested in physics.

Leo Szilard was ahead of everyone. He had this idea five years before. He was still in Europe, a Hungarian refugee. He understood, somewhat mistakenly, that it was a sign of how to make a chain reaction. For four, five years he toured Europe, trying to buttonhole people. Trying to find a place where he could work on it. He acquired a reputation as this crazy guy who has the idea of making energy from the atom. He didn't think of the bomb so much then, but of a source of power. He became a figure of folklore.

He came to the United States to look up Enrico Fermi, who had just come here from Italy. He tried to convince him to get to work on it. Then, Szilard and Wigner persuaded Einstein to write that letter to Roosevelt: the Germans are well ahead on the bomb. Let us do something. Their information on Germany was not very good, but it seemed to them plausible. This was the fall of '39. War had already broken out. With the fall of France in '40, we were already on a war footing.

I was looking for a job. Chicago was the place where I went. I was hired by Fermi the day after the first chain reaction, which took place December 2, '42.

For a year, I had been doing war work at the University of Illinois. There was no physicist able to breathe who wasn't doing war work. Physics was totally mobilized. The U.S. was still not at war, there was plenty of war work. After Pearl Harbor, the campus was immediately mobilized. Classes were accelerated. Students were in uniform. They marched to class singing "Sixpence." I was wildly enthusiastic, 'cause I was a long-time anti-Nazi and this was the war I expected and feared. I was caught up spontaneously and naively in this terrible war. It was the great crusade.

I was an air-raid warden at Illinois. I spent the drills on top of the physics building, with my sand bucket to put out incendiary bombs. We even figured out the Germans would send a little aircraft carrier to Hudson's Bay and try to bomb Chicago. But they would miss Chicago, because the lights were off. And they might find Urbana, which was straight past Chicago. (Laughs.) Really bizarre. There was a great sense of camaraderie, of national unity. Everybody was caught up in it.

The day I joined Fermi at Chicago was suffused with excitement. My friend, who'd been working there, said, "You know what we're doing here?" I guessed that they were working on a chain reaction. He said, "We already did that. Now we're going to make an atomic bomb."

This bomb requires fissionable material. A chain reaction does not. It can be made out of ordinary uranium. The idea was to make plutonium, chemically separable from the other elements. After that, it was alchemy: to turn uranium into plutonium.

In Oak Ridge, Tennessee, two factories were built: one for the New York scientists from Columbia University, under Harold Urey; the other, for the Berkeley people, under William Lawrence. The third plant, in Hanford, Washington, was for Fermi's Chicago laboratory.

We had a tight schedule. We had to decide what the plutonium design would be, train the Du Pont engineers, enlarge the work, and develop it: all leading to fissionable material. Then, it would be taken to another place and turned into a bomb.

It was all one single enterprise, highly divided, highly complex: the Manhattan Project, run by General Groves.

We knew the idea was to make the most destructive of all possible bombs. We believed Hitler was well ahead of us. My own personal experience was colored by a notion that came to me about six months after I joined the project. It occurred to me there were other ways of finding out what the Germans were doing, instead of just shaking prisoners and asking them what was going on. Technical means.

I prepared a careful, lengthy letter, which I sent off to General Groves. The same week it appeared on his desk, there was by chance a remarkable similar letter from a chemist in New York. We had never seen each other or even heard of each other before. This coincidence fitted General Groves's own turn of thought. He called us in and said, "Set it up." He gave us a few officers to work with. We set up a scheme for studying German intelligence. This eventually became known as the Alsace Project. I made myself into an intelligence officer. I just sat and read . . .

We initiated a terrible set of operations, the kind you read about in books. In my present view, it was wasteful, but probably justified by the circumstances. We sent airplanes into all kinds of difficult jobs. We sent young men to do all kinds of difficult tasks. Sometimes they were killed for negligible information. We took photographs galore, penetrating far behind German lines, in our fastest aircraft. We'd taken photographs of a Czechoslovakian uranium mine: was it working? We'd measure the number of trucks that came in and out each day.

We studied literature. We got all the magazines from Switzerland that the Germans published. We collected instrument dials from wrecked airplanes and measured their radioactivity. We even got people to fly up and down the rivers of Austria and Germany, at a very low altitude, dragging cotton wicks into the water, to pick up samples. Was the water radioactive?

We assumed the Germans were well ahead of us. They were our teachers. They had been well organized for war. We had a hard time doing that. Intelligence is an impossible task because it is marred by false information. We had heard innumerable stories from Sweden, from Switzerland, from prisoners of war. Yes, the Germans are testing bombs. Yes, they're well ahead. Yes, they have secret weapons. But now, through our other ways, we knew precisely what they did in all detail. We had their notebooks. Of course they were working on it, but they were far behind us.

By December '44, we learned unmistakably, from the Alsace mission, from people who went abroad to do studies of the Germans, by taking Strasbourg—we seized the laboratory of an important German physicist, Fleischmann—that the Germans were not a threat. They could not make the atomic bomb. It was like an open book. They were far behind and arrogant. They said, "We're well ahead of the rest of the world. The Americans can't do it. Even if Germany loses the war, we'll win the peace, because we alone control this powerful weapon." When we read this, we laughed out loud.

The work at Chicago was becoming more and more an engineering job. The plant at Hanford was ready to go by the summer of '44. I was scheduled to head out there with Fermi to work up this enormous power-generating plant. The biggest thing in the world. But General Groves said, "Don't go." The Normandy invasion was under way. We were preparing to go into German territory to shake down any information they had.

A crisis came up in Los Alamos. Here, in the New Mexican desert, they'd be assembling the bomb, making it. They were already working there, under Oppenheimer. It had been formed in the spring of '43. It began to grow enormously, much more than we had expected. They needed help to solve the problem of implosion, when it became clear that plutonium could not be used in the bomb unless a new method of assembly was developed. They'd better get people there in a hurry. The work in Chicago was slacking off. We began to talk about the postwar world and peaceful uses of atomic energy.

I was quite happy to go to Los Alamos, at first, because I felt a great loyalty to Oppenheimer. Los Alamos was a community of great single-mindedness and intensity. We thought of ourselves as being in the front line. We stood in the breach between Hitler and the world. The only way we could lose the war was if we failed our jobs.

Los Alamos was not a city like Chicago. It was an army post with physicists. When I walked down the street, I knew everyone personally. We never had such a sense of fraternity in a little community before. Of course, it was secret. It was surrounded by guards. We could not go out without permission. Our mail was censored, our telephone calls were interrupted. We consented to all this. The payment that Oppenheimer, quite wisely, elicited for our acceptance of control and isolation was that we be allowed to talk freely, one with the other. You knew all that was going on. Within the community, there was a complete openness. Fermi, Bethe, Neumann, Kistiakowsky, Teller were all there. There were no secrets to which we were not privy. We were inventing the secrets. We were writing the book.

Teller? As Oppenheimer said, "In wartime, he is an obstructionist. In peacetime, he'll become a promoter." Teller had an *idée fixe*. He said, "My work is more important, making a thermonuclear weapon." It was clear to everyone, you had to make the fission one first. It was clearly in the wrong sequence. It wasn't at that moment a moral question. It just wasn't realistic.

We spent a lot of time and risked a lot of lives to do so. Of my little group of eight, two were killed. We were using high explosives and radioactive material in large quantities for the first time. There was a series of events that rocked us. We were working hard, day and night, to do something that had never been done before. It might not work at all.

I remember working late one night with my friend Louis Slotin. He was killed by a radiation accident. We shared the job. It could have been I. But it was he, who was there that day. It was a Saturday, We'd get the material and we'd work from nine in the morning to three the next morning. We worked alone in a shielded laboratory, with a couple of guards. The shadowy night outside. A soldier or two, who was technical.

A very important role was played in the Los Alamos project by young men and women who were taken in the army, sifted out of the draft, graduate students in chemistry or physics or metallurgy. They were sent to Oak Ridge, selected, and sent on to Los Alamos. I was the senior physicist. I was twenty-seven. It was exactly the mean age of Los Alamos scientists. We were all young.

What was the right thing for us to do? It was a critical moment. The Japanese war was not yet over. Our work may bring an end to the war, save many lives, start a new world. We were disappointed that the United Nations did not hear about it. Nobody breathed its possibilities to the UN. Acheson didn't mention the weaponry that could transform the world. That puzzled me.

Then came the terrible news of the sudden death of Roosevelt. I think that ended the possibility that anything novel would happen with the bomb. Yet if Truman had modified the obvious course—going ahead, using it—he wouldn't have had the power to do so. The pressure of his advisers was too much.

I don't say I was antagonistic to its use, not at all. But I wondered: is this the right thing to do? The idea of dropping it was implicit in making it. We were not certain just how. Our task was to get the bomb finished, to find out if it would work. The whole world was depending on that, we felt.

I was appointed one of the people to make sure of the details of the test in the desert. The Trinity test. There was talk of the possibility of its use over Japan. There was another suggestion that the Japanese be invited to see the test. But there was this enormous uncertainty: would it work? If it didn't work, you'd feel pretty embarrassed. (Laughs.) July 16, it went off in the desert.

The shot was set for Monday morning. I went down the Thursday before, guarded in a convoy of automobiles, carrying the core, the little ball of plutonium. I designed the ball. We assembled the bomb in the high explosive only for the second time. We were all afraid. Kistiakowsky was afraid for us. When we tried it on the hill, it worked. We came down in the desert and tried it again. At the base of the tower, we put the plutonium core into the high explosive. That was the end of our job. We were done.

We went to the base camp, exactly ten miles away. We stayed there for a couple of days, hearing gossip, living our lives, getting ready for the day of the test. It began to rain on Sunday evening. The test was uncertain. There was much anxiety. In the morning, just before dawn, the rain subsided.

I had a short-wave set and was responsible for listening to the radio communications from the people who would actually start it. Fermi, all the others were there. But those directly engaged with the instrumentation were scattered all over the desert, some in shelters, some far away. I had a microphone and I relayed the countdown. I announced it: 30 seconds, 20 seconds, 10 seconds, 9, 8, 7, 6 . . .

From ten miles away, we saw the unbelievably brilliant flash. That was not the most impressive thing. We knew it was going to be blinding. We wore welder's glasses. The thing that got me was not the flash but the blinding heat of a bright day on your face in the cold desert morning. It was like opening a hot oven with the sun coming out like a sunrise. It was a feeling of awe and wonder and dismay and fear and triumph, all together. The sound came a minute later. It went off in a dead silence, a great thunder.

Within a few days, I went from Los Alamos to Wendover Air Force Base at Wendover, Utah. The 509th Composite Group was there. And our transport aircraft. With the core of the bomb, I flew to Tinian. That's where the B-29 bases were. They had been attacking Japan for a year.

I loaded the plane called *Bock's Car*. It had two dice, with sixes showing. It was named after Captain Bock. Somebody else loaded the other bomb on the *Enola Gay*. The takeoff was dangerous, because there was no way of rendering it safe. The airplane just had to take a chance. *Bock's Car*'s bomb fell on Nagasaki three days after *Enola Gay*'s fell on Hiroshima.

We heard the news of Hiroshima from the airplane itself, a coded message. When they returned, we didn't see them. The generals had them. But then the people came back with photographs. I remember looking at them with awe and terror. We knew a terrible thing had been unleashed. The men had a great party that night to celebrate, but we didn't go. Almost no physicists went to it. We obviously killed a hundred thousand people and that was nothing to have a party about. The reality confronts you with things you could never anticipate.

Before I went to Wendover, an English physicist, Bill Penney, held a seminar five days after the test at Los Alamos. He applied his calculations. He predicted that this would reduce a city of three or four hundred thousand people to nothing but a sink for disaster relief, bandages, and hospitals. He made it absolutely clear in numbers. It was reality. We knew it, but we didn't see it. After we saw the event . . .

What was the purpose of the Nagasaki bombing? Didn't Hiroshima do the trick?

That's been much debated. From the viewpoint of the leadership, it was the same event. Two bombs were ordered. Admiral Pernell pointed out to General Groves that if you drop one bomb, after four years of war, the Japanese may think you could make only one bomb in that time. So why don't you drop two in quick succession? Then they don't know how many to expect. That fitted the project's plan: they were both being tested. They were two quite different bombs, with different mechanisms. Each one cost billions of dollars, so you used them both. When they cut the orders, they didn't say drop one. They said drop the first one and, as soon as you can, drop the second.

I was of the opinion that a warning to the Japanese might work. I was disappointed when the military said you don't warn.

Realize this: the air force had bombed sixty-six Japanese cities and towns before the end of the war. Ninety-nine big air raids and sixty-six targets. The place was destroyed. From our point of view, the atomic bomb was not a discontinuity. We were just carrying on more of the same, only it was much cheaper. For that war, it was just one more city destroyed. We had already destroyed sixty-six; what's two more? Fire bombs and high explosives did the job on Dresden and Hamburg and Leipzig.

Would the A-bomb have been dropped on Germany?

Oh, you bet. We would have all struck if it hadn't been. If Roosevelt were still there and Germany had not surrendered, it certainly would have been used. The libido of the physicists was to drop it on Germany. Every physicist felt this.

Through the years, we've heard it said that the A-bomb would never have been used on a Caucasian nation.

I think it underestimates the hatred against the Germans and the bitterness that we felt.

 James Franck, a truly wonderful man, produced the Franck Report: don't drop the bomb on a city. Drop it as a demonstration and offer a warning. This was about a month before Hiroshima. The movement against the bomb was beginning among the physicists, but with little hope. It was strong at Chicago, but it didn't affect Los Alamos. As soon as the bombs were dropped, the scientists, with few exceptions, felt the time had come to end all wars.

Two among sixty-six is nothing, but each of these two big ones was only one airplane. That was the real military meaning of Hiroshima and Nagasaki. It was not that the bombs were so destructive. It was not that the bombs created radioactivity. Terrible, of course. It's that the atomic bomb, now the nuclear bomb, is cheap. That's why we're in this big trouble.

At the height of its mobilization in World War Two, the United States could manage to make six or eight hundred big bombers. They could visit a city and do big damage in one night. If these eight hundred came to a city several nights, they could do the damage of an atomic bomb. So, you could manage to knock off, with all your forces, a city a week. But now, a thousand cities in a night! It's the numbers. It's the cheapness.

In World War One, we saw the first application of twentieth-century science to war. In the Battle of the Somme, the worst, the British and the Germans together could mobilize ten kilotons of high explosives; to shoot ten thousand pounds at a time, cannon shot by cannon shot, into the trenches for fifty miles around. That's ten kilotons a day—ten thousand tons. That's a lot of bombs, a lot of shells, right?

A freight train carries 40 tons a boxcar; 40 times 250 is 10 kilotons. That's a train 250 boxcars long. A mile long. Several freight trains of shells were fired off in one day by fifty thousand sweating gunners shooting the shells one by one.

By 1951, the United States could do the whole World War One, which lasted a thousand nights, in one day. By 1952, there was the thermonuclear weapon. By 1958, we could do—not a kiloton as in World War One, not a megaton as in World War Two—a gigaton. A billion tons.

A billion tons?

A thousand million tons. That's where we stand now. It is this inordinate scale of change. Destruction has become so available and so cheap. The world still does not understand it.

The physicists have nothing to do with it any more. It's an industry. It's bought and paid for. There are thousands of jobs. The materials are expensive. It's highly technical. The processes are complicated. And high-paid people are doing it.

This is the legacy of World War Two, a direct legacy of Hitler. When we beat the Nazis, we emulated them. I include myself. I became callous to death. I became willing to risk everything on war and peace. I followed my leaders enthusiastically and rather blindly.

The Germans made the rocket. The cruise missile and the ballistic missile are also German inventions; they came out of Peenemünde. They didn't have the atomic bomb, but I believed they would have it. I thought that's why they were making these missiles.

In my intelligence capacity, I once wrote a letter to somebody in authority: don't let Churchill and Roosevelt meet in the south of England. It's not safe. Any day the Germans will launch an atomic bomb and destroy any place they please. They'll just kill the leadership at once.

There was the feeling that it was justified. Now, of course, I don't think it was justified. But if I had to do it all over again, I honestly say I would do the same. Nationalism is a terrible force. We're nation states, and people follow their leaders. Sure, there is an international community of scientists, but it's weak compared to the national impulse. You see it every day.

We fought the war to stop fascism. But it transformed the societies that opposed fascism. They took on some of its attributes. All these clichés, all these slogans: Total War. No Appeasement. No More Pearl Harbors.

In cold objective fact, Pearl Harbor was the greatest American victory of World War Two. It mobilized the country. A few battleships were sunk, a few thousand sailors were killed. Sure, it's bad. But from the viewpoint of history, no Japanese defeat was as bad for them as their successful attack on Pearl Harbor.

In the same way, I feel all this arming and preparing comes from the same syndrome: we can't afford to be surprised, we can't afford to be weak. That's what the Germans said. And did. They mobilized first. Look what happened to them. The same thing will happen to us if we don't cool it.

As one of Samuel Beckett's tramps asks the other, What's to be done?

End the arms race. It sounds like a slogan, but it happens to be our last best hope. We must wind it down as fast and as far as we can. I'm optimistic. I think there's a great survival instinct. In spite of the cold war, in spite of all the anxiety, the war has remained cold. We've never used the weapons for thirty-eight years. I wouldn't have given it twenty-five years. So we've had, as I see it, thirteen years of grace. Perhaps people will now decide we'd better have a lot more years of grace.

A lot of people went into government, worked at developing these weapons, and came away saying it was the wrong thing to do.

The people who made the H-bomb say it was a mistake. I made only the A-bomb. It took me only one lesson to learn the mistake. I don't know what the future holds. But I do know we're beginning to understand the climate, beginning to understand the oceans, beginning to understand the cell and the nucleus of the cell. We're beginning to understand things we didn't understand before. It is simply not possible to have war and nation states in the old way, with this kind of knowledge and this kind of technology. It cannot work into the next century.

"A Terrible New Weapon"

Yamaoka Michiko, Shin Bok Su, and Matsushige Yoshito

Firsthand witnesses of ground zero at Hiroshima and Nagasaki, interviewed by Haruko Taya Cook and Theodore F. Cook
(from *Japan at War*).

YAMAOKA MICHIKO

She is a hibakusha—*one who was exposed to the atomic bomb. The term
has come to be used frequently to specify this particular kind of victimiza-
tion, as distinct from more general terms applied to those who suffered
from the war. Persons registered with the Ministry of Health and Welfare
are eligible to carry an "A-bomb notebook," which officially identifies them
and today entitles them to receive the relief medical assistance available
only to victims of the bomb.*

*We meet in a corner of a large room in the Hiroshima Peace Memo-
rial Museum, a short walk from the Atomic Bomb Dome at the edge of
the Peace Memorial Park. "These days I talk to groups of schoolchildren
who come to Hiroshima. They seem to listen, but I fear that nobody really
understands our feelings."*

That year, on August 6, I was in the third year of girls' high
school, fifteen years old. I was an operator at the telephone
exchange. We had been mobilized from school for various work

219

assignments for more than a year. My assigned place of duty was civilian, but we, too, were expected to protect the nation. We were tied by strong bonds to the country. We'd heard the news about the Tokyo and Osaka bombings, but nothing had dropped on Hiroshima. Japan was winning. So we still believed. We only had to endure. I wasn't particularly afraid when B-29s flew overhead.

That morning I left the house at about seven forty-five. I heard that the B-29s had already gone home. Mom told me, "Watch out, the B-29s might come again." My house was one point three kilometers from the hypocenter. My place of work was five hundred meters from the hypocenter. I walked toward the hypocenter in an area where all the houses and buildings had been deliberately demolished for fire breaks. There was no shade. I had on a white shirt and *monpe*. As I walked there, I noticed middle-school students pulling down houses at a point about eight hundred meters away from the hypocenter. I heard the faint sound of planes as I approached the river. The planes were tricky. Sometimes they only pretended to leave. I could still hear the very faint sound of planes. Today, I have no hearing in my left ear because of damage from the blast. I thought, how strange, so I put my right hand above my eyes and looked up to see if I could spot them. The sun was dazzling. That was the moment.

There was no sound. I felt something strong. It was terribly intense. I felt colors. It wasn't heat. You can't really say it was yellow, and it wasn't blue. At that moment I thought I would be the only one who would die. I said to myself, "Goodbye, Mom."

They say temperatures of seven thousand degrees centigrade hit me. You can't really say it washed over me. It's hard to describe. I simply fainted. I remember my body floating in the air. That was probably the blast, but I don't know how far I was blown. When I came to my senses, my surroundings were silent. There was no wind. I saw a slight threadlike light, so I felt I must be alive. I was under stones. I couldn't move my body. I heard voices crying, "Help! Water!" It was then I realized I wasn't the only one. I couldn't really see around me. I tried to say something, but my voice wouldn't come out.

"Fire! Run away! Help! Hurry up!" They weren't voices but moans of agony and despair. "I have to get help and shout," I thought. The person who rescued me was Mom, although she herself had been buried under our collapsed house. Mom knew the route I'd been taking. She came, calling out to me. I heard her voice and cried for help. Our surroundings were already starting to burn. Fires burst out from just the light itself. It didn't really drop. It just flashed.

It was beyond my mother's ability. She pleaded, "My daughter's buried here, she's been helping you, working for the military." She convinced soldiers nearby to help her and they started to dig me out. The fire was now blazing. "Woman, hurry up, run away from here," soldiers called. From underneath the stones I heard the crackling of flames. I called to her, "It's all right. Don't worry about me. Run away." I really didn't mind dying for the sake of the nation. Then they pulled me out by my legs.

Nobody there looked like human beings. Until that moment I thought incendiary bombs had fallen. Everyone was stupefied. Humans had lost the ability to speak. People couldn't scream, "It hurts!" even when they were on fire. People didn't say, "It's hot!" They just sat catching fire.

My clothes were burnt and so was my skin. I was in rags. I had braided my hair, but now it was like a lion's mane. There were people, barely breathing, trying to push their intestines back in. People with their legs wrenched off. Without heads. Or with faces burned and swollen out of shape. The scene I saw was a living hell.

Mom didn't say anything when she saw my face and I didn't feel any pain. She just squeezed my hand and told me to run. She was going to go rescue my aunt. Large numbers of people were moving away from the flames. My eyes were still able to see, so I made my way towards the mountain, where there was no fire, toward Hiji-yama. On this flight I saw a friend of mine from the phone exchange.

She'd been inside her house and wasn't burned. I called her name, but she didn't respond. My face was so swollen she couldn't tell who I was. Finally, she recognized my voice. She said, "Miss Yamaoka, you look like a monster!" That's the first time I heard that word. I looked at my hands and saw my own skin hanging down and the red flesh exposed. I didn't realize my face was swollen up because I was unable to see it.

The only medicine was *tempura* oil. I put it on my body myself. I lay on the concrete for hours. My skin was now flat, not puffed up anymore. One or two layers had peeled off. Only now did it become painful. A scorching sky was overhead. The flies swarmed over me and covered my wounds, which were already festering. People were simply left lying around. When their faint breathing became silent, they'd say, "This one's dead," and put the body in a pile of corpses. Some called for water, and if they got it, they died immediately.

Mom came looking for me again. That's why I'm alive today. I couldn't walk anymore. I couldn't see anymore. I was carried on a stretcher as far as Ujina, and then from there to an island where evacuees were taken. On the boat there I heard voices saying, "Let them drink water if they want. They'll die either way." I drank a lot of water.

I spent the next year bedridden. All my hair fell out. When we went to relatives' houses later they wouldn't even let me in because they feared they'd catch the disease. There was neither treatment nor assistance for me. Those people who had money, people who had both parents, people who had houses, they could go to the Red Cross Hospital or the Hiroshima City Hospital. They could get operations. But we didn't have any money. It was just my Mom and I. Keloids covered my face, my neck. I couldn't even move my neck. One eye was hanging down. I was unable to control my drooling because my lip had been burned off. I couldn't get any treatments at a hospital, so my mother gave me massages. Because she did that for me, my keloids aren't as bad as they would have been. My fingers were all stuck together. I couldn't move them. The only thing I could do was sew shorts, since I only needed to sew a straight line. I had to do something to earn money.

The Japanese government just told us we weren't the only victims of the war. There was no support or treatment. It was probably harder for my Mom. Once she told me she tried to choke me to death. If a girl has terrible scars, a face you couldn't be born with, I understand that even a mother could want to kill her child. People threw stones at me and called me Monster. That was before I had my many operations. I only showed this side of my face, the right hand side, when I had to face someone. Like I'm sitting now.

A decade after the bomb, we went to America. I was one of the twenty-five selected by Norman Cousins to be brought to America for treatment and plastic surgery.* We were called the Hiroshima Maidens. The American government opposed us, arguing that it would be acknowledging a mistake if they admitted us to America, but we were supported by many civilian groups. We went to Mount Sinai Hospital in New York and spent about a year and a half undergoing treatment. I improved tremendously. I've now had thirty-seven operations, including efforts at skin grafts.

When I went to America I had a deep hatred toward America. I asked myself why they ended the war by a means which destroyed human beings. When I talked about how I suffered, I was often told, "Well, you attacked Pearl Harbor!" I didn't understand much English then, and it's probably just as well. From the American point of view, they dropped that bomb in order to end the war faster, in order to create more damage faster. But it's inexcusable to harm human beings in this way. I wonder what kind of education there is now in America about atomic bombs. They're still making them, aren't they?

---

*Norman Cousins, longtime editor of Saturday Review, is widely known in Japan for his work in support of the victims of the atomic bombs and other work for the promotion of peace.

SHIN BOK SU

Korea House, an office building in the center of the city, is where she wishes to meet. Her accent is rich in the flavors and vocabulary of Hiroshima. Tears occasionally well up in her eyes as she speaks. Her present husband has been hospitalized for about a year. He was also in Hiroshima on that day.

The number of non-Japanese who became victims of the atomic bombings at Hiroshima and Nagasaki is extremely difficult to determine. But careful estimates indicate that about 50,000 Koreans were exposed to the atomic bomb in Hiroshima. Approximately 30,000 were killed. Of the 20,000 survivors, all but 5,000 were repatriated to Korea after Korean independence. Chinese, from both Taiwan and the continent, people from elsewhere in Asia, Allied prisoners of war, and Japanese Americans caught in Japan by the onset of war also became hibakusha.

It was the time of the "unification" of Japan and Korea. Mr. Minami, the governor general, addressing us, said we were now all Japanese. All of us Koreans were suddenly told to change our names. We adopted a Japanese name, Shigemitsu. The characters meant "thickly-wooded," because our family had been living on a heavily wooded mountain. A new school was founded about four kilometers from our village of two hundred and fifty people. I wanted to go. My parents opposed it since they thought it would be too dangerous for a girl. I beseeched Grandpa and finally he relented, so I became a first-grader at the age of ten.

Seven of the ten teachers were Japanese. Korean kids, even when they wanted to go weewee, didn't know how to say that in Japanese. So some kids ended up wetting themselves. But still, when at that school, I felt we had become Japanese. Many Japanese people came to Korea. There were money-lenders, real usurers who lent money at outrageous rates, and when they weren't repaid immediately, took away people's fields and became rich. They had bathtubs in their own homes! Lived in luxury.

Conversations about marriage came up when I was about

twenty-three years old and working in an agricultural laboratory. I yearned for Japan. At that time the Japanese were gods. Their authority was overwhelming. When we met Japanese we bowed to them. My husband-to-be came back to Korea from Japan for our *o-miai*, our first meeting. I agreed to it. In three days we were married. He was just an ordinary Korean, a simple, straightforward person. That's how I came to Hiroshima in 1937.

I'd believed that Koreans were living the good life in Japan, but that didn't seem to be the case. But my husband was a subcontractor, part of a subsidiary of Mitsubishi which was using Korean labor. I didn't have to worry. We were able to eat white rice. We had cash too. I was quite happy I'd come to Japan. He bought me my first Western dress a week after we arrived. He was one of the leaders of the Kyōwakai, a Korean people's group. I asked him to arrange for a Korean Women's Kyōwakai. He got the needed permission, and when it opened, all the big shots from the city came. Thought it was a great idea. I became its head. We did volunteer work and also civil-defense and air-defense training. I was occupied from morning to night.

We ate breakfast about seven forty that morning when the atomic bomb fell. Then a warning of an imminent air attack sounded. My seven-year-old son warned my husband's mother, who lived with us, "Grandma, take care. Hurry, or you'll die." "Don't worry about me," she answered, "I run well. I'm fine." With this kind of banter we entered the shelter in our backyard. We all had our headgear on. We left the radio on loud until we heard that the skies over Hiroshima were all clear. Then we came out, removed our headgear, and stripped off our outer clothes, down to our underwear. It was so hot in Hiroshima. I took off the baby's diaper cover. Grandma wore only a band around her waist. She put the youngest on her back, tied on with a sash—he was thirteen months old—and went into the kitchen to wash the morning dishes. The other two children were sleepy because air raid warnings the night before had kept them awake. So I told them to nap awhile, and put out their futon.

I hung the mosquito net for them in the six-mat room. From our window I noticed the cistern water was low, so I ran a hose out from our bathtub to fill it up.

Suddenly, *"PIKA!"* a brilliant light and then *"DON!"* a gigantic noise. I looked up. But I couldn't see anything. It was pitch black. I heard Grandma's voice shouting. "Help, help!" "Where are you?" I called. "I'm in the living room. I'm suffocating!"

Gradually, the darkness lightened. I saw that Grandma was on top of the child. Two pillars of the house had fallen on her neck and legs. I looked around and there were no houses to be seen. This can't be a bomb, I thought. I pulled at the pillars, but couldn't lift them off her. They didn't even budge. I shouted to our neighbor, "Help, my child's buried under the house!" He jumped over the ruins of his own house and tried to pull them out. He couldn't move a thing. "I'm sorry," he said, "My grandfather is trapped in the second-floor room. I have to rescue him."

Then Mr. Ishihara, our other neighbor, bleeding himself, gave me a knife with the handle missing. "Mrs. Hirota," he said—that was my Japanese name then—"cut the sash off with this." I ran to them, cut the sash with the kitchen knife, and pulled the baby boy out. The flesh on his left leg was torn. Somehow, with both of us tugging, Grandma managed to wriggle free herself. It took more than an hour and a half. Then Grandma started to run away. She was thinking only of herself! I shouted at her, "Take the baby with you," but she didn't listen. I chased her and caught her. There was a millet field nearby where we grew vegetables because of the food shortage. I got her to sit down and hold the baby in her arms. Then I ran back to the house for the other children.

Where were the children sleeping? Our house was quite large. They had been in the middle. The fire-prevention cistern was still there, so I used that as a point of reference and started digging through the roof tiles. One by one. I shouted, "Takeo! Akiko! Come out!" But I heard no response. I kept pulling off tiles. I heard the droning sound of an airplane! But I no longer cared if I died right there. I just kept digging. Soon it started raining. That was the Black Rain.

My husband returned about the time things started burning. That morning he'd gone to visit someone in the city. He was in a toilet and was buried there. He came back wearing only his shorts. His whole body was covered completely in black soot. I couldn't tell who he was until he said something to me. I cried to him that the kids were still under the house.

The flames were starting to break out from the rubble. He found a straw mat and soaked that in water. He walked over the roof tiles. That straw mat caught on fire while he was trying to move aside as many tiles as he could. A soldier came and insisted that we flee. We were both dragged away. That night we stayed at a city sports ground. All night long people were dying off all around us.

The next morning, we went back to find out what happened to our children. The house had burned completely. All our household goods, so carefully piled up for evacuation, and some rationed food we'd accumulated were still burning. So were the corpses of my children. When I approached, I saw a line of buttons from my son's white shirt. Akiko, my girl, was curled up next to Takeo. Flames were still licking up from them.

I couldn't walk anymore. Pieces of the house were embedded in my back, and I'd been rushing around so desperately that I'd injured my legs. One of my husband's men took me in a cart to get some medicine. Along the street, I saw men and women all red, burned, someone still wearing a soldier's cap but with a body all scorched. You couldn't tell men from women. If there were breasts, that was a woman. Faces hung down like icicles. Skin in strips from arms held out in front of them. "Water! Water!" You couldn't walk the streets without stepping over the dead. I saw girl students, all dead, their heads in a water cistern. It must have been hot.

About a week later, we were notified that we should come to

school to pick up the remains of our children. There we were given two yellow envelopes. When we opened them, my husband said, "These are from the backbones of adults." Our kids were seven and four. So we released those bones into the river.

My husband had only gotten a small scrape on his knee. I thought we were lucky. But from the twenty-fifth of August his hair started falling out. He went to the hospital and got some medicine, but his mouth turned black. He swore he'd die if he stayed there, cried "I have to go to Tokyo. I must get medicine!" He ran off to a train station. I put my baby on my back and followed him. I just left Grandma there. They'd both made it. We jumped on a freight train packed with soldiers and we reached Osaka that night. He looked as if he were going to die right then. A train heading away from Tokyo came by. I lied to him. I said that it was bound for Tokyo and I took him back to Hiroshima. The next morning he died. His body had turned black. Blood seeped from his skin. He smelled awful.

By then, we were living on the one rice ball a day they brought on a truck. A month passed before the wife of a neighbor told me that if you went to city hall, they'd give you money for the ones who'd died of the atomic bomb. That was good news. I went to the city office. The clerk gave me a form to fill out. I put down our names and place of family registration. "You're a foreigner," he said. Until that moment I'd been Japanese. All I'd done was say my registration was in Korea. "We cannot give anything to Koreans," he replied. "Why?" I asked him. My husband and two children had died because we were Japanese. Who had suddenly decided we were aliens? "I don't know," he said. "The orders came from above."

MATSUSHIGE YOSHITO

He is seventy-six years old. He has just given a talk about the atomic bomb to a group of elementary school children at the Peace Memorial Hall in the Peace Park in Hiroshima. He has with him the photographs he took on the day of the explosion. "When I talk looking at these pictures, memories of more than forty years ago come back as if it were yesterday."

I worked for the *Chūgoku Shimbun*, the Hiroshima daily paper. I was a photographer, but I was attached at the time to an army press unit stationed at the army divisional headquarters in Hiroshima. The night before, I went to the HQ by bicycle at the sound of the air-raid warning—about twelve-thirty. It was three point seven kilometers from my house to the division in a straight line on a map. After the warning was lifted, I stretched out on an army chair and caught some sleep. The sun rose and I watched Hiroshima City from the stone walls of Hiroshima Castle, where the headquarters was located. It was a quiet and peaceful morning, so I went home, since it was still too early to go to the newspaper. That became the dividing line between death and life for me. Both the division and my office were nine hundred meters from the hypocenter.

My underwear had gotten sweaty on the trip home, so I hung it out on the clothesline when I got home. I was about to get it when terrific sparks jumped from the spot where the electric lines entered the house. I heard a tremendous cracking noise, like trees being torn apart, and at the same instant there was a brilliant flash of immaculate white, like the igniting of the magnesium we used to use for taking photographs. I couldn't see a thing. I was sitting in a six-mat room, half-naked, my shirt out on the line. I sensed an explosive wind like needles striking me. It seemed only a moment before my wife came in. "A bomb fell," she just said. I grabbed her hand and we ran outside. When I fully came to my senses, we were already squatting down in a hollow in a sweet-potato field across the train tracks from our house. We thought an ordinary bomb had hit our house directly or exploded right near it. It was absolutely black outdoors. I couldn't see my wife's face even though we were pressed right up against each other. I thought my wife and I had been saved, as I felt the warmth of her hand in mine. My heart felt ready to split open, it was beating so fast.

Gradually, the lowest edge of the fog seemed to rise a little, and I could see. A four-story wooden fire station nearby had collapsed in an instant. I had to get to headquarters! I returned to my house to find my camera. The walls had toppled over. I noticed that I, my-self, was bleeding from little bits of glass, from chest to face, but my bleeding soon stopped. My wife seemed all right, so I grabbed my camera, a Mamiya Six, Japanese-made, and walked along the train tracks toward the center of the city.

I approached the City Hall, about one point one kilometers from the hypocenter. Both it and the Western Fire Station were in flames. It was a sea of fire. I couldn't make my way to the newspaper office, so I returned to the western side of the Miyuki Bridge and tried to head towards the city center by passing along the bank of the river. But fireballs were rolling down the road. There was nobody to be seen. If I hang around here, I thought, I'll be swallowed up in these fires, so I returned to the bridge.

You had to weave through the streets avoiding the bodies. People's bodies were all swollen up. Their skin, burst open, was hanging down in rags. Their faces were burnt black. I put my hand on my camera, but it was such a hellish apparition that I couldn't press the shutter. I hesitated about twenty minutes before I finally pushed it and took this first picture. The man in this picture might be a policeman giving first aid to people for burns using cooking oil. A can of oil's behind there. This woman's hair was burned frizzy. They were all barefoot because their shoes had stuck to the asphalt. This woman was holding a baby in the crook of her arm. She was half naked. The baby's eyes were closed. Either dead or in shock. She was running around crying to her child, "Please open your eyes." The baby was probably already dead. You can see in the picture that her legs are slightly blurred. The film was slow then, so you can tell she was running.

I approached and took this second shot. It was such a cruel sight. The viewfinder of the camera was clouded with my tears when I took it. It was around eleven o'clock. The whole area was still under fire and smoke. The bottom of the picture shows the asphalt. People, lying along the upstream railing of the bridge which had fallen onto the surface. They're using it as a pillow. The people on the down-stream side of the bridge didn't have that luxury and were lying directly on the road. Their bodies were burned head to toe. They were covered in asphalt. They mistook me for a soldier. "Please Mister Soldier, give me some water," they'd call out faintly. I had an armband on that said "Military Reporter." I could only reply, "The relief unit will come soon, so please hold on."

I returned home, but left again about two o'clock. The fire was dying out. I set my feet towards the center of town again with a mind to go to the headquarters or the office, but corpses were everywhere and smoldering ruins were still sending up plumes of flame here and there. It was hot, I suppose, but maybe my nerves were paralyzed. I didn't feel a thing.

Japanese homes are made of wood and collapsed easily from the force of the blast. So, too, did most of the shops and other small buildings. Many people were trapped under the wreckage. They couldn't pull themselves out. This area was hit by winds with a velocity of 440 meters per second and thermal waves of several hundred degrees centigrade. Fires began spontaneously. Even had the people gotten out, they couldn't have outrun the flames. Many people burned to death. The corpses I saw on the seventh were black and hardened, but on that day they were still burning from below and the fat of the bodies was bubbling up and sputtering as it burned. That was the only time I've seen humans roasting.

I walked on flames to reach the office building. It was made of reinforced concrete, so I was confident that the inside wouldn't be burned down. I'd left my other camera in my locker there. I was ready to enter the building when I saw piles of ash and red coals glowing inside. I took only a few steps in before I pulled back.

Nearby, I saw a burnt trolley car halfway up on the sidewalk. Probably blown there by the wind. I didn't go near it, but walked toward Kamiyachō. There I saw another burned trolley car at a curve. It looked like people were still on it, so I approached, put my foot on the step and peered inside. Fifteen or sixteen people were there, all dead. Kamiyachō had been only two hundred and fifty meters from the hypocenter. They probably died instantly when the pressure of the blast wind caused their internal organs to rupture. Then they burst into flame and burned, together with the car. All of them were naked. I had my foot on the rear doorstep. I didn't really stare at them, but recoiled in shock. The doors and windows were charred. Only the skeleton of that train remained. I don't remember if it was hot or not. I don't think I grasped the doorframe when I looked in. I thought about taking a picture. I even put my hand on the camera. But it was so hideous I couldn't do it.

I did take a picture of people lined up to register for disaster relief. The seated policeman, his own head wrapped in a dirty bandage, was giving them documents to prove that they had suffered a disaster. With this piece of paper they could get rations, or board a train, as victims. In it you can see they're also passing out hard biscuits, one bag per person. I myself received one. We ate it that night. We had no water, no electricity. We had no idea when airplanes might come again.

I returned home about five o'clock. My niece came to the house. Her face and half her body were seriously burned. She couldn't get back to her own place. Her shoes had gotten stuck in the asphalt and come off, so she'd walked barefoot. The soles of her feet were burned and swollen. We had no medicine, so we just fanned her to cool her some. Maggots, like tiny threads of silk, many of them, were already infesting her wounds. Humans were burned, but flies survived. We spent the night sitting on the wreckage of the fire station. I could see fires burning in scattered places toward the center of town.

The next day we took our niece to the house of my wife's brother a little way out in the countryside. I'd evacuated my own child and my parents there a month previously. Luckily, none of us were seriously injured. We were able to stay overnight with my children. I had my camera on my shoulder, but I didn't take any more pictures those days.

I went back to the newspaper office on the ninth. There was no point in taking pictures, since there was no newspaper for them to appear in. But on the eleventh or twelfth of August I developed these pictures I had shot on the sixth. When the sun set I developed the film outdoors in a simple tray.

They appeared in the evening edition of the *Chūgoku Shimbun* a year later, on August 5, 1946. I was summoned to the Occupation GHQ together with the reporter who wrote the article. Despite what we expected, they weren't angry. We were told that it was all right to print those things, since they were facts, but they wanted us to submit them for review prior to publishing them. The American questioning us then asked me how many pictures I'd taken. I told him five. He asked me for copies of them, so I went back and made him prints in B5 size. When I brought them to him, he asked me to sign them. I started to write my name on the back, but he said, "No, no, sign on the front. It's OK to use Japanese," so I signed my name in characters on the face of the pictures taken August sixth.

I didn't feel any particular hatred toward the American or Australian soldiers who came to Hiroshima. I was actually an A-bomb victim, inside my house, but I never suffered directly from it. I am a shade anemic. I find it strange I haven't fallen ill. I'm often asked why I didn't take more pictures. Some even criticize me for that. It makes me angry. How can they ask such a thing? They didn't see the reality. It was too overwhelming. I wasn't the only one who had a camera that day. Other people walked around with cameras, but nobody else took pictures.

Part V

Postwar

World War II remains the deadliest conflict in history. The human losses and material destruction were so extensive that accurate calculations have been difficult to establish. Over fifty million people died.

The United States—whose own territory was all but untouched by the war itself—emerged as a military and industrial giant after 1945. Yet for millions of people in Europe and Asia, the years immediately following the war's end were marked by displacement, suffering, and even starvation. Over 6.5 million Japanese soldiers and civilians were stranded overseas in July of 1945. In Europe, millions of people had been made homeless, and millions more were refugees.

Here, as a coda to this volume, two of the most distinctive literary voices to emerge from the postwar era recount the immediate aftermath of World War II in Europe.

"*The War* (Rough Draft)"

Marguerite Duras

Here is a partial draft of the manuscript that was to become the celebrated author Marguerite Duras's memoir of World War II, entitled *The War*. Writing in Paris in 1945, Duras recounts the excruciating wait for news of her husband's return from a Nazi concentration camp (from *Wartime Writings, 1943–1949*).

F acing the fireplace. The telephone beside me. On the right, the door to the sitting room and the hall; at the end of the hall, the front door. He might come straight here, he'd ring the doorbell. "Who is it?" "It's me." Or he might telephone as soon as he arrives at a transit center: "I'm back, I'm at the [Hôtel] Lutétia, for the paperwork." There would be no warning. He'd phone as soon as he arrived. Such things are possible. Some people are coming back, after all. He isn't a special case, there aren't any particular reasons why he shouldn't come back. There aren't any reasons why he should. He might come back. He'd ring the bell. "Who is it?" "It's me." Lots of other things like that are happening. They finally crossed the Rhine. They finally broke through the major stalemate at Avranches.* I finally made it

---

*During the Battle of Normandy, in Operation Cobra, the Americans ended several weeks of stalemate by breaking through the German defenses on the western flank of the Normandy beachhead. On July 30, 1944, the Fourth Armored Division seized the strategic prize of Avranches, and Patton's Third Army began pouring through the Avranches corridor to fan out through northwestern France.

through the war. It wouldn't be an extraordinary thing if he came back. Careful: it would not be extraordinary. "Hello?" "Who is it?" "It's me, Robert." It would be normal and not extraordinary. Be very careful not to make it into something extraordinary: the Extraordinary is unexpected. Be reasonable. I am reasonable. I'm waiting for Robert, who should be coming back.

The telephone: "Hello?" "Hello! Heard any news?" Two beats. First one: phones do ring; waiting for it to ring is not a waste of time; phones are meant to ring. Second one: shit. Desire to rip someone's throat out. "No news." "Nothing? No information?" "None." "You know Belsen was liberated yesterday afternoon?" "I know." Silence. Am I going to ask yet again? That's it, too late, I'm asking: "So what do you think? I'm beginning to get worried." Silence. "You must wait, and above all, hang on, don't get discouraged—you're not the only one, unfortunately. . . . I know a mother with four children who . . ." Cut this off: "I know. I'm sorry, I have to go out. Goodbye." Done. I hang up the phone.

I'm still sitting here. Mustn't make too many movements, it's a waste of energy. Saving every bit of strength for the ordeal. She said: "You know Belsen was liberated yesterday afternoon?" I hadn't known. Another camp liberated. She said: "[*illegible*] yesterday afternoon." She didn't say so, but I know that the lists will arrive tomorrow. Go downstairs, pick up a paper, pay for the paper, read the list. No. I hear a throbbing in my temples, getting worse. No, I won't read that list. I'll ask someone to read it and let me know in case . . . First off, the system of lists—I've been using them for three weeks, and it's not the right way. Plus the more lists there are . . . No, no list: the more lists there are, the fewer . . . They'll keep appearing until . . . Until the end. He won't be . . . It's time to move. Stand up, take three steps, go to the window. The École de Médecine: still there, even if . . . Passersby in the streets; they'll still be walking . . . At the instant when I hear the news—still passersby . . . It happens. A notification of death. They're already informing . . . "Who's there?" "A social worker from the town hall." The mother with four

children was notified. If this pounding in my temples keeps up . . .
Above all, I must get rid of this throbbing, it can be deadly. Death
is inside me: it's pounding in my temples, no mistake about that;
must stop the pounding, stop the heart, calm it down—it won't calm
down on its own, it needs help; must keep reason from breaking
down any more, draining away; I put on my coat. Landing. Staircase. "Good afternoon, Madame Antelme." Concierge. She didn't
seem any different. The street either. Outside, April carries on as if
nothing were wrong. In the street, I'm asleep, hands jammed into
pockets, legs moving forward. Avoid newspaper stands. Avoid transit centers. The Allies are advancing along all fronts. Even a few
days ago, that was important. Now, not at all. I no longer read the
news bulletins. Why bother? They'll advance until the end. Daylight, broad daylight on the Nazi mystery. April—it will have happened in April. The Allied armies surge across Germany. Berlin in
flames. The Red Army continues its victorious advance in the south.
Past Dresden. The Allies are advancing on all fronts; past the Rhine,
that was bound to happen. The great day of the war: Remagen.* It
began after that. Ever since Eisenhower was sickened by Buchenwald, three million women and I don't give a fuck how the war turns
out. In a ditch, face turned toward the earth, legs folded, arms flung
out, he's dying. I see. Everything. He starved to death. Through the
skeletons of Buchenwald . . . his skeleton. Warm weather. Perhaps
he's beginning to rot. Along the road next to him pass the Allied
armies advancing on all fronts. He's been dead for three weeks.
That's it. I'm sure of it. The legs keep walking. Faster. His mouth
sags open. It's evening. He thought of me before dying. The exquisite pleasure of pain. There are far too many people in the streets.
I'd like to move across a great plain and be able to think freely. Just
before dying he must have thought my name. All along the road,

*On March 7, 1945, the U.S. Ninth Armored Division captured the Ludendorff
Bridge at Remagen and established the first Allied bridgehead across the Rhine, a
watershed event in the Allies' push eastward across Germany.

along every German road, others are lying more or less as he does. Thousands. Dozens, hundreds of thousands, and him. Him—one of the thousands of others. Him—distinct from those thousands for me alone in all the world, and completely distinct from them. I know everything you can know when you know nothing. They evacuated them, then at the last minute, they killed them. So. Generalities. The war, generality. The war. The necessities of war. The dead, necessities of war, generality.

He died saying my name. What other name would he have said? The war: generality. I don't live on generalities. Those who live on generalities have nothing in common with me. No one has anything in common with me. The street. Some people laugh, especially the young. I have only enemies. It's evening, I'll have to go home. It's evening on the other side as well. In the ditch darkness is taking over, covering his mouth. Red sun over Paris. Six years of war are ending. Big deal, big story, they'll be talking about it for twenty years. Nazi Germany is crushed. The butchers, crushed. So is he, in the ditch. I am broken. Something broken. Impossible for me to stop walking. Dry as dry sand. Beside the ditch, the parapet of the Pont des Arts. The Seine. Just to the right of the ditch. Something separates them: darkness. The Pont des Arts. My victory. Nothing in the world belongs to me except that corpse in a ditch. Childhood, over. Innocence, over. It's evening. It's my end-of-the-world. Shit on everyone. My dying isn't directed against anyone. The simplicity of my death. I will have lived . . . I don't care about that, I don't care about the moment of my death. In dying I don't rejoin him, I stop waiting for him. No fuss. I'll tell D.: "I'd best die—what would you do with me?" Craftily, I'll be dying while alive for him; afterward death will bring only relief. I make this base calculation. Not strong enough to live for D. I have to go home. D. is waiting for me. Eight thirty.

"Any news?" "None." No one asks how I am or says hello anymore, they say: "Any news?" I say: "None." I go sit on the couch near the telephone. I don't say anything. I know D. is uneasy. When he's not looking at me he seems worried. It's already been a week. I catch him puttering around. "Say something," I tell D. Just last week he laughed and told me, "You're nuts, you haven't the right to worry like that." Now he tells me, "There's no reason . . . Be sensible. . . ." He doesn't laugh anymore but he smiles, and his face crinkles. And yet without D. I don't think I could keep going. We turn on the light in the sitting room. D. has already been here for an hour. It must be nine o'clock. We haven't had dinner yet. We don't talk. D. is sitting not far from me; I'm still sitting in the same place on the couch. I stare fixedly out the black window. D. watches me. Sometimes he says, "Enough." Then I look at him. He smiles at me. Then I look at the window. Only last week he was taking my hand, kissing me, telling me impulsively, "Robert will come back, I promise." Now I know he's wondering if hope is still worth it. Once in a while I say, "I'm sorry." He smiles. An hour later I say, "How come we've had no news?" He tells me, "There are still thousands of men in camps the Allies haven't reached yet." "The Allies have reached them all, there are Americans and British everywhere." "How do you expect him to get word to you?" "They can write. The Bernards heard from their daughters." This goes on for a long time, until I ask D. to assure me that Robert will come back. "He'll come back," D. tells me. Then he says we ought to eat something. I go to the kitchen, I put potatoes in a pot, water in the pot, I turn on the gas, I put the pot on the flame. Then I bow my head, lean my forehead against the edge of the stove, pushing harder and harder. I close my eyes. I don't move, leaning against the stove. Silence. D. doesn't make a sound in the apartment. The gas hums, that's all. Where? Where is he? Where can he be? Where, in the name of God where? The black ditch—dead for two weeks. His mouth sags open. Along the road, next to him, pass the Allied armies advancing on all fronts. Dead for two weeks. Two weeks of days and nights, abandoned in a ditch, the soles of his feet exposed. Rain on him, sun, the dust of the victorious armies. For two weeks. His hands open. Each hand dearer to me than life.

Familiar to me. Familiar that way only to me. I shout: "D!" Footsteps, very slow, in the sitting room. D. appears. He comes into the kitchen. Around my shoulders I feel two firm, gentle hands that pull me away from the stove. I huddle against D.

"It's awful," I say. "I know," says D. "No, you can't know." "I know," says D. "Just try. We can do anything. . . ." "I can't do a thing anymore." D.'s arms are around me. The tighter he holds me, the more comforting it is, much better than words. Sometimes, gripped by his arms, I might almost believe I feel better. Able to breathe for a minute. We sit down at the table. Two plates on the kitchen table. I get the bread from the cupboard. Three-day-old bread. Pause. "The bread's three days old," I tell D. "Everything's closed at this hour. . . ." We look at each other. "True enough," says D. We're thinking the same thing about the bread. We start eating. We sit down again. The piece of bread in my hand . . . I look at it. I feel like vomiting. The dead bread. The bread he didn't eat. Not having bread is what killed him. My throat closes up—a needle couldn't get through. The bread, the taste of the bread he didn't eat. We didn't know until a month ago, and then the world was flooded with photographs: charnel houses. The light broke through onto mass graves of bones. We know their rations. While we were eating bread, they weren't. I'm not even going to discuss the Germans. Corpses thick on the ground, millions of corpses. Instead of wheat, crops of corpses: take, eat, this is my body. There are still some who believe in that. In [the posh neighborhood of] Auteuil, they still believe in it. Class warfare. The corpse class. The only relief: dead people of the world, unite! And get that guy down off his cross. The Christians, the only ones who don't share the hatred. During the Liberation, when it was throat-cutting time, they were already preaching leniency and the forgiveness of sins. The little priest's bread: take, eat, this is my body. The farm worker's bread. The maid's always-eaten-in-the-kitchen bread: "We have a maid who constantly eats more than her ration card! Imagine, madame! Such people are simply appalling." Hard-earned bread. Bakery bread bought by the capitalist papa for his dear little offspring who at this very moment is starting to take an interest in the war. The earthy bread of the Soviet partisan, all the trouble it cost him—in short the basic bread of the land of the Revolution. I look at the bread. "I'm not hungry." D. stops eating. "If you don't eat, I don't eat." I nibble so that D. will eat. Before leaving, D. says, "Promise me to . . ." I promise. When D. said, "I have to go home," I wanted it to be over and done with, I wanted him already gone and then I wouldn't have to close the door behind him.

D. has left. The apartment creaks beneath my feet. One by one, I turn off the lamps. I go to my room. I go very slowly. The important thing is to sleep. If I'm not careful I won't sleep. When I don't sleep at all things are much worse the next day. When I have slept, things aren't as bad in the morning for an hour. When I do fall asleep it's in the black ditch, near him lying dead.

Went to the center at the Gare d'Orsay. I had considerable trouble gaining admission for the Tracing Service of *Libres*.* They insisted that it wasn't an official service. The BCRA is already there and doesn't want to relinquish its place to anyone.† To begin with I got us set up on the sly, with forged papers. We have managed to collect a lot of information about the transfers and whereabouts of camp survivors, which has appeared in our paper. A great deal of personal news. "You can tell the Such-and-such family that their son is alive;

*Marguerite Duras was a journalist at Libres (Free), a newspaper in which she passed on whatever relevant information she could glean to those waiting for their loved ones to return. Libres was the newspaper of the MNPGD (National Movement of Prisoners of War and Deportees), a Resistance movement founded by François Mitterrand.

† In June 1940, General de Gaulle entrusted the creation of the London-based Bureau Central de Renseignement et d'Action (Central Bureau for Intelligence and Action) to André Dewavrin, alias Colonel Passy. The BCRA operated its own missions in France and coordinated intelligence from all the Resistance networks there, providing vital information about German military operations to the Allies.

I saw him yesterday." But my four comrades and I were thrown out. "Everyone wants to be here, it's impossible. Only stalag secretariats are allowed here." I protest, saying that 75,000 wives and relatives of prisoners and deportees read our paper. "It's unfortunate, but regulations forbid the operation here of any unofficial services." "Our paper isn't like all the others, it's the only one that publishes special issues of lists. . . ." "That's not a sufficient reason." I'm talking to a senior official in the repatriation service of the Frenay ministry.* Apparently preoccupied, he's distant and worried. "I'm sorry," he says. I say, "I won't go without a fight," and I head for the main offices. "Where are you going?" "I'm going to try to stay." I attempt to slip through a line of prisoners of war that's blocking the corridor. He looks at me and says, "As you like, but be careful—those (he points at them) haven't been disinfected yet. In any case, if you're still here this evening, I'm sorry but I'll have to evict you." We've [spotted] a small deal table that we place at the beginning of the "circuit." We question the prisoners. Many come to us. We gather hundreds of pieces of information. I work steadily, without looking up, without thinking of anything. Now and then, an officer (easily recognizable: young, starched khaki shirt, pouter-pigeon chest) comes over to ask who we are. "Just what is this tracing service? Do you have a pass?" I present my forged passes. Next there's a woman from the repatriation service. "What do you want with them?" "We're asking for news of their comrades who are still in Germany." "And what do you do with that?" She's a perky young platinum blonde, navy blue suit, matching shoes, sheer stockings, manicured nails. "We publish it in *Libres*, the newspaper for prisoners and deportees." "*Libres?* You're not from the ministry?" "No." "Do you have the authority to

*Henri Frenay was a conservative Catholic army officer who turned in disillusionment from the Vichy regime to become one of the first and most important leaders of the Resistance. He was a founder of the movement Combat in 1941; in 1944 de Gaulle appointed him Minister for Prisoners, Deportees, and Refugees, and Frenay served in de Gaulle's first provisional government after the war.

do this?" she says coolly. "We're taking the authority. It's simple."
Off she goes. We keep asking our questions. Our task is made easier,
unfortunately, by the two and a half hours it takes the prisoners to
get to identity verification, the first office in the circuit. It will take
the deportees even longer, since they have no papers. An officer
comes over: forty-five, sweating in his jacket, very curt this time.
"What is all this?" We explain yet again. "There is already a similar
service in the circuit." Boldly, I ask: "How do you get the news to the
families? We hear it will take at least three months before everyone
will have been able to write. . . ." He looks at me and laughs haugh-
tily. "You don't understand. I'm talking about information on Nazi
atrocities. We are compiling dossiers." He moves away, then returns.
"How do you know they're telling you the truth? It's very dangerous,
what you're doing. You must know . . . The militiamen . . ." I don't
reply. He goes away. A half-hour later a general heads directly for
our table, trailed by the first officer, the second officer, and the young
woman. "Your papers?" I present them. "Unsatisfactory. You may
work standing up, but I do not want to see this table again." I object:
it takes up hardly any room. "The ministry has expressly forbidden
the use of tables in the main hall." They call two scouts over to re-
move the table. We work standing up.

   The radio occasionally blasts music that varies between swing and
patriotic tunes. The line of prisoners grows longer. Now and then
I go to the ticket window at the far end of the room. "Still no deportees?" "No deportees." Women in uniform. Repatriation service.
They talk about the prisoners, referring to them only as "the poor
boys, the poor boys . . ." They address one another as Mademoiselle
de Thingummy, Madame de ButtHole. They're smiling. Their work
is just so hard. It's suffocating in here. They're really very, very busy.
Some officers come over occasionally to see them; they swap English
cigarettes and idle banter. "Indefatigable, Mademoiselle de [*illegible*]?" "As you see, Captain. . . ." The main hall [rumbles] with footsteps. And they keep coming. Trucks stream in from Le Bourget.
In groups of fifty, the prisoners arrive, and then—quick, [an army

song on] the loudspeaker: "*C'est la route qui va, qui va, qui va . . .*"
When it's a larger group, they put on the "Marseillaise." [Hiccups
of silence] between the songs. The young men look around the main
hall. All smiling. Repatriation officials herd them along: "All right,
my friends, line up." They line up, still smiling. The first ones to get
there say, "Long wait," but nicely, and still smiling. When asked for
information, the men stop smiling and try to remember. The officers call them "my friends"; the women, "those poor boys," or "my
friends" to their faces. At the Gare de l'Est, pointing to her stripes,
one of these "ladies" scolded a soldier from the Legion: "So, my
friend—we're not saluting? Can't you see I'm a captain?" The soldier
looked at her. "Me, when I see a skirt, I don't salute her, I fuck her."
A prolonged "Ohhh!" greeted those words. "How rude!" The lady
beat a dignified retreat.

April. I went to see S., the head of the center, to sort things out. We
are allowed to stay, but at the tail end of the circuit, over by the luggage checkroom. Really pleased. As long as there are no deportees
I can handle it. (Some are turning up at the Lutétia, but only rarely
at Orsay.) A few isolated cases. At which point I leave the circuit,
my colleagues understand that. I return only after the deportees
are gone. When I do return, my comrades signal across the room:
"Nothing." I sit down again. In the evening I take the lists to the
paper. And go home. Every evening: "I'm not going back to Orsay
tomorrow."

But I do believe that tomorrow I won't be going back there. First
convoy of deportees from Weimar. April 20. I receive a phone call at
home that morning: they won't arrive until the afternoon. No courage. Whenever I pass by Orsay I run away. I run from newspapers.
Outside the Orsay center the wives of prisoners of war clump into
a compact mass. White barriers separate them from the prisoners.
They call out, asking for news of this or that person. Occasionally
the soldiers stop. A few of them know something. Women are there
at seven in the morning. Some stay until three in the morning—and

come back later that day. They're not allowed into the center. The prisoners arrive in an orderly way. At night they arrive in big trucks, and emerge into bright light. The women scream, clap; the men stop, dazed, speechless. Sometimes they reply, usually they go on inside.

At first I used to ask many of them, "Do you know any political deportees?" No. Most of them knew STO workers.* No one knew any political deportees and they didn't really understand the difference. They'd seen some at the transit center "in a terrible state." I admire the women who stay and never stop asking [their questions]. I asked D. to come to the center to see the first deportees from Weimar. After breakfast, I feel like running away again. "Antelme? Oh, yes. . . ." They won't tell me. They'll look at me in a way that . . . I'm working badly. All these names I add up, names of prisoners of war, are not his. Every five minutes I feel like packing it in, putting down the pencil, abandoning my questions, leaving the center. Each truck stopping out in the street: them. No. At around two thirty I get up; I'd like to know when they're arriving. I go looking in the main hall for someone to ask. Ten or so women are in a corner of the room listening to a tall woman, a general in a navy blue suit with the cross of Lorraine on the lapel. She has blue-rinsed white hair, curled with tongs. She gestures as she speaks; the girls watch. They seem spent, and afraid. Their bundles and suitcases are sitting around, and there's a small child lying on one bundle. Their dresses are filthy. But what's remarkable is that their faces are distorted— by fatigue, or fear? And they're quite dirty, young. Two or three of

*By early 1942, Germany needed more foreign labor for its war effort. Many thousands of French workers were sent to Germany, mostly prisoners of war at first, then volunteers enticed by promises of good pay and decent food. By February 1943 the Germans had introduced the Service du Travail Obligatoire (Compulsory Labor Service), an organized deportation of French workers, with the complicity of the Vichy regime—the only European government that legally compelled its own citizens to serve the Nazi war machine. France was the second largest contributor of unskilled labor and the largest contributor of skilled labor to the German wartime economy.

them have huge bellies, pregnant fit to burst. Standing nearby, another woman officer watches the general speak. "What's going on?" She looks at me, lowers her eyes discreetly: "[STO] Volunteers." The general tells them to stand up. They do, and follow her. They look frightened because people jeered at them outside the center. I heard some volunteers being booed one night; the men hadn't expected it and smiled at first, then gradually they understood and took on that same stricken look. The general now turns to the young woman in uniform: "What should we do with them?" She points at the huddled group. "I don't know," says the other officer. The general must have informed them that they were scum. Some of them are crying. The pregnant ones are staring vacantly. They're all working girls, with big hands scarred by German machinery. Two of them may be prostitutes, but they, too, must have worked with machines. They're standing there, as the general had asked, looking at her. An officer comes up: "What's all this?" "Volunteers." The general's voice is shrill: "Sit down." Obediently, they sit down again. That's not enough. "And keep quiet," says the general sternly. "Understood? Don't think you're going to just walk away. . . ." The general has quite a refined voice. Her delicate hand with its red fingernails threatens and [condemns] the volunteers with their grease-stained hands. Machines. German machines. The volunteers don't reply. The man approaches the huddled group to study them with quiet curiosity. Casually, in front of the volunteers, he asks the general, "Have you any orders?" "No," she says, "do you?" "I heard something about six months' detention." The general nods her lovely curly head: "It would serve them right." The senior officer blows puffs of cigarette smoke over the bunch of volunteers following the conversation open-mouthed, watching with haggard eyes. "Right!" says the senior officer, a horseman, pirouetting elegantly, Camel in hand, and off he goes. The volunteers watch everyone and look for some sign of the fate that awaits them. No sign. I snag the general as she's leaving: "Do you know when the convoy from Weimar is arriving?" She looks me up and down. "Three o'clock." Another once-over and then, a delicate, threatening finger: "But I warn you, it's not worth your getting in the way here, only generals and perfects will be coming." I look at the general. "Why? What about the others?" I wasn't being careful, my tone must not have been appropriate to use with a lady of such quality. She draws herself up: "Oh-oh-oh. I detest that kind of attitude! Peddle your complaints elsewhere, missy." She's so indignant that she reports this to a small group of women, also in uniform, who listen, take offense, and look my way. I approach one of them. I hear myself say: "So she's not waiting for anyone, that woman?" I get a scandalized look: "She has so much to do, her nerves are in a state." I return to the Tracing Service at the end of the circuit.

Shortly afterward, I go back to the main hall. D. is waiting for me there with a forged pass.

Around three o'clock there's a rumor. "They're here!" I leave the circuit to go stand at the entrance to a small corridor opposite the main hall. I wait. I know that Robert A. won't be among them. D. is beside me. His job is to find out from the deportees if they've seen Robert Antelme. He's pale. He pays no attention to me. There's a great hubbub in the main hall. The uniformed women are busy with the volunteers, making them sit on the floor somewhere out of the way. The main hall is empty. No prisoners of war are arriving at the moment. Some officers bustle about. I hear: "The minister!" I recognize Frenay among the officers. I'm still in the same place, at the mouth of the little corridor. I watch the main entrance. I know Robert Antelme hasn't a chance of being among them.

Something's wrong: I'm shaking. I'm cold. I lean against the wall. Two scouts emerge abruptly from the entryway, carrying a man. His arms are wrapped around the scouts' necks. The scouts carry him with their arms crossed beneath his thighs. The man's [head] is shaved, he's in civilian clothes, and he seems in great pain. He's a strange color. He must be crying. You can't call him thin—it's something else: there's hardly anything left of him. And yet he's alive.

He looks at nothing—not the minister, not the room, not anything. He grimaces. He's the first deportee from Weimar to arrive at the center. Without realizing it, I've moved forward, into the middle of the hall, with my back to the loudspeaker. Two more scouts appear, supporting an old man, who is followed by about ten other men. They are guided to garden benches that have been brought in. The minister goes over to them. The old man is weeping. He's very old, at least he must be—it's impossible to tell. Suddenly I see D. sitting next to the old man. I feel very cold. My teeth are chattering. Some-one comes over to me: "Don't stay there, it's making you sick, there's no point." I know him, he's a guy from the center. I stay. D. has started talking to the old man. I go over everything rapidly: there's one chance in ten thousand that he knows Robert Antelme. But I've heard they have lists of the survivors of Buchenwald. So. Aside from the [skeletal deportee] and the weeping old man, the others don't seem too badly off. The minister is sitting with them, along with some senior officers. D. talks to the old man for quite a while. I look only at D.'s face. He seems to be taking too long. So I go toward the bench, into D.'s field of vision. He notices, looks at me, and shakes his head. I gather that he's saying, "Doesn't know him." I go away. I'm very tired. I feel like leaving the center and taking a rest. I'm sure that I could manage to sleep this afternoon. Now the uniformed women are bringing the deportees some mess tins. They eat, and while they eat, they answer [questions]. But what's striking is that they don't seem interested in what's said to them. The next day I'll read in the papers that the group included General Challe; his son Hubert Challe (who would die that night), a former cadet at Saint-Cyr; General Audibert; Ferrières, the head of the State Tobacco Department; Julien Cain, the director of the Bibliothèque Natio-nale; General Heurteaux; Professor Suard of the faculty of medicine in Angers; Professor Richet; Claude Bourdet, [a writer and jour-nalist]; the father of Teitgen, the Minister of Information; Maurice Nègre, [an agricultural engineer]; Marcel Paul, [a union activist], and others.

• • •

I go home toward five in the afternoon, walking along the Seine.
It's lovely weather, a beautiful sunny day. Once I've left the embank-
ment and turned onto the rue du Bac, I've left the center far behind.
I'm going home, I'm eager to be home. Maybe he will return. I'm
very tired. I'm very dirty, I spent part of the night at the center.
I intend to take a bath when I get home. I must wash; not washing
doesn't solve anything. But I'm cold. I don't feel like washing. It
must be at least a week since I last washed. I think about myself: I've
never met a woman more cowardly than I am.

I think about the wives and mothers I know who are waiting for
deportees. None is as cowardly as that. Absolutely none. I am very
tired. I know some who are quite brave. The fortitude of S., R.'s wife,
I'd call simply extraordinary. Although I am a coward, I know it.
My cowardice is so bad that no one dares discuss it around me. My
colleagues in the service speak to me as if I were sick in the head. So
do M. and A. Me, I know I'm not sick. I'm cowardly. D. tells me so
sometimes: "One never, ever, has the right to destroy oneself like
that." He often tells me: "You're a sick woman, you're crazy." When
D. also says to me, "Take a look at yourself: you don't look like anything anymore," I can't understand. Not for one second do I grasp
the need to have courage. Maybe being brave would be my way of
being a coward. Why would I have courage? Suzy is brave for her
little boy. Why would I husband my strength, for what? If he's dead,
what good is courage? There's no battle out there for me to fight.
The one I do fight is invisible. I struggle against a vision: the black
ditch, the corpse stone-dead for two weeks. And it depends—there
are moments when the vision takes over. I don't care to live if he's
no longer alive. That's all. "You must hold on," Madame Cats tells
me. "Me, I hang on; you have to hang on, for him." I feel sorry for
Madame Cats. Why fight it? In the name of what? I have no dignity.
My dignity—can go to hell. No shame at all anymore. My shame
has been suspended. "When you think back on it," says D., "you'll
be ashamed." There's just one [thing]: we're talking about me. People

who wait with dignity—I despise them. My dignity is waiting too, like the rest, and there's no rush for its return. If he's dead, my dignity can't do a thing about it. What's my dignity compared to that?

People are out in the streets as usual. Lines in front of stores. There are already a few cherries. I buy a paper. The Russians are in Strausberg and perhaps even farther along, on the outskirts of Berlin. I'm waiting for the fall of Berlin too. Everyone, the whole world, is waiting for that. All governments agree. The heart of Germany, the papers say. And the wives of deportees: "Now they'll see what's what." And my concierge. When [the heart of Germany] stops beating, it will be all over. The streets are full of murderers. People dream the dreams of murderers. I dream about an ideal city, its burned ruins flooded with German blood. I think I smell this blood; it's redder than ox blood, more like pig blood and wouldn't coagulate but flow a long way, and on the banks of these rivers, there would be weeping women whose butts I would kick, sending them nose-diving into their own men's blood. People who at this moment, today, feel pity for Germany, or rather, feel no hatred for it, make me pity them in turn. Most especially the holier-than-thou bunch.

One of them recently brought a German child to the center, explaining with a smile: "He's a little orphan." So proud. Leading him by the hand. Of course, he wasn't wrong (the disgrace of people who are never wrong). Of course he had to take him in: this poor little child wasn't to blame. The holier-than-thou types always find an occasion for charity. His little German Good Deed. If I had that kid I'd probably take care of him, not kill him. But why remind us that there are still children in Germany? Why remind us of that now? I want my hatred complete and untouched. My black bread. Not long ago a girl said to me: "Germans? There are eighty million of 'em. Well, eighty million bullets can't be hard to find, right?" Anyone who hasn't dreamed that bloodthirsty dream about Germany at least one night in his life, in this month of April 1945 (Christian era), is feebleminded. Between the volunteers impregnated by the Nazis and the priestling bringing back the German boy, I'm for the volunteers. First off, the little priest, he'll never be a volunteer, he was a war prisoner, and then, no question, the clerical life pays well enough so that he doesn't have to choose—and he can easily forgive every sin: he's never committed any, he's real careful about this. That he could believe he has the right to forgive—no.

More news: Monty has crossed the Elbe, it seems; Monty's aims aren't as clear as Patton's. Patton charges ahead, reaches Nuremberg. Monty's supposed to have reached Hamburg. Rousset's wife phoned me: "They're in Hamburg. They won't say anything about the Hamburg Neuengamme camp for several days."

She's been very worried lately, and rightly so. In these last days, the Germans are shooting people. Halle has been cleaned out, Chemnitz taken, and they've swept on toward Dresden. Patch is cleaning out Nuremberg. Georges Bidault is talking with President Truman and Stettinius about the San Francisco conference.* Who cares? I'm tired, tired. Under the heading "Wurtemberg Occupied," Michel [*illegible*] says in *Libération Soir:* "We'll never hear of Vaihingen again. On every map the delicate green of forests will sweep all the way down to the Enz. . . . The watchmaker died at Stalingrad. . . . The barber served in Paris, the village idiot occupied Athens." Now the main street is hopelessly empty, its cobblestones belly-up like dead fish. "Regarding deportees: 140,000 prisoners of war have been repatriated, but so far, few deportees. . . . Despite all the ministerial services' efforts, the question requires action on a grander scale.

---

* *The United Nations Conference on International Organization, known informally as the San Francisco Conference (April 25–June 26, 1945), was attended by delegations from the nations that had signed the 1942 Declaration of the United Nations (a statement of the Allies' objectives in World War II). The conference concluded with the signing of the Charter of the United Nations.*

    U.S. secretary of state Edward Stettinius, Foreign Secretary Anthony Eden of Great Britain, and French foreign minister Georges Bidault, an important Resistance leader, headed their respective national delegations to the conference.

The prisoners wait hours in the Tuileries gardens." [And:] "Cinema Night will be a particularly brilliant affair this year." I feel like holing up in my apartment. I'm tired. They say one in five hundred will come back. 600,000 political deportees. 350,000 Jews. So 6,000 will return. He might be among them. It's been a month; he could have sent word. It seems to me I've waited long enough. I'm tired. I don't know if it's the arrival of those deportees from Buchenwald—I can't wait anymore. This evening I'm not waiting for anything.

I'm very tired. An open bakery. Maybe I should buy some bread for D. It's not worth it anymore. I won't wash, I don't need to wash. It must be seven o'clock. D. won't come before eight thirty. I'll go home. Perhaps I shouldn't waste my [bread] coupons. I remember [the refrain]: "It's criminal to waste food coupons these days." Most people are waiting. But some aren't waiting for anything. Others have stopped waiting, because he came home, because they've received word, because he's dead. Two evenings ago, returning from the center, I went to the rue Bonaparte to alert a family. I rang, I delivered my message: "I'm from the Orsay center. Your son will return, he's in good health, we've seen one of his friends." [I'd hurried up] the stairs, I was out of breath. Holding the door open with one hand, the lady heard me out. "We knew that," she said. "We had a letter from him five days ago. Thank you anyway." She invited me in. No. I went slowly downstairs. D. was right there waiting for me at home. "Well?" "They knew, he'd written. So, they can write." D. didn't answer. That was the day before yesterday. Two days ago. In a way, every day I wait less. Here's my street. The dairy store is packed. There's no point in going there. Every time I see my building, every time, I tell myself: "Maybe a letter came while I was out." If one had, my concierge would be waiting for me in front of the door. Her lodge is dark. I knock anyway: "Who is it?" "Me." "There's nothing, Madame Antelme." She opens her door each time. This evening, she has a favor to ask. "Listen, Madame Antelme? I wanted to tell you: you should go see Madame Bordes, she's in a bad way over her sons, won't leave her bed anymore." Am I going to go there now?

No. "I'll go tomorrow morning. Tell her there's no reason for her to worry herself sick. Today it was Stalag VII-A that came back. It's too early for III-A." Madame Fossé puts on her cape: "I'll go. Pitiful, she is; nothing for it—won't leave her bed anymore. Doesn't read the papers. Can't make head or tail of 'em." I go upstairs. Madame Bordes is an old woman, the school concierge, a widow who raised six children. I'll go tomorrow morning. This whole business has hit Madame Fossé hard. I used to go see her occasionally, the last time was only three weeks ago. "Sit yourself down, Madame Antelme." I don't go there anymore. Whenever I see her, though, I'm tempted—just a little—to stop by. "No need to say it, I know what it's like." When I tell her, "I have no one to be there for," she replies, "How well I know, Madame Antelme." Madame Fossé had her first husband taken prisoner of war in 1914–18. He died a prisoner. "That day I just set out blindly with my two brats, wanted to kill myself and them too. Walked like that with them all night, and then the feeling passed. Told myself I shouldn't. I went back to the factory." She has told me that story ten times but since Robert's arrest, tactfully, she hasn't mentioned it. I go home. I'm not expecting anything. I'm cold. I go wash my hands. The water is frigid. I go sit once more on the couch, near the phone. I'm cold. I hear the street bustling down below. It's the end of the war. I don't know if I'm tired. I believe I am. For some time now, I haven't truly slept. I wake up, and then I know I've been asleep. In a ditch for two weeks now, day and night. He said my name. I should do something. I stand up and go to the window, lean my forehead against the glass. Night falls. Below, the Saint-Bênoit is lit up. The Saint-Bênoit, literary café. The world eats, and always will. They have a secret menu for those who can [afford it]. "Madame Bordes—won't leave her bed anymore." Madame Bordes doesn't eat anymore. 350,000 men and women are waiting, and bread makes them feel like vomiting. Two weeks in that ditch. It isn't normal to wait like this. Women waiting behind closed doors for their lovers: "If he's not here by eleven, it's because he has betrayed me. . . ." Mothers waiting for the child due home from school who is two hours late: "He must have been run over"—and they clutch their bellies because the thought gives them shooting pains. But in the next few hours, these women will know. Madame Bordes has been waiting for almost three weeks now. If her sons don't return, she'll never know anything. I'll never know anything. I know that he was hungry for months and died without having eaten, that he didn't have a morsel of bread to ease his hunger before dying. Not even once. The last cravings of the dying.

Since April 7 we've had a choice. Perhaps he's among the two thousand shot dead in Belsen the day before the Americans arrived. At Mittel Glattbach they found fifteen hundred in a charnel house, "rotting in the sunshine." Everywhere, huge columns on all the roads, where they drop like flies. Today: "The 20,000 survivors of Buchenwald salute the 51,000 dead of Buchenwald" (*Libres*, April 24, 1945). We have a choice. It's no ordinary wait. *They've* been waiting for months. Hunger ate into their hope. Their hope had become a fantasy. Shot the day before the Allies arrived. Hope had kept them alive, but it was useless: machine-gun fire on the very eve of their liberation. An hour later, the Allies arrived to find their bodies still warm. Why? The Germans shot them, and then left. The Germans are in their own country, you can't reach out to stay their hands and say, "Don't shoot them, it's not worth it. . . ." Time is different for them: they're losing the war, fleeing. What can they do at the last moment? Bursts of machine-gun fire, the way you break dishes in a tantrum. I'm no longer angry at them, you can't call it that anymore. For a while I was able to feel anger toward them; now I cannot tell the difference between my love for him and my hatred for them.

It's a single image with two sides: on the one, him facing the German, a [bullet hole] in his chest, twelve months' hope drowning in his eyes at this very moment, in a moment; on the other, the eyes of the German aiming at him. That's the image—two sides between which I must choose: him crumpling into the ditch; the German swinging the machine gun back onto his shoulder and walking off. I don't know whether I should concentrate on taking him in my arms and let the German run away (forever), saving his skin, or whether I should grab the German and with my fingers dig out those eyes that never looked into his—thus abandoning [Robert] to his ditch. Everything, every image, matches [that conundrum]. I have only one head, I can't think of everything anymore. For three weeks, I've been thinking [the Germans] should be kept from killing them. No one has dealt with that. We could have sent teams of parachutists to "secure" the camps for the twenty-four hours before the Allies' arrival. Jacques Auvray began trying to arrange that in August 1944. It wasn't possible, because Frenay didn't want any such initiative to come from a resistance movement. Yet he, the Minister for Prisoners of War and Deportees, had no way of doing it himself. It wasn't possible. That's what interests me, in the end. I don't understand why; I can't think of everything. It wasn't done, that's all. They'll be shot down to the last concentration camp. There's no way to prevent it. Sometimes, behind the German, I see Frenay, but it doesn't last.

I'm tired. The only thing that does me good is leaning my head against the gas stove, or the windowpane. I cannot carry my head around anymore. My arms and legs are heavy, but not as heavy as my head. It's no longer a head, it's an abscess. The cool windowpane. D. will be here in an hour. I close my eyes. If he did come back we'd go to the seaside. That's what he'd like best. I think I'm going to die anyway. If he comes back I'll still die. If he rang the bell: "Who is it?" "Me, Robert." All I could do would be open the door and then die. If he comes back we'll go to the beach. It will be summer, the height of summer. Between the moment when I'll open the door and the one when we're at the beach, I'll have died. Surviving somehow, I see a green ocean, a pale orange beach; inside my head I feel the salt air; I don't know where he is while I'm looking at the sea but he's alive. Somewhere on this earth he is breathing; I can stretch out on the beach and relax. When he returns we'll go to the shore. That's what he'll like the best. He loves the sea. Plus it will do him good. He'll be standing on the beach looking at the sea, and it will be enough for me to look at him looking at the sea. I'm not asking anything for myself. As long as he's looking at the sea, so am I. My head against the windowpane. My cheeks become wet. I might well be crying. Out of the six hundred thousand, here's one who's crying. That's him by the sea. In Germany the nights were cold. There on the beach he'll be in shirtsleeves and he'll talk with D. I'll watch them from a distance. Absorbed in their conversation, they won't be thinking of me. Anyway, I'll be dead. Killed by his return. Impossible for it to be otherwise. That's my secret. D. doesn't know this. One way or another I will die, whether he returns or not. My health isn't good. Many times in my life I've had to wait as I'm waiting for him. But him—I've chosen to wait for him. That's my business.

I return to the couch, I lie down. D. will arrive. He rings the doorbell. "Nothing?" "Nothing." He sits down next to the couch. I say: "I don't think there's much hope left." D. looks exasperated, he doesn't reply. I continue: "Tomorrow is April 22. Twenty percent of the camps have been freed. I've seen Sorel at the center, he told me that about one in five hundred will come back." I know that D. no longer has the strength to answer me, but I continue. The doorbell rings. D. looks at me: "I'll get it." I stay on the couch. I hear the door opening. It's Robert's brother-in-law. "Well?" "Nothing." He sits down, he tries to smile, he looks at me, then he looks at D. "Nothing? . . ." "Nothing." He nods, reflects, then says: "If you ask me, it's a question of communication. They can't write."

D.: "Marguerite is crazy. Practically speaking—let's be practical—Robert isn't in Besançon, right? There's no normal mail service in Germany, right?"

Michel: "The Americans have other things to do, unfortunately."

Me: "Well, we've definitely had news from people who were in Buchenwald. There's a chance he was in the August 17 convoy that reached Buchenwald."

D.: "And what tells you he stayed there?"

Me: "If he left on a transport, there's not much hope."

Michel: "No one's told you that he left at the last minute; he might have been transferred elsewhere earlier in the year."

D.: "If Marguerite keeps this up, when Robert comes back . . ."

I'm tired. I'd like M. and D. to go. I lie down. I hear them talking, then after a while, the conversation flags, with some long pauses. I couldn't care less what they're talking about. Whatever happens will happen. I'm tired. . . . Suddenly D. grips my shoulder: "What's the matter with you?" "I don't know." Michel is standing next to him: "Why are you sleeping like that?" "I'm tired, I'd like you to go." They continue talking. I go back to sleep. Then D. again. "What is it?" I ask where M. is. He's gone. D. fetches a thermometer. I've got a slight fever. "It's fatigue, I wore myself out at the center."

"Refugees"

Charles Simic

Poet Charles Simic, the former United States Poet Laureate, remembers a life in transit, in the aftermath of the German surrender (from *Letters of Transit*).

Mine is an old, familiar story by now. So many people have been displaced in this century, their numbers so large, their collective and individual destinies so varied, it's impossible for me or anyone else, if we are honest, to claim any special status as a victim. Particularly since what happened to me fifty years ago is happening to someone else today. Rwanda, Bosnia, Afghanistan, Congo, the endlessly humiliated Kurds—and so it goes. Fifty years ago it was fascism and communism, now it's nationalism and religious fundamentalism that make life miserable in lots of places. Recently, for instance, I was translating the work of a woman poet from Sarajevo for an anthology, and its editors had great difficulty locating her. She had vanished. She was not a young woman, she had plenty of friends, but no one seemed to know what had happened to her in the confusion of the war. It took many months to find her sweeping floors in a restaurant in Germany.

"Displaced persons" is the name they had for us back in 1945, and that's what we truly were. As you sit watching bombs falling in some old documentary, or the armies advancing against each other, villages and towns going up in fire and smoke, you forget about the people huddled in the cellar. Mr. and Mrs. Innocent and their families paid dearly in this century for just being there. Condemned by history, as Marxists were fond of saying, perhaps belonging to a wrong class, wrong ethnic group, wrong religion—what have you—they were and continue to be an unpleasant reminder of all the philosophical and nationalist utopias gone wrong. With their rags and bundles and their general air of misery and despair, they came in droves from the East, fleeing evil with no idea where they were running to. No one had much to eat in Europe and here were the starving refugees, hundreds of thousands of them in trains, camps, and prisons, dipping stale bread into watery soup, searching for lice on their children's heads and squawking in dozens of languages about their awful fate.

My family, like so many others, got to see the world for free thanks to Hitler's wars and Stalin's takeover of Eastern Europe. We were not German collaborators or members of the aristocracy, nor were we, strictly speaking, political exiles. Small fry, we made no decisions ourselves. It was all arranged for us by the world leaders of the times. Like so many others who were displaced, we had no ambition to stray far beyond our neighborhood in Belgrade. We liked it fine. Deals were made about spheres of influence, borders were redrawn, the so-called Iron Curtain was lowered, and we were set adrift with our few possessions. Historians are still documenting all the treacheries and horrors that came our way as the result of Yalta and other such conferences, and the subject is far from finished.

As always, there were degrees of evil and degrees of tragedy. My family didn't fare as badly as others. Thousands of Russians whom the Germans forcibly brought to work in their factories and on their farms were returned to Stalin against their will by the Allies. Some were shot and the rest packed off to the gulags so they would not contaminate the rest of the citizenry with newly acquired decadent capitalist notions. Our own prospects were rosier. We had hopes of ending up in the United States, Canada, or Australia. Not that this was guaranteed. Getting into the United States was especially difficult. Most Eastern European countries had very small quotas, unlike the Western European ones. In the eyes of the American genetic experts and immigration policymakers, South Slavs were not highly desirable ethnic material.

It's hard for people who have never experienced it to truly grasp what it means to lack proper documents. We read every day about our own immigration officers, using and misusing their recently acquired authority to turn back suspicious aliens from our borders. The pleasure of humiliating the powerless must not be underestimated. Even as a young boy, I could see that was the case. Everywhere there are bureaucrats, the police state is an ideal.

I remember standing in endless lines in Paris at police headquarters to receive or renew resident permits. It seems like that's all we ever did when we lived there. We'd wait all day only to discover that the rules had changed since the last time, that they now required, for instance, something as absurd as my mother's parents' marriage certificate or her grade-school diploma, even though she was in possession of a French diploma since she did her post-graduate studies in Paris. As we'd stand there pondering the impossibility of what they were asking of us, we'd be listening to someone at the next window trying to convey in poor French how the family's house had burned, how they'd left in a hurry with only one small suitcase, and so on, to which the official would shrug his shoulders and proceed to inform them that unless the documents were produced promptly, the residence permit would be denied.

So what did we do? Well, if the weather was nice we'd go and sit outside on a bench and watch the lucky Parisians stroll by carrying groceries, pushing baby carriages, walking their dogs, even whistling. Occasionally a couple would stop in front of us to smooch while we cursed the French and our rotten luck. In the end, we'd trudge back to our small hotel room and write home.

The mail didn't travel very swiftly, of course. We would go nuts every day for weeks waiting for the mailman, who couldn't stand the sight of us since we were always pestering him, and finally, somehow, the documents would arrive thanks to a distant relative. Then they had to be translated by an official translator who, of course, couldn't make heads or tails out of the dog-eared fifty-year-old entry in a provincial Balkan school or church registry. In any case, eventually we'd go back to the long line only to discover that they were not needed after all, but something else was. Every passport office, every police station, every consulate had a desk with a wary and bad-tempered official who suspected us of not being what we claimed to be. No one likes refugees. The ambiguous status of being called a DP made it even worse. The officials we met knew next to nothing about where we came from and why, but that did not prevent them from passing judgment on us. Having been driven out by the Nazis brought us a measure of sympathy, but having left because of the Communists was not as well received. If the officials were leftists, they told us bluntly that, ungrateful wretches that we were, we had left behind the most progressive, the most just society on the face of the earth. The others figured we were just riffraff with fake diplomas and a shady past. Even the smiling dummies in store windows on the elegant Avenue Victor Hugo regarded us as if we were out to steal something. It was actually all extremely simple: either we were going to get a foothold here or somewhere else, or we were going back to a refugee camp, prison, or, even worse, to "the embodiment of man's dearest longing for justice and happiness," as the communist world was described in certain quarters.

Immigration, exile, being uprooted and made a pariah may be the most effective way yet devised to impress on an individual the arbitrary nature of his or her own existence. Who needed a shrink or a guru when everyone we met asked us who we were the moment we opened our mouths and they heard the accent?

The truth is, we had no simple answers. Being rattled around in freight trains, open trucks, and ratty ocean-liners, we ended up being a puzzle even to ourselves. At first, that was hard to take; then we got used to the idea. We began to savor it, to enjoy it. Being no-body struck me personally as being far more interesting than being somebody. The streets were full of these "somebodys" putting on confident airs. Half the time I envied them; half the time I looked down on them with pity. I knew something they didn't, something hard to come by unless history gives you a good kick in the ass: how superfluous and insignificant in any grand scheme mere individuals are. And how pitiless are those who have no understanding that this could be their fate too.

I stepped off the boat in New York City on August 10, 1954, with my mother and my brother. The day was hot, the sky was cloud-less, and the streets were full of people and cars. My father, who was already in the United States, put us up in a hotel just off Times Square. It was incredible, astonishing. The immigration officers didn't torment us and rip up our papers. They didn't send us back. Our being here and breathing was perfectly legal. Watching TV, ordering room service, and taking a shower broke no laws. Every half hour, we asked my father again if this was true. When he told us yes, we literally jumped for joy. No New Year's Eve, no birthday celebration, no party afterward ever gave me as much happiness. A fear had lifted.

"My love of the country follows from my love of its freedoms," Lewis Lapham said, and I know that's true. I felt that the first day I came to America and I still feel the same.

I was sixteen, old enough to take walks by myself. The city, which I had seen in so many movies, felt strangely familiar. I'm a big city boy and all large cities resemble one another in a fundamental way. Walking around confirms what one already knows. Here's where the rich live, here the poor. Here is where business is conducted and the expensive stores are to be found. And finally, here is the neigh-borhood where one goes to have a good time. Nobody had to explain to me the difference between the young women I saw on Madi-son Avenue and the ones hanging around a candy store on Eighth

Avenue. It was the same in Paris and in Belgrade. Of course, New York is also unlike any European city. Its bright colors were startling after the grayness of Europe. Guys in pink shirts, wearing neckties with palm trees on them, getting into yellow taxis on a street of huge neon signs and billboards showing smiling, rosy-cheeked faces drinking tea and puffing cigarettes. That was really something.

Architecturally, too, the city was full of surprises. A skyscraper in midtown next to a three-story building with a hot dog stand. Water towers, fire escapes, trash on the sidewalks, a street with a dozen movie houses all showing films twenty-four hours a day and then a building seemingly made entirely of glass and a park with car-riages pulled by horses. The question a newcomer asks, inevitably, is, Where am I going to live? Is it going to be a tenement in Hell's Kitchen or one of the brownstones on some quiet side street on the Upper East Side?

Our initial needs and worries were few and basic. First, and most importantly, we wanted new clothes and an American haircut to take away that look of a hopeless loser that comes with being a DP. We spent the first few days in New York changing our disguises. Jeans, Hawaiian shirts, cowboy belts, colorful T-shirts, sneakers, and other such items, procured cheaply in the vicinity of Times Square, appeared to me to be the height of elegance. To my great surprise, the natives still gave me funny looks on the street. Unwittingly I had transformed myself from a European schoolboy to a country hick, the kind you often saw around the Port Authority Bus Terminal or outside a 42nd Street movie house showing westerns.

Then there was the problem of language. I had studied English, could read it more or less, but speaking it was a different matter. I remember asking for directions the second or third day in New York and not being understood. I wanted to know how many blocks to the Empire State Building. A simple question, except that in-stead of "blocks," I said "corners." The astonishment and the em-barrassment of speaking and not being able to communicate are deeply humbling. Every day in America, I realized, I would have a fresh opportunity to make a complete fool of myself. Quickly, I learned to keep my mouth shut except when absolutely necessary. In the meantime, I read the movie marquees, I tried to follow the TV and radio programs. In secrecy I repeated words and phrases I overheard: Hey, smart aleck! Crackerjack. Okeydokey. Chase butterflies. Hogwash. Hold the phone. Go to the dogs.

Then there was food. All these burgers, cherry Cokes, hot dogs, grilled cheese sandwiches, apple pies à la mode, and dozens of different candy bars had to be sampled. If you've grown up on thick soups and casseroles, American fast food has the advantage of being portable. It's hard to eat spaghetti or goulash in bed or in a car; it's much easier with a bag of chips or a can of peanuts. It's a perfect invention for someone hungry all the time, as I was. It sounds nice intellectually to claim that an expatriate can never feel at home anywhere again. It's definitely not true of a sixteen year old. I was more adaptable than a cat or a goldfish would have been. I was eager to see and taste everything.

Once, my father's rich boss invited us to his house for a Sunday meal. We expected a huge feast and were astonished by the canned vegetables and the thin, overcooked slices of roast beef served in small portions. No spices; no hot peppers; not even a proper amount of salt and pepper. We couldn't get over it. Whatever inferiority complexes we had about entering American homes were quickly cured by the poorly cooked food we were given to eat. Banana splits at some drugstore counter were nothing to sneer at; the tasteless, soggy white bread they served at home made no sense. When we wanted to eat well, we'd seek out a Hungarian or German restaurant in Yorkville or an Italian place down in the Village.

Of course, we always had the option of getting together with other Yugoslavs for some home-style food. However, there was a heavy price to pay. The talk made it difficult to enjoy the cuisine. Exiles usually imagine that theirs is a temporary situation. It was just a matter of days before communism collapsed and their homes and their lives would be restored to them just as they were. Nostalgia is big on the menu at such gatherings, and so is anger at how events turned out. My parents were tired of Balkan squabbles; they wanted a breather. Also, they didn't think there was a likelihood of ever going back. They turned out to be right. The Communists, thinly disguised as democrats, are still in charge at home and so is the old secret police.

To want to be an American, which I certainly desired, made us strangers even to our own kind. They eyed us suspiciously. Without the superiority one's own ethnic group readily provides, what do you have? It's terrible when collective sentiments one is born with begin to seem artificial, when one starts to suspect that one's exile is a great misfortune but also a terrific opportunity to get away from everything one has always secretly disliked about the people one grew up with.

I now understand the big choice we made without quite realizing that we were making it. We stopped seeing our fellow Yugoslavs. Already in those early days, I realized that America gave me an opportunity to stop playing the assigned roles that I inevitably had to play around my fellow Serbs. All that deferring to tradition, clannishness, and machismo, with their accompanying vocabularies, I happily gave up. Nor did the role of the professional exile, forever homesick, forever misunderstood, attract me. Adventure lay elsewhere. America and the Americans were far more interesting to me and so was the anonymity that came with full-scale assimilation.

Actually, that's not entirely accurate. Many of my early friends were Italian, Jewish, Irish, and other immigrants. One of the great experiences of a city like New York was the exposure to so many other ways of life. The ideal of the times was, of course, the melting pot. Still, what did I know about the Blacks, Chinese, Cubans, Lebanese, Hungarians, Russians, Sicilians, before I lived in New York? There is no school as good as the life that takes you one day from a Hungarian butcher on Second Avenue, to an Irish bar in Chelsea, an Italian coffee shop on Macdougal Street, and a jazz club off Sheridan Square in the company of a young woman who hails from Texas. No wonder nationalists of all stripes hate cities. It's hard to remain the faithful and obedient son of your own clan when so many other attractive options offer themselves. One has to be a fool or a hypocrite to sing the praises of one's native customs to the exclusion of every other, after one has lived in New York City. The cities are, indeed, agreeably corrupting. They produce free individuals and that, as every state and religious institution the world over will tell you, is an unpardonable heresy.

If the choice, then, was between deepening my own displacement and trying to belong, I made my situation even more complicated by moving away from home when I was eighteen. In other words, exactly two years after I stepped off the 44th Street pier, I found myself again adrift. My parents were not getting along and life at home was most unpleasant, so I had no alternative. I broke a few more ties I still had to my old identity. I had no other relatives or friends. I had no fixed address or purpose. There was no question of college, because my parents were not able to support me and my grades were not good enough to get me a scholarship anywhere. But if you think that I cried myself to sleep every night over my predicament, you're wrong. It was one of the happiest times of my life. Finding a job and making ends meet—as I discovered quickly—was very easy. Both in Chicago and New York, I could find decent work in a matter of hours. I did everything from being a mail clerk at a newspaper to selling shirts in a department store. I worked in several offices as a bookkeeper. I met all kinds of interesting men and women. Best of all, I felt safe in this country from the persecutions we were accustomed to, and that was more than enough to make a young man permanently cheerful.

In the meantime, there were Charlie Parker, Thelonious Monk, Billie Holiday, Bessie Smith, Duke Ellington, the Five Spot, Birdland, rhythm and blues, country music, film noir, Scott Fitzgerald, Wallace Stevens, William Carlos Williams and the entire New Directions list, the Gotham Book Mart, MoMA, Willem de Kooning, Jackson Pollock, *Partisan Review*, the Brooklyn

Dodgers, the Yankees, boxing at Madison Square Garden, "The Honeymooners," Sid Caesar, "I Love Lucy," and literally hundreds of other things to learn about. I was astonished to encounter other recent arrivals who had little or no interest in any of this.

To fall in love with a country or another human being requires some gullibility, and I had plenty to spare. It took me at least fifteen years to appreciate the full extent of our political corruption and to see the problems and injustices this country is faced with. Early on, I was living a version of the American Dream, ignorant of the simple fact that a white boy with an accent is more readily employable than a person of color. There has always been a kind of see-no-evil, let's-pretend demeanor about this country. It needs fresh supplies of true believers to keep it going, and that's what I was. In addition, there was the generosity that I and so many others found here. Every cliche about getting a second chance and reinventing oneself turned out to be true. It gave one confidence—America did that. Who could resist that sudden burst of optimism? I could not.

The clearest proof I had that I've become "an American" came to me in 1962 when I found myself in the U.S. Army in Europe, first in Germany and then in France. The little towns and small cities with their closely knit, insular societies frightened me. It was very pleasant to dine in one of the fine restaurants in Nancy or Colmar, but the silence of the streets after eight o'clock in the evening gave me the creeps: closed shutters, locked doors, lights out almost everywhere. I could well imagine what being a refugee there would be like.

More recently, during the break-up of Yugoslavia, I reexperienced my estrangement from the old world. I found myself, for example, incapable of taking sides or seeing any attraction in being a nationalist. The advantage of the melting pot is that it undermines tribalism. One gains a distance from one's own national folly. Fashionable present-day multiculturalism with its naive calls for ethnic pride sounds to me like an attempt to restore me to precisely that state of mind my parents ran away from in Europe. The American identity is a strange concoction of cultures, but at its best it is a concoction prepared and cooked by each individual in his or her own kitchen. It ought not to come in a package with a label and a fake list of wholesome, all-natural ingredients.

There's an old Soviet poster picturing Comrade Lenin standing on the planet earth holding a broom. He's sweeping off "undesirable elements," men and women easily identified by their clothes as belonging to the bourgeoisie. That was us. For that very reason, every project for betterment of humanity, every collectivist ideology, no matter how chaste it sounds, terrifies me. Barbarism, intolerance, and fanaticism have been the by-products of all utopian projects in this century. Infallible theories of history and human progress brought about the most repellent forms of repression. The noble-sounding attempt to make the whole of society accept a particular worldview always leads, sooner or later, to the slaughter of the innocents.

We, displaced persons, were caught between two rival intellectual projects: fascism and communism. Our persecution was justified because we lagged in our understanding of the laws of history. We stood in the way, and so our misfortune was unavoidable and not to be greatly regretted. This harsh view, as we know, had the enthusiastic support of many of the leading writers and intellectuals in Europe. The violence and injustice may have been regrettable, but were in the service of messianic hopes for future happiness. The political writings of the times—both on the left and the right—consist of endless justifications for inflicting death and suffering on the innocent.

If you think I'm exaggerating, consider this. While we stood in lines at the Prefecture, Sartre, Aragon, de Beauvoir, and their kind were dining in style or attending some gala at the Russian or Yugoslav embassy, celebrating Stalin's or Tito's birthday. In this century, the executioners' best friends have often turned out to be writers and intellectuals. The last remaining myth of our age is the myth of the intellectual's integrity and independence. The true enemy continues to be—to return to what I said at the very beginning—the innocent bystander. Or, more precisely, the antagonist has always been the individual conscience. It's that part of ourselves that remains stubbornly suspicious of mass enthusiasms, the one that makes us sleep badly at night. At 3 A.M., the proposed means that are justified by the lofty ends look pretty nasty. For the "lunatics of one idea," as Wallace Stevens called them, that has always been the supreme obstacle on the way to Utopia. Millions perished or lost everything while huge intellectual and military efforts were being made to obliterate and circumvent the conscience of countless human beings.

Speaking as one of the laboratory animals used in a series of famous historical experiments, I'd say I ended up, for better or for worse, with a clearer idea of how the world works—and that's no small matter. I prefer that solitary knowledge to the jubilation of the masses in Red Square or at some Nuremberg rally. I have a firm conviction that the ideologues on the left and on the right are interchangeable. I have a contempt for all shepherd-and-flock theories, all euphorias of thinking the same thought with hundreds of others, all preaching and moralizing in art and literature. Besides, I am a poet, the kind they call a lyric poet. A lyric poem is the voice of a single human being taking stock of his or her own existence. If it works, we speak of its "originality," meaning it is without precedent, it doesn't fit preconceived notions. The poem is both a part of history and outside its domain. That is its beauty and its hope. A poet is a member of that minority that refuses to be part of any official minority, because a poet knows what it is to belong among those walking in broad daylight, as well as among those hiding behind closed shutters.

Sources

Adams, Ansel, "Entrance to Manzanar, Manzanar Relocation Center." Photographic print, 1943. Manzanar War Relocation Photographs. Courtesy of the Library of Congress. LOT 10479–2, no. 1. http://hdl.loc.gov/loc.pnp/ppprs.00286.

————, "Mr. and Mrs. Henry J. Tsurutani and baby Bruce, Manzanar Relocation Center, California." Photographic print, 1943. Manzanar War Relocation Photographs. Courtesy of the Library of Congress. LOT 10479–1, no. 30. http://hdl.loc.gov/loc.pnp/pprs.00251.

————, "Roy Takeno reading paper in front of office." Photographic print, 1943. Manzanar War Relocation Photographs. Courtesy of the Library of Congress. LOT 10479–7, no. 2. http://hdl.loc.gov/loc.pnp/ppprs.00407.

————, "Manzanar street scene, clouds, Manzanar Relocation Center, California." Photographic print, 1943. Manzanar War Relocation Photographs. Courtesy of the Library of Congress. LOT 10479–2, no. 5. http://hdl.loc.gov/loc.pnp/ppprs.00284.

"Caputured Japanese photograph taken aboard a Japanese carrier before the attack on Pearl Harbor, December 7, 1941." Photographic print. Courtesy of the National Archives and Records Administration. 80-G-30549.

"Captured Japanese photograph taken during the December 7, 1941, attack on Pearl Harbor. In the distance, the smoke rises from Hickam Field." Photographic print. Courtesy of the National Archives and Records Administration. 80-G-30550.

Cook, Haruko Taya, and Theodore F. Cook, *Japan at War: An Oral History* (New York: The New Press, 1992).

Dellinger, David, "Statement on Entering Prison," from *Home Fronts: A Wartime America Reader,* edited by Michael S. Foley and Brendan P. O'Malley (New York: The New Press, 2008).

Dr. Seuss & Co. Go to War: The World War II Editorial Cartoons of America's Leading Comic Artists, André Schiffrin (New York: The New Press, 2009).

Duras, Marguerite, *Wartime Writings, 1943–1949,* edited by Sophie Bogaert and Olivier Corpet, translated by Linda Coverdale (New York: The New Press, 2008).

Freund, Elisabeth ("Flight"), from "Waiting," from *Hitler's Exiles: Personal Stories from Nazi Germany to America,* edited by Mark M. Anderson (New York: The New Press, 1998).

Hobsbawm, Eric, *Interesting Times: A Twentieth-Century Life* (New York: The New Press, 2002).

Hollem, Howard R., "With a woman's determination, Lorena Craig takes over a man-size job, Corpus Christi, Texas." Color transparency, August 1942. America from the Great Depression to World War II: Color Photographs from the FSA-OWI, 1939–1945. Courtesy of the Library of Congress. LC-USW36–59. http://hdl.loc.gov/loc.pnp/fsac.1a34877.

Jirosik, Joe, interviewed by John Henry Faulk for the American Folklife Center. Courtesy of the Library of Congress. Sound disc, 1941. AFS 6454. http://hdl.loc.gov/loc.afc/afc1941004.sr21.

Kook, Hillel, interviewed by David Wyman from *A Race Against Death: Peter Bergson, America, and the Holocaust,* edited by David S. Wyman and Rafael Medoff (New York: The New Press, 2002).

Levi, Primo, from *The Voice of Memory: Interviews, 1961–1987* (New York: The New Press, 2001).

Miller, J. Howard, "We Can Do It." Color poster, 1942. World War II Photos. Courtesy of the National Archives and Records Administration. 179-WP-1563.

One World or None, edited by Dexter Masters and Katharine Way (New York: The New Press, 2007).

Palmer, Alfred T., "Women at work on bomber, Douglas Aircraft Company, Long Beach, California." Color transparency, October 1942. America from the Great Depression to World War II: Color Photographs from the FSA-OWI, 1939–1945. Courtesy of the Library of Congress. LC-USW36–109. http://hdl.loc.gov/loc.pnp/fsac.1a35341.

———, "A candid view of one of the women workers touching up the U.S. Army Air Forces insignia on the side of the fuselage of a 'Vengeance' dive bomber manufactured at Vultee's Nashville division, Tennessee." Color transparency, February 1943. America from the Great Depression to World War II: Color Photographs from the FSA-OWI, 1939–1945. Courtesy of the Library of Congress. LC-USW36–143. http://hdl.loc.gov/loc.pnp/fsac.1a35370.

"Pearl Harbor, T.H. taken by surprise, during the Japanese aerial attack. U.S.S. West Virginia aflame." Photographic print, December 1941. A World in Flames. Courtesy of the National Archives and Records Administration. 80-G-19947.

Peery, Nelson, *Black Fire: The Making of an American Revolutionary* (New York: The New Press, 1995).

Pittsburgh Courier, "Double V Campaign" (1942) from *Home Fronts: A Wartime America Reader,* edited by Michael S. Foley and Brendan P. O'Malley (New York: The New Press, 2008).

Schoenheimer, Ellen, "Refugee Life in France" from *Hitler's Exiles: Personal Stories from Nazi Germany to America,* edited by Mark M. Anderson (New York: The New Press, 1998).

Simic, Charles, "Refugees," from *Letters of Transit: Reflections of*

Exile, Identity, Language, and Loss, edited by André Aciman (New York: The New Press, 2000).

Terkel, Studs, *"The Good War": An Oral History of World War II* (New York: The New Press, 1997).

"USS *Shaw* (DD-373) exploding during the Japanese raid on Pearl Harbor." Photographic print, December 1941. A World in Flames. Courtesy of the National Archives and Records Administration. 80-G-16871.